The Trouble-Makers at Frankfurt
A Vindication of the English Reformation

The Trouble-Makers at Frankfurt

A Vindication of the English Reformation

George M. Ella

Go *publications*

Go Publications
Gibb Hill Farm, Ponsonby, Cumbria, CA20 1BX, ENGLAND

© Go Publications 2018
First Published 2003

British Library Cataloguing in Publication Data available

ISBN 978-1-908475-12-1

Cover design: Peter Cooper.
Cover photograph: The old city of Frankfurt is now largely restored
and blends with the modern architecture of business and commerce.
Photograph courtesy of Tourismus + Congress GmbH.
Photographer: Jochen Keute.

Printed and bound in Great Britain
by Lightning Source UK Ltd.

Dedication

This book is dedicated to my dear wife Erika and my fine sons Mark and Robin, especially for their continued support over the years for my endeavours to vindicate wronged saints of the past and the faith for which they lived and in which they died.

Acknowledgements

This is a good opportunity to thank the staff of the Duisburg University Library, in particular Alfons Ballweg of the History Department and Ingrid Kuta of the Lending Department, for their most helpful cooperation. Inge Becker and Gerd Meiselbach of the university's Inter-Library Loans Department also worked wonders in tracing the documents and books I needed. I am also much indebted to Regina Jesse of the Duisburg City Archives who helped me to trace Prof. Withof's works, long thought lost, and also the staff of the Frankfurt Archives for loaning me most important books, not the least being Archive Director Rudolf Jung's account of the English exiles. I would also like to thank Derek Scales, General Secretary of the Protestant Reformation Society, for his sound advice on the period covered and his loan of books appertaining to the problems of the exiles. Above all, my grateful thanks go out to Peter and Gill Meney, of Go Publications, for their kind encouragement, patience and help with the MS but especially for their deep friendship, fellowship and hospitality.

Two magazines have greatly encouraged me in my work on the British Reformation; these are *New Focus* with its fine Reformed stance and the *English Churchman* with its faithful presentation of Evangelical Anglicanism and its brotherly dialogue between Presbyterians and Episcopalians. My deep gratitude must be expressed here for the annual Banner of Truth conferences and those of the Protestant Reformation Society which place Biblical and Historical Theology, experimental Christianity and brotherly fellowship before narrow denominational claims.

Dr George M. Ella
June 2002

Table of Contents

List of Illustrations

FOREWORD

Picture a refugee. He is a fugitive and a stranger, far from home in a foreign land. He has fled his country in fear of his life. A new monarch is in power. New politics prevail. Old prejudices demand his imprisonment, perhaps even his death and the confiscation of all his property. Who is this man? What is his crime? He is a minister of the gospel, or a university professor, a student of the Word of God or a merchant-trader. His crime is to have been a Protestant in England during the reign of Mary the Bloody.

He is not alone. His family have left their home too. England is no place for those of reformed faith and practice. There are others also, hundreds, perhaps thousands, seeking refuge at a time of political and religious persecution and intolerance. They have come to Europe and the relative safety of protestant countries such as Switzerland, Holland and Germany. They are seeking asylum in the cities of Geneva, Zurich and Frankfurt.

In this book Dr Ella opens up a period of great importance in the history of the Reformation in the United Kingdom and particularly England. It is often assumed that the Reformation was uniquely or mainly a continental European phenomenon. Some writers have even encouraged this wrong assumption to serve their purpose of tracing reforming zeal and purity of worship to a particular movement or denomination. Yet, this is to misrepresent the testimony of historic evidence and underestimate the fine contribution British churchmen made to the reformation of their own national church and the wider reformation in Europe. Throughout the sixteenth century, British ministers of the gospel were in no degree lagging behind the reforming efforts of Luther in Germany and Calvin and Beza in Switzerland.

It was precisely because of the great reforms of church and state begun in England under Henry VIII and honed by Edward VI that Mary's reign, when it came, had to be so reactionary and brutal if Rome was ever to recover its lost influence and domination in Britain. The Marian exiles were the cream of British evangelicals with reforming ardour and credentials second to none. This made them a thorn in Queen Mary's side and an impediment to her re-Romanising activities. Their flight from England and their presence in Europe demonstrates their dedication to the cause of reformation.

Yet their period of exile was not without controversy as The *Troubles at Frankfort* shows. The nature of these troubles, the identity of those involved and the role they played have long been discussed and debated. However, there has been too, a tendency for some commentators to use the events in Frankfurt from 1553 to 1560 to support their own interpretation of history, particularly with reference to later church disruptions and schisms.

The existence of this revisionist writing and the practice of back-projecting later controversies onto the Frankfurt troubles has been of special interest to Dr Ella in his research and study of this period. Though a Yorkshireman by birth Dr Ella has lived and worked in Germany for many years and his familiarity with the language, and his librarian and archivist experience have been invaluable to him in his search for source material and relevant city records from the period, including Senate correspondence and minutebooks. This original research alone makes this book a valuable contribution to the subject.

But it is not, perhaps, the most significant contribution. That honour goes to Dr Ella's fine vindication of those English reformers who have too frequently been maligned and vilified by later writers. Some readers may complain that redressing the balance of responsibility and blame for the troubles that beset the British exiles in Frankfurt casts shadows of reproach upon their heroes. Yet what injustice allows one man's reputation to be sullied for generations while the true perpetrator of strife marches on without criticism?

This aspect of Dr Ella's work is especially close to his own heart because of the high regard in which he holds the stalwarts of the pre-Laudian Reformed Church of England. As readers of his earlier works such as *Mountain Movers* and his historical essays in such magazines as *New Focus* will know, Dr Ella has re-introduced worthies such as Archbishops Edmund Grindal, John Whitgift, and George Abbot to the Christian public. These men, together with others equally astute in reformed theology and spiritual application such as John Bale, Richard Cox, John Jewel, John Fox and David Whitehead are just as much part of the reformation in Britain as their successors and better known puritan counterparts.

It is with great pleasure that I commend this work to you the reader with the shared hope of the author that in considering the evidence laid before us some of the brightest lights in the early history of the reformation in Britain will be recognised and acknowledged for their Christ glorifying service and their genuine commitment to Christian liberty and freedom of worship.

One final point. To a man, these individuals of whom Dr Ella writes would eschew the prominence their labours have earned. Their Christ-centred preaching, their spiritual stature and the brave convictions with which they faced persecution and adversity helped to establish the Christian legacy we possess today. They secured access to the scriptures, endowed a formidible body of reformed doctrine and gained the freedom of worship from both Rome and state involvement that we continue to be blessed with. Yet the same men were themselves outcasts and refugees; homeless, stateless, often jobless and reliant on the generosity and accommodation of others.

The theological and ecclesiological testimony of the Marian exiles remains strong and should be the study of all those interested in discerning the true harbingers of reformation in Britain during the sixteenth century. Their real life experiences and tenacity in the face of trial and opposition should inspire all believers to rise to the challenge of their own time; to witness and serve our Lord despite personal cost and against overwhelming odds.

Peter L. Meney

Richard Cox

Introduction:
Reformers, Puritans, Precisians, and Presbyterians

The origin of the Vatican sect

Anyone reading such sound and instructive books as Bungener's *History of the Council of Trent*, Miles' *The Voice of the Glorious Reformation* and Collette's *The Novelties of Romanism*, will realise how the Vatican sect, erroneously known as the Roman Catholic Church, is a pseudo-religious movement of a relatively young age. Indeed, it is a rebellious, anti-Christian, revolutionary, political institution of which communism, fascism, the Mafia and the lodges are mere pale reflections. It arose amongst the militant ranks of those who wished to force a worldwide, man-made, occult, pseudo-religious, political tyranny onto the masses. This society of unrepentant sinners now claims total power over all nations, property and wealth. Theirs is an absolute, tyrannical aim to enslave all men's bodies, souls and spirits and make them willing but servile pawns in the hands of a hierarchy of self-styled eunuchs. These theoretical half-men[1] proclaim themselves as the universal Church outside of which is no hope, no faith and no charity. Yet they build their system on the blood of the martyrs, shutting out the very faith, hope and charity they pretend to possess.

---

[1] A friend who was for many years an administer of RC funding, informs me that they had a special financial department for the support of priests' 'common law' wives and their joint offspring.

This separatist and worldly movement, taking over the super-stitions of the ancient Roman Empire, declare their ruler to be *Pontifex Maximus* and proclaim themselves the very Body of Christ, the offspring of the Queen of Heaven and the sole interpreters of God's will for mankind. Thus, in 1545, this anachronistic sect called their people together at the notorious Council of Trent to constitute their new religion in opposition to Biblical Christianity. Throwing the Word of the True and Living God aside as being secondary to their own position, this self-appointed clerical elite instituted their new pseudo-religion. They drew up fifteen novel decrees, backed by one hundred and twenty-five curses to make them effective. These have remained the basic superstitions of the Vatican sect ever since. They proclaim that the salvation of the sinner is en-tirely dependent on their clergy's intention or lack of intention to save. The sinner, they add, can never know in this life if the priest who granted absolution was 'pure' in his intention. Thus, the Vati-can clergy as a body are raised to the Godhead, professing to be lords over life, death and destruction. No less a notorious hench-man of this blasphemous cause than Cardinal Bellermine tells us that the decrees of Trent were not of divine origin because the Bi-ble proscribed them nor even because tradition upheld them but simply because the Papal Council itself decreed them.

One worthy Scotsman has inscribed on the inside cover of my copy of Bungener:

> Roman Catholicism is not suited to deliver men from their sinful condition, rather is it designed to allow men to gratify their evil propensities. This is not the religion of Jesus Christ.

May this sad fact instruct our hearts and minds as we seek to guide people along the old paths of traditional Biblical Christian-ity, knowing that Christ alone is the Way, the Truth and the Life.

Separating the corrupt from the pure
Faced with the innovations of Romanism, the English Reformers, whether they were a Grossetête, Bradwardine, Wycliffe, Tyndale,

Latimer, Hooper or Jewel, did not seek to go Rome's way and bring in a new church outward structure with new orders and a new discipline. Their greater task was to deal with the essentials of true spiritual life, cleaning up the apostolic, catholic church of the Roman dross that had been lately accumulated in it by a clergy who had become mere worldly, indeed, earthly, despots. All the occult and pseudo-magical traditions of the papists' extra-biblical dogmas and ceremonies had to go. All that taught sect-wise that salvation was to be found within the new cults of the Roman clergy, and within that tight enclosure only, was to be rejected with the contempt such machinations of men deserved. In this, the English Reformers were greatly successful. Thus, the Reformed Church of England as it was renewed in the days of Edward VI whom Englishmen, at least, ought to call Edward the Great, became second to none in the world for true doctrine and evangelical expansion. They clearly showed that popery was not catholic, was not apostolic and was certainly not the primitive faith of the Church.[2] But few or none of these Reformers were prepared to rest on their laurels. They realised that church reformation must be a continuing and progressive process as long as sinful man remained on earth and the Resurrection Dawn had yet to brighten the universe.

Demands for a new mixture of Rome and Reform
Riding in the rear shadow, of this faithful and courageous vanguard, was a group of men who wished to combine much of the old with the new. They wanted sound doctrine but they wanted it presented in a way that melted their love for Christ into an outward mould of solid, steadfast forms that could be seen, touched and felt and which gave them a sense of political as well as spiritual security. They wanted a Church which was identical with the State. This Church, for them, should not merely reflect a spiritual sense of oneness in Christ, but become the badge and banner of a mili-

---

[2] See Jeremy Taylor's excellent essay *Popery not Catholic, Apostolic, or Primitive* in his 'A Dissuasive from Popery to the People of Ireland', in *The Whole Works of the Right Rev. Jeremy Taylor*, Longman, Brown, Green, and Longmans, Vol. VI, 1849.

tant, politico-social organisation. This society would then not only offer man the New Birth, but also provide him with a politico-religious cradle and concept of a state-church in which he could be born, grow up, live, move and have his being.

Being under Moses as a sign of being in grace

These men were called by the doughty Reformers 'Precisians', a modern man would call them parsimonious or perhaps even nit-pickers. The secret of the church, they argued, is to be found in the exactness of its order, discipline and ceremonies and nothing must be decreed and done unless it were lawful according to their highly questionable view of the Scriptures. Indeed, for these Precisian pedants, one must prove oneself in Christ by going back and taking up the yoke of Moses again. Old Testament case law now became the substitute for New Testament grace and the rule of faith and they, outdoing even the Mosaic Law of shadows, pronounced the death penalty on all who did not follow their Precisian ways.

Seeking for new structures, corsets and indeed, straight-jackets to bind in their beliefs, these Neo-Romanists used the freedom the Reformers had gained to plot their new superstructure and plans of church and state rebellion. The first Precisian decree, they maintained, must be to abolish the Episcopacy. This ancient apostolic utility had been the backbone of the English Reformation. The cry was for an entirely new hierarchy. But what could replace New Testament Episcopacy and yet claim to out-do it in Scriptural origins? The answer was found in the New Testament word 'presbyter'. Superintendents called bishops must go, a superintendence called the Presbytery must take its place. The old order must have a new name. Most of the English Reformers could not have cared less whether their Episcopal duties were given a new name or not. They were, however, alarmed to see that their brethren in Christ were giving a new meaning to their new word and claiming divine rights for their presbyteries. They also claimed that every single little detail of their new order was Scriptural and that the English had been under unscriptural orders from the dawn of Christian times. The Church was now first being established on English soil! Such pompous, far-fetched claims caused no great alarm at first as the English Reformers during Elizabeth's glorious reign, did not waste their time on the Precisians' trifles which were inessential to true faith. Richard Cox, Edward VI's tutor, argued that the main business of the Reformation was at best to win people for Christ or at least rescue them from Rome. Once true Christianity was preached and believed in the nation, they could attend to lesser matters. However, Cox was prepared to put up with the Precisians for the gospel's sake, even refraining to kneel in worship at the Lord's Supper when fellowshipping with those who believed, wrongly, that Christ and the Apostles had sat at table on four-legged chairs. He was shocked to find, however, that the Precisians called those 'devilish' who argued that in Christ's day, one reclined at meals. Such haggling about what the Precisians obviously either did not understand or stressed in a totally exaggerated way, led Cox, Jewel and Horn to ask them why, though they claimed to have the grain of the wheat, they spent their time contending about the chaff.

Continental warnings against the English Precisians

The Continental Reformers, however, quickly warned their English brethren of the dangers developing in the Presbyterian system. This rigid institutionalisation had become co-equal with Biblical doctrine in expressing the Precisians' faith and thus they were not reforming the Church but adopting the stance of Rome. Bucer, Calvin, Martyr, Zanchy, Bullinger, Gualter and even Beza who was closest to the British Precisians, denounced the growing crypto-Romanist claims placed on the office of a Presbyter and argued that they themselves had no quarrel whatsoever with the Episcopacy. It was papist abuses of the office which they had deplored; abuses which sadly could and did affect Presbyterianism as easily as any of the many other denominations that Presbyterianism eventually produced. It is one thing to find a Biblical word. It is quite another to fill it with a false content.

Writing from Zürich to Richard Cox, one of the foremost men in the English Reformation, his Swiss counterpart Rudolf Gualter warns his English brother:

... not (to) give encouragement to those promoters of dis-
order, whom either ambitious emulation or even ignorance
has so beguiled, that they are unable to see what makes for
the preservation of our common church. They wish to re-
vive, as you tell me, that ancient presbytery which existed
in the primitive church: but I wish they would think about
reviving that simplicity of faith and purity of morals, which
formerly flourished, and not attack the commonwealth, the
ancient rights and constitution of which Christ does not
change.[3]

The Swiss Reformer stressed the need for purity of religion rather
than precise ceremonies, orders and laws as by this time (March,
1574) the Precisians were claiming for themselves the sole right to
be called Puritans as a result of their outward structure. Gualter is
especially shocked by the Presbyterian policy of redefining the roles
of magistrates and clergy. They thus not only did away with ancient and proved church structures, but also planned an entirely
new system of jurisprudence, though they had not the slightest Biblical precedent for such radical moves, neither in the Old Testament nor the New. Clearly, to Zwingli's successor and son-in-law,
Gualter, the new British Presbyterianism concealed a love for forms
of earthly rule that could very quickly degenerate into tyranny at
which, as he argued clearly, even Romanists would marvel. Gualter
pointed out that both Zwingli and Oecolampadius had warned
against such radical abuses of church power.

Again, this time writing to Bishop Sandys, a former exile under
Mary, Gualter tells his friend:

Many parties now-a-days are insisting upon, I know not
what plan of church government, under the plausible name
of ecclesiastical discipline; and they tell us that no church
can exist without it. But I am greatly afraid, lest they should

---

[3] *Zürich Letters*, Second Series, Letter C. p. 251.

give birth to an aristocracy, which will shortly degenerate into an oligarchy, and be the beginning of a new papacy. [4]

He then gives clear examples of church tyranny practised in Presbyterian circles which illustrate that a new name may disguise an old papist face.

In another letter to Cox, Gualter again condemns the Presbyterians' innovations in the strongest language but advises Cox to deal with them with caution, saying:

> Nevertheless, it should be your endeavour to oppose these troublesome parties with meekness and prudence, lest some more grievous danger may at last arise out of these contentions; or lest those, who are still opposed to purer religion, may find an opportunity of effecting what they have long desired.[5]

Henry Bullinger, one of the main Continental allies of the English Reformation, also wrote to Edwin Sandys, a man known by Rome as 'the greatest heretic in England', warning him of such developments. He explained how the left and right extremities of the Reformation in both the Lutheranism of Germany as it had developed after Luther's death and Presbyterianism as it had been brought to birth in Britain, were but steps back to Rome. Describing the dangers of both extremes, Bullinger links them together and sees the exaggerations of the Lutheran position reflected in England in the exaggerations of Presbyterianism. He tells the balanced bishop:

> Those parties are endeavouring to erect a church, which they will never raise to the height they wish; nor if they should erect it, will they be able to maintain it. I have seen the heads of their fabric as delineated by you, with respect

---

[4] Ibid, Letter XCVI, p. 238.
[5] Ibid, Letter CIV, p. 259.

of which I have long since declared my sentiments. The first proposition, that the civil magistrate has no authority in ecclesiastical matters; and also the second, that the church admits of no other government than that of presbyters, or the presbytery; these two, I say, they hold in common with the papists, who also displace the magistrate from the government of the church, and substitute themselves alone in his place. Whose opinion I have confuted in my refutation of the pope's bull, and in my defence of the queen of England and her noble realm, &c., which I sent two years since. I wish there were no lust of dominion in the originators of this presbytery![6]

Sadly, after a century of sound church rule under Cranmer, Parker, Grindal, Whitgift and Abbot, broken only by the brief tyranny of Mary the Bloody, Rome, the Arminian Laudians and Laudian Presbyterians joined hands to promote what Gualter and his Continental colleagues in their wisdom had foreseen and warned against. Then, for a very brief time of inquisitorial terror, Erastian Presbyterianism was established in England as the state-cum-church, until Pride's Purge brought in a different tyranny claiming an even purer national religion called Congregationalism.

The more direct cause of complaints by Cox, Sandys, Gualter and Bullinger were the novelties of Beza who as he broke away from a strict adherence to Calvin's more lenient principles went over to a more institutionalised view of the Church-at-large, seeing its centre at Geneva which he viewed as '*orbis Christiani oraculum*'. This idea had thrilled such English High Church Presbyterians as Thomas Cartwright[7] and Walter Travers who, caught by the inter-

---

[6] Ibid, Letter XCVIII, pp. 241-242.

[7] Cartwright's form of militant, all-embracing Presbyterianism which included the death penalty for heretics even if they 'repented' was first made public in 1570 through his lectures on Acts given at Cambridge. Cartwright was no Separatist, however, and was to modify his views considerably, eventually returning to the hand he had bitten to be fed. Puritan Archbishop Whitgift, whom Cartwright had made the main target of his slander, gave him a good position with a good salary.

national ideology of a Genevan controlled world-Church went to great extremes to force England, recently free from Rome, to put on the Neo-Genevan, or, as some call it, a Neo-Calvinist, yoke and fill the vacuum left by the ousted papists.

As Beza grew in power, enforcing an external uniformity of Reformed discipline through Europe, he was not without some limited success in England. That land, however, had had enough of foreign tyranny. The English Reformers loved Christian pragmatism rather than dogmas, be they Roman or post-Calvinist Genevan. Calvin's Presbyterian principles were tolerable but the Presbyterianism of Beza was too rigid to tolerate the love of liberty and freedom of conscience that the English loved. This is the reason why Presbyterianism never had much success in claiming the obedience of English independent Christian thought and even when Presbyterian ideology was forced on that land during the Great Rebellion, it did not even last a generation as a spiritual force and soon faded from the political scene.

Seeing that Beza was the greatest single influence on the English rebels, Gualter wrote to him most diplomatically in 1566, but leaving him to read between the lines. In this way Gualter showed Beza that in using his influence so negatively, he was forcing good men to leave the Reformed Church of England over such secondary matters as caps and gowns thus playing into the hands of the enemy who would strive to fill those vacancies with pro-Roman or pro-Lutheran clergy.[8] Gualter (with many other protesters) appears to have been successful in his warning as in 1571 Beza confessed that the English Presbyterians were going to extremes and he wanted no part in their 'indiscreet proceedings'.[9]

Knox and Goodman's books banned in Geneva
Beza wrote to Bullinger on 3 September 1566, asking for his cooperation in sending a peace delegation from the Zürich and Genevan churches to patch up old quarrels with Elizabeth and the Reformed

---

[8] *Zürich Letters*, Letter LVII, pp. 142-146.
[9] See Collinson's *The Elizabethan Puritan Movement*, p. 121.

Church of England. Indeed, developing a common wish to have stronger ties with the English Church drew the Swiss churches, well-known for their bickering past, gradually together. Beza had been upset to find that Queen Elizabeth had not acknowledged a work of his and concluded that he was considered 'hateful' to her. He told Bullinger:

> The reason for her dislike is two-fold: one, because we are accounted too severe and precise, which is very displeasing to those who fear reproof; the other is, because formerly, though without our knowledge, during the lifetime of Queen Mary two books were published here in the English language, one by master Knox against the government of women, the other by master Goodman on the rights of the magistrate. As soon as we learned the contents of each, we were much displeased, and their sale was forbidden in consequence: but she notwithstanding cherishes the opinion she has taken into her head. If therefore you think the present cause worthy of being undertaken by us, it would seem the most suitable plan, and most useful to the brethren, that someone should be chosen from your congregation, if not by the express authority, at least with the permission or connivance of your magistrates, to proceed to England on this special business, and openly solicit from the queen and bishops a remedy for these evils. This would be indeed an heroic action, worthy of your city, and, as I think, very acceptable to God, even though it should not altogether succeed according to our wish.[10]

Naturally the massive support coming from both the major Swiss Reformed churches caused as much alarm amongst the Precisians as it caused joy amongst the Reformers and Anglican Puritans. This caused Miles Coverdale to strive to now bring peace between the Swiss churches and those Precisians who had formerly almost idol-

---

[10] *Zürich Letters*, Second Series, p. 131.

ised their Swiss brethren. On 10 September 1566, Bullinger wrote to Coverdale to defend his position but also to ask him not to use private letters as public ammunition in the vestiarian debate. On this matter, Bullinger maintained:

> My chief object was this, to convince those who think it better to desert the churches than to adopt those habits, that it would be more advisable for them to adopt the habits, and at the same time remain with the churches committed to their charge. But I had no wish to obtrude even this advice upon the brethren inconsiderately, but only to state to them what appeared to me most advisable in this matter, leaving it in the mean time free to themselves to follow what might seem best.[11]

The Precisian-Presbyterian split with the English Reformers back-dated to 1554

Apparently oblivious to the downgrading of the Reformed position demonstrated above, a number of modern critics of the English Reformation love to trace the origin of their political form of Presbyterianism, which they injuriously call Puritanism, to another source. This source, they trace back to the affairs of a relatively small congregation of English exiles in Frankfurt during the brief months of the autumn and winter of 1554-55. Here they see the beginnings of a second Reformation, which, they feel, was more powerful than the first. Here, at Frankfurt, they maintain, the true allegedly Puritan Nonconformist Reformers, whom they call Knoxians, separated from the supposed High Church Conforming Anglicans, whom they call Coxians. These critics of the 16th century Reformation are, however, far from united in their approach to the subject. Some find that the Anglican reforms were higgledy-piggledy, incomplete and inadequate because they put too much faith in experimental doctrine and too little in church order and discipline. However, this view united all the members of the Frank-

---

[11] Ibid, p. 136.

furt congregation and caused no strife whatsoever. There was no separation on such issues. The entire group of Anglicans in Germany sought to unite their gifts and callings in the work of continual renewal and progressive reform. Other fierce critics of the Reformed Church of England, and these seem to become more numerous as Presbyterian influence grows once again and Anglican influence declines, do not see any reformation in the Anglican Church at all. The simple, naive reasons given are that it was not a Presbyterian movement, it was not carried out by political motives, it did not upset the on-going church and state, it did not enforce case law and did not cause an all-cleansing rebellion. What it *did do* is simply ignored. Thus hard-line critics of the English Reformation such as Dr Martyn Lloyd-Jones[12] virtually write off the great victories of the Reformation against popish innovations because they did not bring in the equally innovating factors of Presbyterianism, separatism, and, one would suspect, revolutionary Republicanism. Happily, however, there are modern writers such as Packer, Hindson, Martin and Murray[13] who give a far more balanced and comprehensive picture of the Puritans. Nevertheless, in recent years there has developed a highly alarming, superstitious adherence to Dr Lloyd-Jones' political and revolutionary interpretation of true Reformation. Such enthusiasts who follow this line are so keen to persuade men of the validity of their para-Reformation, revolutionary ideas that history is being steadily, though possibly unwittingly, re-written concerning the so-called *Troubles at Frankfort*. The great challengers of Rome such as Cox, Grindal, Whitehead, Sampson, Jewel, Sandys, Lever and Fox(e) are depicted as if they were dyed in the wool papists at heart. Yet the extreme forms of liturgical, disciplinary and political novelties introduced by the Precisians, embodied in Frankfurt by John Knox are praised as true Reformation indeed. Yet these Precisians would not budge an inch on secondary, and even tertiary matters, and even rejected as a child of the devil their brother in Christ who could not adopt their ill-founded ceremonies

---

[12] See Lloyd-Jones' extraordinarily naive and badly documented work *The Puritans*.
[13] See Bibliography.

and legalism. Andrew Lang warns of such hagiographical commentators on Knoxian principles, stating that the shocking writings of Knox are not, as a rule, set before the public by biographers of the Reformer, and adds:

> Mr Carlyle introduced a style of thinking about Knox which may be called platonically Puritan. Sweet enthusiasts glide swiftly over all in the Reformer that is specially distasteful to us.[14]

Tackling the distasteful to demonstrate the truth

It is high time, however, that modern day Christians should tackle things 'specially distasteful' in Presbyterian history in order to test the claims of this movement which sees true Reformation as being only in their ranks. It might be thought all very well for a fan to adore his idol if it were not for the fact that such blandishment shown by believers in Knox's policies seems to be invariably accompanied by a denigrating of his fellow-Reformers. It is as if the latter must be placed in the shadow so that their hero might shine. This principle, of course, distorts the true picture of our Reformers and not only exaggerates the differences and ignores the similarities between them but creates artificial contentions which seriously harm church unity and fellowship in Christ. If this writer appears to be rather hard on the single person Knox in comparison to his view of the bulk of English Reformers, it must be realised that the latter have been given such a bad, even wicked and criminal image by recent lovers of Knox. It is high time that the balance was rectified. Such Anglicans and fellow-exiles as Lever, Becon, Bale, Grindal, Jewel and Fox must be seen as meeting the needs of Nonconformist Puritans to a far greater extent than Knox.

The following story of the trouble-makers at Frankfurt, is an attempt to peep behind the myth-building which has been going on for centuries in the Episcopalian-Presbyterian controversy and look at the early leaders of the English Reformation as they were and

---

[14] *John Knox and the Reformation*, pp. ix-x.

not as they have been made to appear. This can only be done by digging out contemporary documents and studying these people as they lived and died in their day rather than view them through the eyes of modern secondary literature. Happily, this task is none too laborious as this period is one of the best documented in church history, though, nowadays, one of the most ignored. Here then is my attempt to wipe off the patina, rust and rot of days gone by. I wish also to rid my story of the anachronistic juggling of some party-minded modern authors. This will be done chiefly by viewing the English exiled Reformers in the light which shone from their own personalities and callings and through the descriptions found in their own writings and in the records of those who knew them.

Queen Mary
(Mary the Bloody)

Chapter One:
A Brief Analysis of the Situation

The exiled church finds a home from home

Acting under the words of our Lord concerning shaking off the dust and moving on where the gospel falls on barren ground, many English, Scottish and Irish Christians fled their countries when the tares of Mary's bloody reign and French influence in Scotland choked true religion. Most of these exiles journeyed to Holland, Germany and Switzerland though others moved to far-away Scandinavia, Austria, Spain, Italy and Poland. In these countries, they received various stages of asylum ranging from suspicious tolerance to enthusiastic support. Anywhere, it seemed, was safer than in Britain. Sadly, the British exiles were often less tolerated in states which professed to be Protestant than by those which owned their allegiance to Roman Catholic princes and dukes. This was chiefly because of the prevailing view of consubstantiation on the Continent and the watering down of Luther's doctrine which occurred under Melancthon.[1]

The foreign churches which had been licensed by Edward to be constituted freely in England also fled the country during Mary's tyranny, often to meet their English brethren again on the same church premises abroad. Many of the most prominent scholars of the Reformation settled in Zürich[2], those with affluent friends

---

[1] Melancthon himself was very gracious to the English exiles and gave them a degree of protection.
[2] Called Tigury by the English exiles.

amongst the merchants fled to Emden and others made for Wesel, Duisburg[3], Strasburg[4], Aarau[5] and Frankfurt[6]. The latter imperial city, ruled by Charles V through a Senate, had already provided asylum for the French Church and warmly invited the English to join their French brethren, providing them with spacious accommodation in the formerly papist Church of the White Ladies (Weißfrauenkirche). Because of its relatively easy access from England and its centrality in Continental Europe, the exiles' congregation at Frankfurt was larger than the gatherings of exiles in other towns and on 29 July 1554 became the first organised and constituted church amongst the refugees. However, the church's membership never remained stable as Frankfurt functioned as an initial gathering place before the English found employment elsewhere or received invitations to other regions. Also, a number of members travelled extensively amongst the exiles of the Continental Diaspora doing evangelistic and courier work. Indeed, the wanderings of Thomas Lever are typical of this time. His letters to the Swiss Reformer, Henry Bullinger, show that he moved regularly between Wesel, Aarau, Zürich, Basle, Geneva and Frankfurt. Fuller tells us that the travels and travails of the British exiles proved that Christians have no biding cities.

The disappointments but also sturdy hopes of those forced into exile are beautifully expressed in a fragment of a letter preserved in the British Museum. John Fox, safely harboured amongst friends in Germany, welcomes a young, once rich, newly married couple who had gone through terrible hardships because of Mary's purge of their family. The saint, whose works are esteemed as one of the greatest pillars of the English Reformation, writes:

> When I understood, by your friendly letters sent to my brother, what our good God and most sweet Father hath done for you and other members of his mystical body, in

---

[3] Called Densborugh by the English exiles.
[4] Called Argentine by the English exiles.
[5] Called Arrow by the English exiles. Aarau is in Switzerland.
[6] Spelt Frankfort by the English exiles.

delivering you out of that miserable land, from the danger of idolatry and fearful company of Herodians; I was compelled, with a glad heart, to render unto his Divine Majesty most humble thanks, beseeching him that as he hath delivered you from their contagious venom and deathly sting with safe conscience, so he will vouchsafe to protect and preserve it still undefiled. To forsake your country, to despite your commodities at home, to contemn riches, and to set naught by honours which the whole world hath in great veneration, for the love of the sweet gospel of Christ, are not works of the flesh, but the most assured fruits of the Holy Ghost and undeceiveable arguments of your regeneration, or new birth, whereby God certifieth you that ye are justified in him, and sealed to eternal life. And therefore ye have great cause to be thankful; first that he hath chosen you to life, and, secondly that he hath given you his Holy Spirit, which hath altered and changed you into a new creature, working in you through the word such a mind, that these things are not painful but pleasant unto you.[7]

The Frankfurt documents
The story of this dark patch in the history of the Reformation can be traced in the two Parker Society volumes entitled *Original Letters* from 1537-1558 and in the society's large volume of *Zurich Letters (1558-1602), Second Series*. The name given the controversy is taken from that unique and fascinating collection of documents and comments, *A Brief Discourse of the Troubles at Frankfort (1554-1558)*. David Laing, in his six-volume collection *The Works of John Knox*, has placed most of these documents in his fourth volume and assisted his readers further by providing copious notes and helps for further reading. A much neglected, indeed, totally neglected, source in the revived modern debate of the troubles at Frankfurt is the Church Service Society's 1905 publication of the *Second Prayer Book of Edward VI* of 1552 and the *Liturgy of Compromise* drawn up at Frankfurt in 1554. The latter MS was considered lost

---

[7] *Writings of John Fox*, RTS, p. vii.

for centuries until it was rediscovered in an old cabinet by a Mr and Mrs Collis, Leicester dealers in antique furniture, around 1865. Other 16th century documents were found in the cabinet in Thomas Sampson's handwriting. Sampson, a Nonconformist, had opposed Knox at Frankfurt and obviously had the *Liturgy of Compromise* MS in his possession when he returned to England. The Reformer and Puritan died in Leicester in 1589 and was probably the former owner of the cabinet which had remained in Leicester over the centuries. A lawyer named Nevinson purchased the documents and both Professor Lorimer and George Sprott sought permission to publish them but Mr Nevinson always claimed he would publish them himself. Nevinson died in 1900 without fulfilling his ambition and the documents came into the possession of his brother who was too ill to enter into negotiations concerning the MS. A year later, this gentleman died and a near relative wrote to George Sprott to say that she was willing to sell the documents. Sprott tried to obtain them for a Scottish library but the British Museum bid higher. However, Sprott was allowed to transcribe and photograph the *Liturgy of Compromise*. He was able to publish the liturgy in 1905 and commented extensively on the historical and theological situation in the Frankfurt church.

There is much material on the German side which has also been totally neglected in English-speaking appraisals and evaluations of the troubles at Frankfurt. The *Bürgermeisterbücher* (Lord Mayor's Records) the *Ratsprotokolle* and the *Ratschlagungsprotokolle* (corporation minutes and records) give most interesting background and inside information to the troubles, recording all the dealings of the English with the Senate or Corporation, their business transactions, their building proposals, their complaints, the occupations they followed and the taxes they paid. Other facts are revealed, not available in the English records such as the large numbers of refugees from Britain during the 1550s which ran into several thousands and not a few hundred as commonly supposed. Also, it is clear from the records that the term 'English' covered all the refugees from England, be they French, Dutch or English and that particularly the Dutch were often called English in the town records. Furthermore, completely unmentioned in the English accounts is that the Dutch initially worshipped with the British until they received their own church at the end of 1555 through the auspices of Jan Laski, also called John Alasco or à Lasco. This much neglected man of God pioneered the Reformation in Poland, then moved to East Frisia where he became the First Superintendent of the Reformed Church in 1543, then he helped to pioneer the English Reformation and established the Church at Wesel before moving to Frankfurt in 1555 where he founded a Dutch Reformed Church. It might easily be that after further research, we shall find that Laski was as great a Reformer as Wycliffe, Luther, Calvin, Latimer and the other stalwarts who have the sole advantage over Laski that we know more about them at the present time. Other detailed works by German and Dutch authors on this period are Karl Bauer's *Die Beziehung Calvins zur Frankfurt am Main*, Leipzig, 1920 and his *Valerand Poullain*, Elberfeld, 1927; Hermann Dalton's *Johannes a Lasco: Beitrag zur Reformationsgeschichte Polens, Deutschlands und Englands*, Gotha, 1881; G. A. Besser's *Geschichte der Frankfurter Flüchtlingsgemeinden 1554-1558*, Halle, 1906; Rudolf Jung's *Die englishche Flüchtlings-Gemeinden in Frankfurt 1554-1559* and the German sources listed in the Bibliography at the end of this book.

Most important for dating the arrival of the English refugees in Germany is the work of Professor J. H. Withof of Duisburg University. In 1752, whilst doing research on the history of Duisburg, Withof found that a large number of English exiles (viele Engländer) had visited that city in 1553, after the death of Edward and on Mary's becoming Queen. This party then left for Frankfurt that winter. Thus we have one of the earliest indications that the English were in Frankfurt long before the *Troubles at Frankfort* indicate. Withof collected together all the MSS he could find relating to the Frankfurt refugee churches and commented on them briefly in the City Chronicles and in detail in five consecutive issues of the *Wochentliche Duisburgische Adresse- und Intelligentz-Zettel* (Nr. XII-XVI, 1752), which was a continuation of his *Duisburger Chronik* (1740/42). Withof relates how the troubles at Frankfurt were still being debated by 'many thousands' and that 'countless documents' on the subject had come to light. It appears from

Withof's account that the theological and political problems involved when the German Lutherans in Frankfurt and other German cities were confronted by the Reformed refugees from England had enlivened European-wide theological debate for two hundred years, though today few apparently know of the struggles Reformed believers had during their exile. Withof, who sides strongly with the Anglicans and Valerand Poullain, lays much of the blame for the refugees' sufferings on the Continent at the feet of Lutheran Joachim Westphal who, Withof says, 'screamed blue murder'[8] at the Reformed men from England.[9] Withof's work entails a defence of Valerand Poullain in a similar way to my defence of the Anglican refugees in this book. He has thus much to say concerning the pastor of the French-speaking refugee church in Frankfurt, giving insight into the quite unfounded rumours that eventually caused Calvin to turn from Poullain. I had the privilege of visiting the Duisburg City Archives and digging out Prof. Withof's own notes on the subject and his corrected proofs of his *Duisburger Chronik* and *Adresse- und Intelligentz-Zettel*, though I was disappointed to hear that the numerous original documents which Withof had compiled were 'within reasonable certainty' lost in a subsequent fire which devastated parts of Duisburg. In 1754 Whithof re-published in full Poullain's first Frankfurt *Liturgia Sacra* and Confession of Faith with other relevant documents under the title *Wahrhafte Liturgie Und Bekänntniß Des Glaubens, Wie solche von den zu Franckfurt am Mayn Angekommenen Reformirten Vor 200 Jahren überreicht worden, Nach dem ersten authenticken Lateinischen Druck Auf Begehren wieder ans Licht gegeben, Und mit einer Teutschen Uebersetzung samt Vorrede versehen, Von Johann Hildebrand Withof, Professor der Universität zu Duisburg am Rhein. DUISBURG, Gedruckt bey Johann Sebastian Straube, Universitäts-Buchdrucker, 1754.* I had set my heart on finding this publication but sadly, the Duisburg archives on searching diligently, pronounced the collection, 'missing

---

[8] Zetter-Geschrey (Zeter-Geschrei).
[9] *Duisburger Chronik* entry for 1554. Unpaginated proofs interspersed with blank pages and Withof's notes. *Addresse- und Intelligenz-Zettel*, XII, double page 592 (pagination stamped in at later date).

believed lost'. However, the research done at the Duisburg Archives and City Library relied on modern catalogues which, I found, had dropped many ancient documents. My 'last resort' was thus to Dr Alfons Ballweg, the Duisburg University Library resident historian who had helped me find ancient, unrecorded documents in the past. Using older catalogues, he was able to trace a copy of Withof's compilation back to the Frankfurt City Archives who kindly loaned me their copy. Dr Ballweg also discovered copies of the *Liturgia Sacra* of Poullain's Frankfurt church at the Göttingen Niedersächsische Staats- und Universitätsbibliothek; at the Augsburg Universitätsbibliothek; at Frankfurt Stadt- und Universitäts-bibliothek; at the Württembergische Landesbibliothek at the Regensburg Staatliche Bibliothek at the München Universitäts-bibliothek (storeroom) and at the Leipzig Stadtbibliothek. There is also a copy in the British Library, British Museum.

Relevant to our subject, Günter von Roden was authorised by the City of Duisburg in 1973 to bring the city's history up to date. In his subsequent work *Geschichte der Stadt Duisburg, Band I, Das alte Stadt Duisburg von den Anfängen bis 1905*[10], von Roden records a number of interesting details concerning the Marian refu-gees from England. Of note is the fact that it was the Anglicans who first introduced the 'Calvinistic Lord's Supper' to Duisburg in 1553[11]. Amongst these early refugees was Richard Cox who passed through the city on route to Frankfurt[12]. The Knoxians were later to argue, quite against such evidence, that the Coxians were anti-Reformed in their view of the Lord's Supper and that Cox was a member of the anti-Reformed Strasburg group of English refu-gees. Actually, the fact that a relatively large group of Anglicans had fled to Strasburg showed that they were highly Reformed as Strasburg was the home of the Reformation which gave rise to Calvin's Calvinism. Furthermore, Poullain with whom the Angli-cans were on the best of footings, had co-pastored with Bucer at Strasburg where Reformed giants such as Paul Fagius, John Sturm

---

[10] Walter Braun Verlag, Duisburg, 1973.
[11] Op. cit. p. 264.
[12] Ibid, p. 264.

and Peter Martyr also taught, strengthened by the support of the politically influential Jacob Sturm. Bucer, Fagius, Martyr and John Sturm were all highly influential in promoting the Reformation in England. When Calvin, already much indebted to Bucer, was ousted from Geneva from 1538-1543, he sought asylum at Strasburg, and obviously relied heavily on Strasburg teaching in developing his own forms of worship and theological system.

Another work of great importance to students of the Marian refugee churches in Germany is Petrus Dathenus' study, published by Löw in 1598, entitled *Kurtze und warhaftige erzelung, welche massen den Frantzösischen und Niderländischen der wahren Religion halben verjagten Christen in der Stadt Franckfurt im vier und fünffzigsten und etliche volgende jar die offentliche predig Göttliches worts und ausspendung der H. Sacramenten in ihrer sprach verstattet und auß was ursachen ihnen nachmals solches verbotten worden ist.* Copies are available in the ancient Wolfenbüttel Library of Lessing fame and at the Jena University Library, but they may not be copied or loaned from there.

A book which ought not to be neglected in a study of the Protestant exiles of 1553-59, though it is more of a curiosity than a helpful history, is Christina Hallowell Garrett's book *The Marian Exiles*, published in 1938 and reprinted by Oxford University Press in 1966. Actually, Garrett has put a good deal of sound research into her book concerning Aarau, Basle and Strasburg, which, however, has little bearing on the extraordinary conclusions she makes, but a number of her mini-biographies are helpful. Though Garrett deals almost entirely with theologians and theological issues, she insists that she will only judge them politically and thus decides that all the protestant refugees were engaged in active treason or sedition when Mary came to the throne. Yet, because of the magnanimity of the Queen, they were kindly permitted to migrate, whereas any less gracious monarch would have put them all in irons or worse. Thus there can be no talk of a 'flight' and really no talk of an 'exile'. Indeed, Queen Mary, quite contrary to the evidence, most of which Garrett thinks is 'sham', gave the refugees 'ample time' to gather their belongings together and book ships and, merely for form's sake, first sent officers to apprehend them after she knew they had already left the country. Thus, Garrett concludes, 'Naive stories of their hairbreadth escapes from England carry no conviction with them.'[13]

Once the Frankfurt refugees had found a new home, Garrett tells us, Valerand Poullain obtained an authorisation from the city's council on 18 March 1554 *'to organise their cult.'*[14] Apart from this reference, Garrett says very little indeed about the real troubles at Frankfurt. According to her, the entire mix-up was caused by political intrigues managed by various rival lords in England who sent leading churchmen of different persuasions to Germany on political missions. She tells us 'If Frankfurt aimed at democratic unity, Strasbourg was looking to aristocratic hegemony among the English colonies, preparatory to a struggle against the royal prerogative. Independency at Frankfurt, whiggery at Strasbourg, found such a fertile soil for growth in the freedom of exile.'[15] Though Garrett claims that Northumberland and Cecil were behind the troubles between the Knoxians and Coxians, the available sources, including those that Garrett uses, show this to have been of most secondary significance, if any at all. Her idea that Cox was also acting under the orders of less influential Ponet also appears to be sheer speculation.[16]

Garrett's perhaps most interesting comment is that she believes that the *Liturgy of Compromise*, worked out traditionally before the Strasburg contingent reached Frankfurt and now preserved in Sprott and Wotherspoon's joint work *Second Prayer Book of Edward VI*, is not what it appears to be but the work of Cox, Coverdale, Sampson and other 'chief Edwardian divines' after Knox's expulsion.[17] The circumstantial evidence, she gives, e.g. chiefly Whitehead's letter to Calvin of 20 September 1555, does not even hint at such a possibility.

Another most unusual book is entitled *John Knox and the Troubles Begun at Frankfurt* which was photo-copied and bound at

---

[13] Op. cit, 'Migration or Flight', pp. 4, 11-13.
[14] Ibid, p. 48. My emphasis.
[15] Ibid, p. 329.
[16] Ibid, p. 135.
[17] Ibid, p. 135.

Econoprint, Edinburgh and distributed privately in type-script format in 1975 by its author M. A. Simpson, the Assistant Editor of the *Edinburgh Source Book for British History 1603-1707*. The work is introduced as a critical commentary on the 1846 reprint of the *Troubles at Frankfort*, John Knox's narrative of the events and Rudolf Jung's 1910 account of the Frankfurt refugees. As will be seen below, there is just cause to suspect the motives behind the compilation of records known as *A Brief Discourse of the Troubles at Frankfort (1554-1558)* and there has also been some careful editing of the original sources. However, Simpson, finds the collection so riddled with interpolations and re-writings from the 1570s that they are historically worthless apart from giving insight into the dubious ways later anti-Anglicans carried out their attempts to discredit the English Prayer Book. However, Simpson extends this scepticism concerning documents, not only to the collection of texts included in the *Troubles at Frankfort* but to the writings of Calvin, Grindal, Ridley and other Reformers and exiles, in fact to all documents and writers which have anything whatsoever to do with the Marian exile and Elizabethan Settlement, including the Parker Society records. The result is that not only does Simpson argue that there were no troubles at Frankfurt, he also argues that the entire Cox-Knox issue never took place, or, if it did, it was not in the form recorded. Indeed, if Simpson's 'findings' were true, we would be left with a nigh historical blank concerning the Frankfurt church during the years 1553 to 1559.

It might be supposed that one who so radically deals with the records has a mass of counter evidence at his disposal. This is far from being the case. We are told without any substantial evidence whatsoever that the 1575 editor cut out pages of the original accounts and inserted 'what suited his purpose better'[18]. Simpson finds 'cause for suspicion' in almost every record, finding them riddled with 'late insertions'[19]. Every time he finds a, for him, puzzling statement or what he thinks is an 'irrelevant argument' he states

---

[18] Op. cit. p. 68.
[19] Ibid, p. 67.

that, 'the passage appears to us to be an interpolation'[20]. The author even doubts whether the signatures under letters used in the accounts are genuine.[21] Simpson repeatedly argues that there was no debate about the Prayer Book at all and anything put into Knox's mouth, or anybody else's against it was a falsification.[22]

Needless to say, Simpson builds very much on Garrett but extends her speculations enormously. This is a pity as Simpson has also done good research into sources and biography but has allowed his convictions to overcloud his interpretative judgement. I am fully in agreement with Simpson's basic conviction that the *Troubles at Frankfort* was a highly polemic work, but this conviction hardly justifies suggesting that there was no trouble at Frankfurt at all and all the documents which might be thought able to shed light on the story are either forgeries or documents applying to later controversies partly rewritten and back-dated to the Marian exile.

Most commentators who are antagonistic to the position taken by Knox's Frankfurt critics, rely almost exclusively on the first part of *A Brief Discourse of the Troubles at Frankfort, 1554-1558 A.D.*, published in 1575 and commonly called *Troubles at Frankfort*, for brevity's sake. Horton-Davies tells us that 'It is written by a contemporary and from the radical Puritan standpoint of a member of Knox's party.'[23] He argues that 'with considerable probability' McCrie is correct in attributing the authorship to William Whittingham who was one of the founder members of the Frankfurt church of English exiles.

This early Reformer and Puritan was one of the main characters in the story of the troubles. He was born in Westchester of a Lancastrian family around 1524 and entered Brazenose College, Oxford at fifteen or sixteen years of age, eventually becoming a Fellow of Cardinal Wolsey's college, Christ Church. Whittingham left England in May, 1550 to travel through France and Italy but stayed for two or three years at Orleans where he fell in love with

---

[20] Ibid, p. 40.
[21] Ibid, p. 146.
[22] Ibid, p. 42.
[23] *The Worship of the Early Puritans*, p. 27.

Louise Jacqueman who accepted his proposal of marriage. His knowledge of French and good bearing caused Ambassador Sir William Pickering to use him as interpreter and agent at the French court. Whittingham continued his studies whilst in France and then travelled to Germany and Geneva before returning to England shortly before the death of Edward. On hearing that Mary had been proclaimed Queen, Whittingham returned to France where he stayed for almost a year. When he heard that the English exiles were setting up a church at Frankfurt, he decided to join his fellow-countrymen in Germany.

Nothing is known of Whittingham's spiritual or doctrinal background up to this period, though the fact that he did not wish to live in England under Mary suggests that he was of Reformed persuasion. Whittingham, however had had no call to the ministry and had not received ordination. He became pastor of the Genevan English Church for a short time in 1559 and may have had some kind of ordination then. On returning to England, Whittingham was given the Deanery of Durham through the influence of the Earl of Warwick. Though not ordained in the Church of England sense, Whittingham's position was never seriously challenged. He did have trouble in later years, however, through a competence controversy with his bishop.

Patrick Collinson, however, claims that Whittingham had little to do with the authorship of *Troubles at Frankfort* apart from providing the transcript of one letter from Calvin. He suggests that a more probably author is found in Thomas Wood, his evidence being:

> The materials were drawn from the archives of the English congregation at Geneva, which apparently included documents which the puritan group had taken with them in their secession from Frankfort in 1555. These had been in the possession of Thomas Wood, one of the elders, when the congregation dispersed after 1559.[24]

---

[24] *The Elizabethan Puritan Movement*, p. 153.

This theory, however, cannot be taken as conclusive. The facts show that either there were a variety of different compilers, editors and annotators, or if the book was the work of one editor, he must have altered his opinions from ultra radical in 1554 to moderate and flexible by 1559. What is most definite is that the documents thus collected were written by several authors in different areas who were by no means in agreement with one another. Relatively few of the documents in the book deal with the period between the summer of 1554 to the summer of 1555 i.e. the period between the church's constitution and the departure of the so-called Knoxians for Basle and Geneva. The bulk of the material traces the controversies in the church from Knox's departure from Frankfurt up to Elizabeth's early reign. Furthermore, contrary to the accounts of a number of writers who seek to discover the first Anglican-Puritan split at Frankfurt, the departing group did not consist of the main body of Puritans (as opposed to Anglicans) in the Church at all but was composed of a very small mixed minority. Neal's argument, and that of the many who use him as their authority, is quite wrong in affirming that the entire original Frankfurt church, before Cox's party joined them, departed in 1555 on the grounds that the 'Anglicans' would not keep to the original church order. The editor of the 1837 Tegg edition of *The History of the Puritans*, reprinted in 1979, states that in Neal's original work, due to a faulty reading of *Troubles at Frankfort*, the author thought that the Frankfurt church had continued two years with the same order before 1555.[25] After being corrected, probably by Bishop Maddox, Neal altered this to nine months. In reality, the early order, if ever one was indeed drawn up, must have been revised almost immediately and cannot have lasted more than a few weeks. Indeed, the evidence is that before Knox's arrival there was no formal and complete order of service and mutual agreement in the church was first obtained in November, 1554, Knox alone being the one who refused to comply. No sooner had Knox arrived at Frankfurt that November than the troubles started and we read:

---

[25] *History of the Puritans*, Vol. I, p. 81.

At length, it was agreed that the Order of Geneva which then was already printed in English, and some copies there among them, should take place, as an Order most godly, and farthest off from superstition. But Master Knox, being spoken unto, as well to put that Order in practice as to minister the Communion, refused to do either the one or the other . . . neither yet would he minister the Communion by the Book of England.[26]

It would be thus more probable that the author was one who had not left Frankfurt in the early days but continued there for some years. Moreover, it is difficult to trace Wood's movements from leaving Frankfurt in 1555. Collinson repeatedly claims that Wood was an elder of the English church of exiles in Geneva, but the list of office-bearers who penned a letter of reconciliation to the Frankfurt brethren on 15 December 1558, the only letter from the Genevan church recorded in *Troubles at Frankfort*, does not include Wood's name.

In an 1846 reprint of *Troubles*, McCrie suggests Whitehead continued the narrative after Whittingham's departure from Frankfurt but Garrett disagrees, naming Thomas Cole, the former Dean of Sarum.[27] However, the reference which Garrett gives merely refers to a private letter of Cole's which gives no indication whatsoever that he was 'continuing the narrative'.[28] Simpson suspects that John Field, who took no part in the Frankfurt story, was the man, possibly because Field was a radical opponent of the Prayer Book and had collected a number of documents, known as his 'Register' appertaining to the Anglican-Precisian controversies. Field had also a reputation for not keeping to the objective truth. Simpson, however, admits that his opinion is a mere 'conjecture'.[29]

---

[26] See *Troubles at Frankfort*, p. 42.
[27] Garrett, p. 1 n.
[28] Ibid, pp. 94-95. Garrett is using the 1846 edition.
[29] Simpson, p. 13.

The different stages in the history of the troubles

a. The Coxian-Knoxian controversy

Indeed, the material provided in *Troubles at Frankfort* and the variety of views expressed in the book suggest that at least three authors took part in the compilation, editing and annotating the work. The first documents covering the period 1554-5 are aggressively anti-'Anglican' and pro-'Knoxian' and most biased in their selection of documents. Even this earlier part of the book may, however, have a multiple authorship as the compiler looks on Cox as the disturber of peace but the pro-Knox texts produced virtually exonerate Cox and Knox is presented as viewing pastor Thomas Lever, as his chief opponent.

b. Financial strife

The following accounts, outlining the financial controversies which plagued the supposed non-Puritan church, can hardly have been written by an outsider and show that the commonly held idea that all the supposed Puritans left in 1555 and all the High Church remained is quite untrue. The remaining church, a body of some hundred men, not including their families and servants, had a pastor, preacher, elder, deacon ministry who were elected by a common vote. Their ministers wore no vestments, did not use an 'altar' or even candles on the Lord's Table, and neither made the sign of the cross nor did they decorate their church with a crucifix. The church up to the summer of 1555 had suffered greatly under controversies ranged around the order of worship, now the controversies were between the poorer of the church and the richer and their various representatives.

The only controversy that arose here on worship was in the baptismal service. One group wished to keep Godparents as a practical utility should true parents die. It must be remembered at this time that the lives of the exiles were often in great peril. Another faction maintained that only true parents were able to perform the rights of those in covenant with God and not Godparents, therefore the latter were superfluous.

c. Problems concerning discipline

A third stage in the history of the Frankfurt church was the question of discipline. In 1557, during a period when the church had no officers, the Senate dictated that a so-called Second New Discipline should be drawn up, which became the centre of heated debate. This debate was a most petty business and did not deal with the fundamentals of the Reformed faith as did the earlier. Indeed, one can hardly imagine sound Christian men arguing as they did. Apparently, the task of drawing up the order of discipline was given to fifteen of the congregation. Of this number, two, Robert Horn(e) and Richard Chambers, opted out whilst the finishing touches were being made. Thereafter the order was presented to the church and forty-two further members, including their one-time pastor David Whitehead said they would accept it. Immediately Horn and Chambers protested that the opinion of twenty-four of the members could not be respected. These were poor members of the congregation, the two men argued, and thus would naturally vote with those who were assisting them financially. This was tantamount to both saying that the bulk of those whom Horn and Chambers opposed were open to bribery and also that poor members of the congregation should not be allowed to vote. Horn and Chambers also complained that the democratic way the congregation was being run undermined the status of pastors and elders. Whitehead asked the two if they wished to abolish what he called 'the authority and liberty of the congregation', which it seemed they did. He furthermore accused the two of wishing to run the congregation between them with Horn as the pastor and Chambers as the man with the money. On 21 December a further twenty-eight exiles joined the church and subscribed to the New Discipline, which left approximately 85-90 members in favour and 12 against. The 12 led by Horn and Chambers subsequently left Frankfurt for Geneva.

The point here is that in the first section, Whitehead is shown as being one of the major instigators against Knox and 'right' religion, whereas, in this section, though there is hardly any editor's comment as in the first section, Whitehead is certainly displayed as having the better arguments and supporting the general body of the church. Edmund Sutton, too, comes off here very well, though he is labelled as being 'on the wrong side' in the earlier section. More interesting still is the fact that Horn and his party had always represented the more High Church and Prayer Book Conformist party at Frankfurt but they now moved not to Basle but joined those former brethren at Geneva who had left Frankfurt, for allegedly totally different reasons. The Genevan brethren obviously welcomed this move and the compiler of this section of *Troubles at Frankfort* writes:

> Not long after this, (the New Discipline dispute) Master Horne and Master Chambers came by Aarau to Geneva; seeming at the time, to like very well of those Congregations, as the Church of Frankfurt then did, as appeareth by their Letters afore: insomuch that the said Masters Horne and Chambers did distribute largely to the necessity of those Churches. So that it appeared that the old grudge, which had been between the Churches of Frankfurt and Geneva, had been clean forgotten.[30]

d. The period of reconciliation
The reader is left to presume that if what might be called the right and left flanks of the Frankfurt church were now amiably united, then there was no question of the more moderate on both sides being in agreement. This proved to be the case. It is worthy of note that in these sturdy efforts at reconciliation, Knox is nowhere mentioned, though his signature does appear below Goodman's and Coverdale's in Geneva's Eirenicon to the churches of Aarau and Frankfurt. These facts go to show that much modern black and white interpretation of the troubles at Frankfurt is quite contrary to the facts and that highly artificial lines of demarcation have been drawn up between supposed 'Puritans' and supposed 'Anglicans'.

The final section of *Troubles at Frankfort* emphasises this reconciliation and shows clearly how full fellowship between the quarrelling churches was restored. Indeed, the compiler highly exoner-

---

[30] P. 222.

ates Thomas Lever who was seen, wrongly, of course, as the principle instigator of High Church practices in the first section. Here, we find Lever doing his successful best to promote peace amongst the exile churches and the general tone of the documents produced show that Frankfurt and Geneva are as close together as seems to make no difference. In other words, from a most anti-Anglican position at the beginning of the book, the authorship proceeds to show that the estranged factions, if they ever were as estranged as the writer of the first section indicated, gradually came to drop their differences in the united hope that Elizabeth would usher in a new time of peace and true Reformation. Indeed, the author or authors of the *Troubles at Frankfort* comes very near to ending with the words, 'and they all lived happily ever after'. Thus Thomas Fuller, who merely relates the story more or less verbatim from *Troubles at Frankfort*, is not saying too much when he concludes *Troubles at Frankfort* is 'a book composed in favour of the opposers of the *English discipline*; and when the *Writer* is all for the *Plaintif*, the discreet Reader, will not only be an unpartial Judge, but also somewhat of an *Advocate* for the *Defendant*.' This is very true. Though the volume-long account of what went on at Frankfurt starts as a defence of the alleged Knoxians, the total facts given clearly produce an acquittal for the so-called Anglican Party. John Strype in his biographies of Grindal and Parker as also in his *History of the Reformation*, gives excellent primary and secondary evidence concerning the troubles which thoroughly endorse this positive, optimistic conclusion.

Finally, it must be understood that the last editor of these documents wrote in 1575 at a time when the Precisian revolt against the Reformed Church of England was weakening and they were losing face not only in England but also on the Continent. This brought a concerted attempt amongst the Precisians to establish their position on historical grounds, attacking not only the Coxians who were now, on the whole, fully established in the Reformed Church of England, but also the 'turncoats', i.e. those Precisians and Romanists who had now also adopted the forms of worship as proscribed in the Elizabethan Settlement. Thus the editor, without revealing his name, writes:

Considering then, how many ways we are unjustly burdened, and brought into hatred without cause; I suppose that no godly man would be offended, if by such lawful means as I might, I sought both to purge myself and the rest of my brethren from such heinous and odious crimes as some would seem to charge us. And that could I not do so well any way, as by the gathering together of this Discourse: wherein the indifferent (impartial) Reader shall find, That the Religion which we hold and profess is not only the true and sincere Religion of Christ, and the self-same with all the Reformed Churches in Christendom; but also (with) that which this Realm hath established, touching the true Doctrine commonly taught therein.

By this Discourse also, it may be seen, both When, Where, How, and By whom, this Controversy first began: Who continued it, Who was on the suffering side, and Who (was) readiest to forget and forgive, that godly peace and concord be had.[31]

The editor goes on to affirm that he had kept these matters secret for twenty years for the sake of peace but now he must unburden his heart. Professor Arber, taking the editor to be Whittingham, comments that the additional information he himself supplies 'puts a very different light to that which Whittingham's honest, but incomplete, History would do.'[32] May the information supplied by this book also serve to present a fuller, balanced and honest picture of the events during 1554-58 in the imperial city of Frankfurt.

---

[31] Ibid, pp. 233-34.
[32] Ibid, p. xxviii.

A Brieff difcours

off the troubles begonne at Franck
ford in Germany AnnoDomini 1554. Abowte
the Booke off off common prayer and Ceremonies / and conti=
nued by the Englishe men theyer / to thende off Q. Maries
Raigne / in the which difcours / the gentle reader shall see
the very originall and beginninge off all the
contention that hathe byn / and what was
the cause off the same.

Marc. 4.

For there is nothinge hid that shall not be o=
pened neither is there a secreat but that it shall co=
me to light / yff anie man haue eares to heare / let
him heare.

M. D. LXXV.

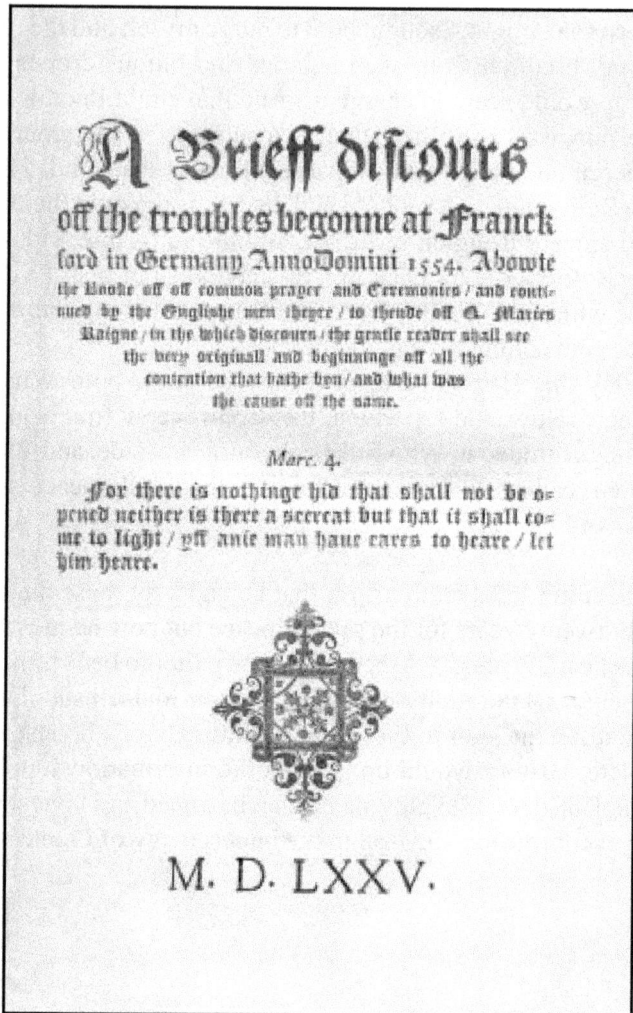

Title page of *The Troubles at Frankfort*

Chapter Two:
Back-projecting Later Controversies

Alleged Nonconformist Puritans versus Conformist Anglicans
Writing in 1656, the Church Historian, Thomas Fuller, opens up his study of the English Maryan exiles with the words:

> Come we now to set down the sad troubles of Frankford, rending these banished exiles asunder, in several factions. This I dare say, if the Reader takes no more delight in perusing, than I in penning so dolefull a subject, he will show little mirth in his face, and feel less joy in his heart. However we will be somewhat large, and wholy impartial in relating this sorrowfull accident; the rather, because the penn-knives of that age, are grown into swords in ours, and their writings laid the foundation of the fightings now adays.[1]

Fuller is referring to the petty differences which arose between 1554-5 in the Frankfurt church of the English exiles and which became so magnified and distorted throughout the following century. This was not merely a foible of the 17th century. The late Martyn Lloyd-Jones,[2] respected and well-known as a Christian leader,

---

[1] *The Church History of Britain*, 1655, Book VIII, p. 27 (p. 727 in 1656 complete volume).
[2] See Lloyd-Jones' chapter *John Knox – The Founder of Puritanism*, in his *The Puritans* for a most biased, unhistorical 'popular' account.

church historian and preacher, traces a direct link between the troubles at Frankfurt and the Great Rebellion at the time of Charles I and Oliver Cromwell. Regarding Knox's politics at Frankfurt and Geneva, Lloyd-Jones comments:

> Here he was ahead of Calvin, and this is again a sign of true Puritanism. I maintain that one cannot truly understand the revolution that took place here in England in the next century except in the light of this teaching. Here was the first opening of the door that led to that later development.[3]

Thus, according to Lloyd-Jones, the troubles at the relatively tiny church at Frankfurt in the middle of the 16th century, sparked off the terrible bloodshed of the civil, Commonwealth and denominational wars of a century later.

Peter Lewis, who in many ways can be called Lloyd-Jones's pupil, perpetuates this view of Knox as an arch-rebel rather than a man of peace, quoting Jasper Ridley with strong approval that 'The theory of the justification of revolution is Knox's special contribution to the theological and political thought.' Knox's genius is seen in the fact that 'As none of the established leaders of the Protestants dared to do it the task fell to Knox and Goodman.' Lewis sees Goodman as sounding in the 16th century the 'death-knell of Charles I of England' which occurred in the next and shows how Knox taught that treason against kings is not necessarily offensive to God.[4] However, Lloyd-Jones and Lewis' revolutionary politics make too much of the Reformer who was still in his developing years as a Christian when he hatched his plans to bring down kings, but especially queens. Knox's bark was far worse than his bite. Though he preached the death of Mary, he fled the country and barked at her from the peaceful safety of Frankfurt and Geneva. Though he pleaded strongly for the death penalty for heretics in his home country, he barked at them

---

[3] *The Puritans: Their Origins and Successors*, p. 275.
[4] *The Christian and the State in Revolutionary Times*, The Westminster Conference, 1975, pp. 61-62. Lewis does not add that Goodman publicly repented of his hot-headed political past.

from the pulpit and not the bench. He was perhaps only directly responsible for one death throughout his time of power, not including those who died as a result of military skirmishes under his indirect command. In comparison, Calvin whom Lloyd-Jones and Lewis feel was outdone by Knox in his militant scourging of heretics, if we can rely on Piette and Goyau, managed to put 58 to death between 1542-46 alone by the most horrific of means and in the same brief period banish 76 'heretics'.[5]

The urgent need to make a balanced study of contemporary sources

Indeed, quite a number of later denominational Church Historians interpret the events which occurred at Frankfurt through the eyes of later fiery spirits of revolutionary times, and their latter day sympathisers, rather than through a balanced study of contemporary sources. Such contemporary records present a totally different picture. Indeed, instead of portraying a picture of growing strife, they portray a picture of growing unity. This hardly suits the argument of these commentators who wish to believe that an essential element in the spiritual make-up of those they call Puritans was a politically rebellious spirit. It is, however, equally clear that the revolutionary Puritans of 1640-1660, who in no way represented the bulk of spiritually-minded men otherwise associated with Puritanism, distorted the troubles at Frankfurt in an effort to show that their revolution was not a sudden outbreak by malcontents against the monarchical and Episcopal status quo but was an essential development of the Reformation process which began in Frankfurt and led to the rise of Puritanism. This theory entirely shuts its eyes to the great Reformation which transformed England long before state-enforced Presbyterian Puritanism made its temporary debut in England. One is amazed that what actually happened at Frankfurt should be stood on its head and used as an excuse for the anti-Episcopalian and anti-Nonconformist bickering which has gone on ever since and has not yet been resolved in these modern times.

---

[5] Maxim Piette, *John Wesley in the Evolution of Protestantism*. See his chapter 'The Calvinist Movement' and pp. 514-515.

It has thus become traditional amongst certain denominational writers to look upon the troubles at Frankfurt as a watershed between the alleged Anglican, Episcopalian, Conforming Churchmen on the one side and the Puritan, Presbyterian, Dissenting Nonconformists on the other. Neal tells us that the troubles at Frankfurt 'made way for the distinction, by which the two parties were afterwards known, of Puritans and Conformists.'[6] A more modern writer, James Heron in his book *A Short History of Puritanism* (1908) tells us under the heading *The Conflict between Anglicanism and Puritanism begins at Frankfort*, 'It is the exiles at Frankfort-on-the main who first demand our attention, for among them a conflict began which ended in a cleavage that continues to this hour, with the Anglicans on one side and the Puritans on the other.' He goes on to say that at Frankfurt, a permanent division occurred of momentous consequences i.e. here we have the historic dividing of the line between 'Anglicans' and 'Puritans' these parties now forming Anglican Conformists on the one side and 'Puritan' Nonconformists on the other.

Reversing the Reformation's role

The trouble with this black and white picture of the highly exaggerated troubles at Frankfurt is that it whitens sepulchres and paints white black. It views the work and testimony of England's Reformers as being counterproductive to the welfare of the state and to the development of Erastian church principles. It condemns the work of the Reformation on two issues, a. the lack of political rebellion amongst them and b. their adherence to the Biblical and traditional order of church government known as the Episcopacy. The critics of the alleged Anglican and Conformist party (which we shall see was far more Nonconformist than the alleged 'Puritan' side) define their use of the word 'Puritan' solely in terms of church order and politics and not in terms of experimental doctrine. Indeed, they even empty the term 'Calvinism' of its doctrinal content, arguing that to be a Calvinist is to be a political agitator, a separatist and a

---

[6] *History of the Puritans*, Vol. I, p. 81.

Presbyterian.[7] Thus, the role that such alleged 'High Churchmen' as Bale, Grindal, Cox, Lever, Becon, Sampson, Whitehead, i.e. the cream of the cream of England's Reformers and early Puritans, played in this controversy is describes as 'evil' and showing 'papist dregs' and 'the mark of the beast' by Knox[8] and their more Laudian but non-Anglican critics.

Bearing this in mind, it is no surprise to find the affairs at Frankfurt summarised by T. M. Lindsay in his *History of the Reformation* (1907-8)[9] in the words:

> The years 1554-58 . . . witnessed the trouble in the Frankfurt congregation of English exiles, where Knox's broad-minded toleration and straightforward action stands in noble contrast with the narrow-minded and crooked policy of his opponents.

A. M. Renwick in his *The Story of the Scottish Reformation*, mistakenly fits the story into the reign of Emperor Charles I and not Charles V, and tells us that:

> The peace was rudely disturbed by the arrival of Dr. Cox (formerly Chancellor of Oxford University), and a fresh band of English refugees. Although received with every mark of Christian generosity, they immediately became exceedingly aggressive, insisted on a full-fledged Anglican service, and paid no attention to the contract made with the French Church, or the agreement reached in the congregation itself.[10]

---

[7] See for instance Martyn Lloyd-Jones' *The Puritans*, p. 255 where the author maintains that true Puritanism "must always end in Presbyterianism or Independency." Lloyd-Jones quite overlooks the fact here that Presbyterianism and Independency became literally deadly enemies when they both left the Church of England.

[8] See Strype's *History of the Reformation*, p. 121.

[9] My copy, a 1951 reprint of the 1908 edition.

[10] P. 61.

On first reading this, the present author thought that Renwick had not only mixed up his emperors but also confused Cox with Knox as there is ample evidence to show that Cox was fully willing to accept the French orders and live with compromises set up by Thomas Lever and Valerand Poullain etc. but any such evidence suggesting that Knox might have agreed with Cox is very slight indeed and rather points in the opposite direction as will be discussed below. Indeed, Knox's contemporary opponents such as Whitehead have gone down in history as blaming the Scotsman for such a total misrepresentation of the situation and the facts that he must be judged a perverter of the truth and an enemy of the Reformation. This contemporary witness has been thoroughly revised in modern anti-Anglican studies, without new evidence being produced. Sadly, there have been scarcely any modern attempts to analyse, never mind defend, the 'Anglican' side in this controversy and the many supporters of the Knox party have either refused to accept evidence from the opposition or ridiculed it as the deceitful cunning of hypocrites.

Andrew Lang, writing in 1905, believes he can divide the Puritans and Protestants from the Anglicans and the Churchmen by viewing the former as the tiny minority who supported Knox and the latter as the majority who opposed him. For Lang, too, it is a question of Scotland versus England. The Caledonian patriot tells us:

> The quarrel between Knox and them (the English Reformers in exile) definitely marks the beginning of the rupture between the fathers of the Church of England and the fathers of Puritanism, Scottish Presbyterianism and Dissent.[11]

Many writers have simplified the matter further and, taking Richard Cox as the leader of a supposed pro-papist, High Church, ritualistic faction, speak only of the Coxians and the Knoxians. Thus

---

[11] *John Knox and the Reformation*, p. 53.

Dickens and Carr entitle their collection of documents on the Frankfurt controversy *Knox and Cox at Frankfurt*,[12] whereas Lang entitles his section on the topic *Knox and Cox*. Here, it is significant to note that Dickens and Carr merely quote texts from the Knoxian side thus giving a most lop-sided slant on the Frankfurt affairs of 1554-55. Cox's arguments and defence against misrepresentation are not given. Neal blandly tells us that 'Dr. Cox and his friends were the aggressors' and that they had 'an ill spirit' and were guilty of 'breaking a congregation to pieces.'[13] Actually, as this paper will seek to prove, Neal has reversed all the arguments which point against the Knox faction and applied them to Cox. He has also jumbled the chronology and sequence of events to a great extent and accused the church majority of beliefs that many of them abhorred and none practised.

Lord Percy is surely flying high on flights of fancy when he comments concerning Cox's move to Frankfurt:

> He may not have met Knox before but he had an old feud with him; he had not forgotten his famous sermon of September 1552, nor the origin of the Black Rubric. Moreover, he had brought with him from England a copy of the Admonition, and was all afume at the trouble that this meddlesome Scotsman had made for sober Anglicans. He had, in fact, made up his mind to drive Knox out of Frankfurt and it took him less than a fortnight to do it.[14]

The facts show clearly that Cox was far less 'churchy' in his view of the Lord's Supper than Knox. He was not only fully of one mind with Knox concerning the thought behind the Black Rubric but was obviously influential at Frankfurt in persuading the Anglicans not to kneel on receiving communion for the sake of the

---

[12] *Documents of Modern History: The Reformation in England to the Accession of Elizabeth I*, Edward Arnold, 1967.
[13] *History of the Puritans*, Vol. I, p. 81. See pp. 76-82 for a most coloured account of the 'troubles'.
[14] *John Knox*, p. 195.

Precisians who confused prayerful worship of Christ with the adoration of the sacrament. The 'fuming' that Lord Percy refers to
would be difficult to relate to any of the records and Knox himself
singles out Isaac rather than Cox as his main opponent on the *Faithful Admonition* question, as he singles out Lever, rather than Cox
concerning modes of worship. Indeed, Knox is very quick to criticise individuals for wronging him, as he supposed, but he makes
no mention of Cox having introduced his work to the church members. As this work was published in Poland on 20 July, 1554, it was
probably circulated on the Continent before it reached England and
Polish Christian refugees often called in at Frankfurt, making it
possible, if not probable, that they brought printed copies of the
Admonition with them. However, Goodman knew Knox's work in-
timately and had most likely helped him in its composition. He was
a member of Cox's party and reached Frankfurt with him. Goodman
was most open in his criticisms of governments so that it is most
likely that he had informed his fellow Strasburg Christians of this
work when he joined them in the Autumn of 1554. We have still not
dealt with the main suspect concerning who let the *Admonition* cat
out of the bag at Frankfurt. Pro-Knoxian writers have for centuries
discussed who the culprit was who made Knox's revolutionary ideas
common knowledge. They have invariably looked for someone outside the Knoxian camp, as if Knox had written out his views to be
ignored by the general Christian public. Obviously, though Calvin
told Cecil and Elizabeth I that he was kept in the dark by Knox
concerning the *Admonition*, Knox wrote to convince others. It is
therefore very much more than likely that Knox himself, rather than
anybody else, spread the news in Frankfurt of his highly revolutionary, indeed, treasonable politics.

When is a Puritan not a Puritan?
Though a number of modern commentators see the troubles and
Frankfurt as being a dividing of the ways between 'Anglicans' and
'Nonconformists', or papists and Puritans, each of these writers
tends to draw the line of demarcation in a different place. This
reminds the present author of his Hebrew studies at Uppsala Uni-

versity when the subject was the authorship of Isaiah. It was found that though many critics tore the prophesies into three parts, supposing a triple authorship, few agreed on where the lines of demarcation were to be made. In fact, their theories so contradicted one another that they clearly provided evidence against the Trito-Isaiah theory. This is also the case concerning the troubles at Frankfurt. Thomas Fuller, though an Anglican, writing in 1656, is mostly on the side of anti-Anglican Knox and depicts him as adhering to the original order of the church. He thus looks upon those whom Knox opposed, such as Richard Cox, as well deserving his rebuke. On the other hand, writing in 1710, Anglican John Strype believed the Frankfurt church was divided from the start but Knox became 'the chief Raiser of Discontent', whereas Anglicans such as Cox, Grindal and Chambers brought peace to the church. On examining the sources these men used, it is easy to follow the grounds for their reasoning. Fuller seems to have relied almost solely on the first section of the Anti-Anglican, pro-Knox work *Troubles at Frankfort*, written in 1575, which presents a very sympathetic view of Knox and a most antagonistic view of Cox, whereas Strype uses the private letters of English Reformers who, though more balanced in their language, reverse the picture. Likewise, Dissenting writers are greatly divided in their appreciation of Knox. One can hardly expect Baptist writers to honour a man who wrote so bitterly against their alleged 'maist horrible and absurd' beliefs.[15] On the other hand, Presbyterian writers in general, as we would naturally suppose, support Knox to the hilt, even if the question as to whether Knox was truly a Presbyterian or not is still open.[16]

---

[15] See *History of Baptists in Scotland*, Ed. Geo. Yuille, Baptist Union Publications Committee, Glasgow, 1923, especially p. 25 and passim. See also Stephen Brachlow's *The Communion of Saints*, OUP, 1988, for deep-sighted comments on the radical politics of certain 'Calvinists', including Knox, especially chapters Six and Seven.

[16] See entries under Knox, Cox, Germany, Frankfurt etc. in Neal's *History of the Puritans* and definitive biographies of varying scholarly contents such as McCrie's, Lang's and Barnett Smith's. See also Knox's own accounts in *Troubles at Frankfort* and in his *History of the Reformation of Religion in Scotland*.

Opposition to Knox came from Nonconformists rather than 'High Churchmen'

There are many anachronisms used in this debate. One thing is certain: modern Non-Anglicans, obviously influenced by the weak, if not apostate state of the present Church of England, tend to thrust such later views onto the Frankfurt opposition to Knox. In doing so, they forget that for centuries, both the English Presbyterians and Congregationalists kept a very low spiritual flame in England, especially during the 18th century awakenings. Moreover, the facts show, as will be documented throughout this work, that opposition to Knox did not come from a High Church, Conformist party but principally from Nonconformists, several of whom were quite radical. Yet such as Lever, Becon, Humphrey, Whitehead, Sampson, Grindal, Jewel and Cox are paraded as frightening examples of anti-Puritan, pro-papist, High Churchmen! Furthermore, since McCrie's days, there has developed a most patriotic, nationalistic identification of Protestant Scotsmen with John Knox so that to question Knox's policies and politics, even at this very early stage in his development, is tantamount to denigrating Scotland. This is a very sad, unbalanced state of affairs as Knox was neither the first nor the last Scottish Reformer and between them all they did a marvellous work of reforming the land whether they were Episcopalians such as Leighton or Marrow Men such as the Erskines. Each were bricks in the Reformation edifice and none must be mistaken for the whole. Furthermore, such great Scottish men of grace as Robert Traill have left a lasting mark in England; Alexander Comrie laid the foundation of a great work in Holland and George Scott became the father, under God, of a great revival work in Scandinavia.

Basic to modern definitions of Puritanism appears to be a socialistic, democratic idea that true reform must always start from the people at the grass-roots and work up to the top. Invariably the 'top' is seen as an establishment worthy of nothing but great suspicion, until the lower forces overcome it and become a new establishment themselves. Though such an idea has brought many political gains to the so-called common man, the history of the church shows that the Spirit moves where He will and is not the agent of an earthly political manifesto. This work of the Spirit is perhaps nowhere more better illustrated than in the work of the English Reformation and the development of Puritanism which invariably started, not from the political masses but from their shepherds, pastors and bishops. Thus Douglas Campbell can write with the work of the Spirit confirmed by history at his side:

> But Puritanism in England began at the top and worked downwards. For years after Elizabeth ascended the throne, some of the most prominent statesmen, many of the most learned bishops, and almost all of the most distinguished divines, were Reformers or Puritans, who, even if they outwardly conformed, yet advocated changes in the discipline and ceremonial of the establishment. These men, and others like them, laid down the doctrines of the Anglican Church on lines so strictly Calvinistic that John Knox, or even Calvin himself, could have found little in them of which to disapprove.[17]

Sadly, that 'little' was so magnified by Knox that it overshadowed all else and hid the real work of reform from his eyes. Thus we have his ideological followers such as Hoeksema Presbyterian Herman Hanko in his *Portraits of Faithful Saints* and Fullerite Baptist David Gay in his *Battle for the Church* who do not seem to have noticed respectively that there was a Reformation in England at all until Scottish Presbyterianism was enforced by violence in England during the Great Rebellion or Andrew Fuller took over Dutch Grotianism and combined it with American New Divinity. Incidentally, such men's idols, on the whole, lack the Calvinistic Puritanism of a Hall, Usher, Featley, Ward, or Balcanqual whom they overthrew and persecuted in what can justly be called the Precisionist Counter-Reformation of the seventeenth century.

---

[17] *The Puritan in Holland, England, and America*, p. 482.

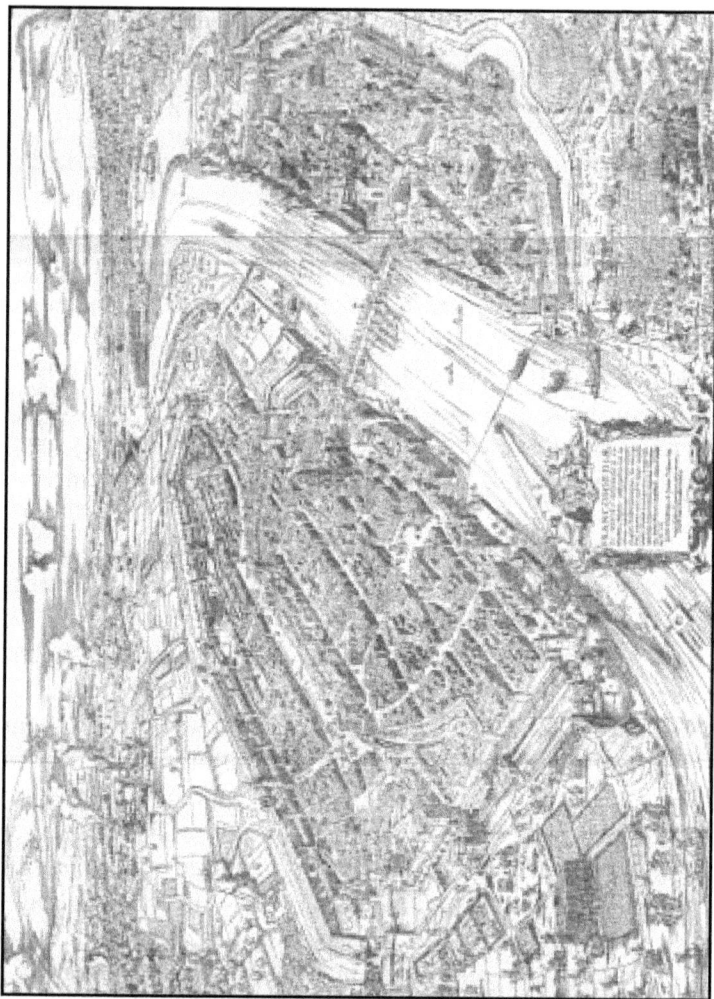

Frankfurt 1552

Chapter Three:
The Founding of the
Frankfurt Church

Initial Senate-imposed restrictions

In order to understand how these wild theories of Anglican Conformity versus Puritan Non-Conformity arose, we must closely examine the founding of the Frankfurt church as it is here that interpretations start to differ. Once the English exiles gathered in Frankfurt and had decided to constitute a church, they applied to the Imperial Senate for permission. The Frankfurt magistrates required the English to draw up a form of worship and a declaration of faith, suggesting that, in the interest of unity and peace, it should differ as little as possible from the French form of service. This was no problem as the French forms had found much approval with the English Reformers which had led to the French Reformed brethren being given freedom of worship in England. The two churches arranged to use their premises on alternate days, with alternate services on Sundays. Plans, however, were made for some form of joint worship and the Englishmen drew up their forms in both English and French. It is obvious that Valerand Poullain, the French pastor, also served in the English church as an advising elder.[1] Though a very modified form of the Second Prayer Book of 1552 became the basis of the English service, agreement was reached with the French to omit certain elements and add others 'according to the State and Time'. In his *Church History of Britain* VIII Book, p.727, Fuller rightly states:

> What is meant by framing their Confession according to the State and Time, I understand not (must our confessions, as our clothes follow the fashions of the State, and place we live in?)

---

[1] *Troubles at Frankfort*, p. 56 and passim.

The historian concludes that the authorities wanted a Confession which was not so much tailored to suit the needs of *sinners* but *foreign exiles* whom they felt compelled to treat with caution. Some of the restrictions placed on the church such as omitting lay responses in worship and the public reading of God's Word, as also the novel idea that the State ruled the Church rather than the Church ruled itself were seen to be a step away from the Reformation by a number of Englishmen who would have found Fuller's strictures applicable to their situation. However, beggars cannot be choosers and the English, on the whole, considered their lot a fair one. The decision to omit lay responses must have been dictated by the Senate as the French pastor, Poullain, was well-known for his insistence on such active participation by the congregation and the responses he used in his service to the reciting of the Ten Commandments were incorporated into the 1552 English Prayer Book. Poullain had pastored the French Church in Glastonbury during Edward's reign and had been given full freedom to draw up his own order there. Knowing Poullain's fine character and love for the English Reformers, it would hardly seem possible that he would deny them the same liberty which they had given him.

The English subscribed readily to the Senate's ruling, having had enough of religious strife in England. They also agreed with the French to discard ecclesiastical robes and introduce prayers for all countries including England. They then drew up a public declaration of faith which was on the lines of the Edwardian *Forty-Two Articles*. However, the exiles soon gained a friend in Senator John Glauburg who gave them more and more freedom to manage their own affairs as the churches grew and became respected. Fuller, and other church historians following him, conclude, without producing evidence, that the English at Frankfurt did not originally use the Litany, though this was used by the Strasburg churches, with responses, and anchored in the English church's 1555 *Liturgy of Compromise* before the arrival of Cox and his party.

It is exceedingly difficult to trace the exact development of the Frankfurt church's growth in independence from the Senate's initial injunctions as these changed not over a matter of years, nor months as is so often stated but within weeks and even days. On the whole, the Senate showed a leniency which can only be described as admirable. Sadly, over the next few years, the Lutheran princes put pressure on the neutral city to clamp down on the foreign Reformed churches. In November, 1561 when Grindal, a former member of the Frankfurt church, wrote to the Frankfurt magistrates in support of the exiled Dutch church there, he mentions his own experiences of the Senate's former hospitality and tolerance. The Dutch brethren were under criticism from the Senate for not accepting the Lutheran view of consubstantiation and had appealed to Grindal who was supervisor of the Dutch exiled churches in England. Grindal was a nigh Zwinglian in his view of the Eucharist. Grindal tells the Frankfurt magistrates:

> I indeed, most illustrious and worshipful sires, have willingly seized this opportunity of writing, not only for the sake of gratifying them, but also that in my own name, and the name of the English exiles, I might return thanks to your honours for your great kindness and pity towards us in the time of our greatest affliction. No time shall ever remove this your benefit from the minds of Englishmen. England owes it to Strasburg, Zürich, Basle, Worms, but above all to your renowned republic, that she has so many bishops and other ministers of God's word, who at this day are preaching the pure doctrines of the gospel. You hospitably received them, and having received you embraced them with the utmost benevolence and protected them by your authority. Did we not therefore with grateful minds acknowledge and proclaim that your piety, we should be of all men most unthankful.[2]

The relation of the earlier church members to Calvinism and church order

It is also very difficult to judge the exact position of the earliest members to doctrine, forms of worship, order and discipline as many, such as Professor Edward Arber, present interpretations as facts and give a most coloured and unbalanced picture of the times.

---

[2] *The Remains of Archbishop Grindal*, pp. 249-250.

This has three major reasons apart from the writers' personal bias: first the English records that we have were put together long after the incidents occurred. Secondly, they were obviously compiled for highly polemic purposes and thus presented one-sidedly. The third reason may well have influenced English-speaking writers the most, namely the lack of ability on the part of those doing research to read the original records which are in Latin, French, Nether-German, Late Middle High German and Dutch. This is illustrated by all the non-Continental studies cited in this book. However, if we take Karl Bauer's history of the Frankfurt churches in his biography of Valerand Poullain, as a Continental example, we find him quoting German, French, English, Dutch and Latin with never a translation, the author obviously thinking that those interested in his subject would have a command of these languages. Also, on the European Continent, it is considered scholarly to quote in the original languages. Rosalind Marshall is something of a British exception as she cites French works translated for her by a colleague but though she received a scholarship to study records relating to Knox's life, she appears not to have used any of the Frankfurt sources apart from a few museum exhibits.

Prof. Arber says, 'Of the original four leaders of the Frankfurt church, only one, Edmund Sutton, was a Prayer Book man; the other three being Calvinists.'[3] Such judgement depends wholly on whom Arber thought were the churches leaders, what he understood by Calvinism and what he understood by 'Prayer Book men'. Arber is obviously basing his argument on the wide-spread belief that Sutton, William Whittingham, William Williams and Thomas Wood were the *first* English exiles to reach Frankfurt, which is hardly an argument for them being the first church officers. However, the information which Arber relies on in *Troubles at Frankfort* gives the arrival in Frankfurt of these men as late as 27 June, 1554, whereas contemporary records affirm that the English had been arriving since the winter and early spring. Some authorities even say that Whittingham arrived with Knox as late as November of that

---

[3] *Troubles at Frankfort*, p. xiii.

year.[4] On taking all the facts into consideration it would appear that the early Frankfurt exiles were all Prayer Book men of sorts and all Calvinists. Even Knox was a Prayer Book man before he started to change his mind in Frankfurt. It is also obvious that a relatively large number of exiles, the bulk of them being moderate Prayer Book men, followed immediately on the heels of Sutton and his friends before ever a church was constituted. The validity of Arber's conclusion can therefore only be assessed by examining the list of founding members.

This is by no means an easy task. Poullain came ahead of the main body of the Anglo-Walloon group he had pastored in Glastonbury, Somersetshire as early as January, 1554 with a number of his church.[5] He formally applied to the Senate for permission to form a church of refugees in March, 1554 which was speedily granted. However, Poullain was only treading in the footsteps of other refugees who had applied before him. For instance, Bauer records how the refugees in Strasburg and Augsburg had sent Jan Utenhove to Frankfurt as early as 4 May, 1546 with a view to setting up a church there. Even in October, 1528, we read of a Johann Wyttingk, also of Belgium, applying for asylum in Frankfurt because of persecution in his home town. So Frankfurt had obviously already a tradition of granting foreign refugees asylum.[6] There was a strong connection between the refugees in Strasburg and the Frankfurt Senate from Henry VIII to Mary I.

The *Ratsprotokolle* for Tuesday, 3 April, 1954 mentions 40 (further?) refugees who had come from England and requested the use of the White Ladies Chapel for worship, but these are referred to as 'Flemming' i.e. Flemish. However, the Lord Mayor's records of Thursday, 26 April say that those worshipping at the White Ladies Chapel were 'Engel und Niederlender', i.e. English and Dutch and that there was much protest from the citizens and women at the

---

[4] A. M. Renwick in his *The Story of the Scottish Reformation*, argues that Whittingham joined the Frankfurt church with Knox in November, 1554.

[5] Accounts vary but it appears that between 21-24 'fathers of families' accompanied Poullain. See, for instance, Dalton, p. 462.

[6] Bauer, pp. 175-176.

'allerlei ungeschicklichkeiten' i.e. 'all kinds of clumsiness or lack of tact' that occurred. Complaints of this kind recorded in the minutes are revealed as being instigated by the Lutheran pastor Mathias, so obviously the Reformed worship of the English and Dutch had caused quite a sensation and the Lutherans were on the defensive. Further references are made to the English throughout April, May and June, so they were obviously in Frankfurt months earlier than the English records suggest. Bauer quotes the French writer Doumergue as saying that the English, in fact, were already established in Frankfurt and had taken over the Weißfrauenkirche a year before the Belgians and Dutch came.

Bauer points out that this may be because Doumergue understands the reference to 'Engländer' in the city records to mean English only, whereas the term was used of all the refugees who came from England, whatever their nationality. However, as both the terms 'Flemish' and 'English' used in the city records obviously included English, we can only conclude that the English were at least in Frankfurt as early as the Belgians, which was several months before Sutton and his friends arrived.[7] That the Senate had little concern for stating the exact nationality of the refugees is illustrated by the *Ratsprotokoll* for 15 March, 1554 where the French-speaking Belgians and English who followed Poullain are called 'Niderlender'. Von Roden, obviously using material culled from Withoff and the Duisburg archives, states that the first English refugees moved to Frankfurt in 1553.

The Liturgia Sacra[8] compared with other Reformed orders
David Laing, mentions a document entitled *Liturgia Sacra*, dated September, 1554 to show that John Mackbray, John Staunton, William Hammond, John Bendall and William Whitingham had joined their French brethren in signing a common statement of faith. This order, Laing argues, is, 'with some changes' similar to the Strasburg Order used by Poullain's church before he left in 1551.[9]

---

[7] Ibid, p. 185.
[8] See Appendix for an overview of the Frankfurt *Liturgia Sacra*.
[9] *The Works of John Knox*, Vol. 4, pp. 144.

This form of worship was influenced strongly by Bucer. As Poullain was a disciple of Bucer's and pastored the French-speaking church at Strasburg, one could understand his interest in preserving Strasburg's theological traditions. Poullain translated the order into Latin and took it with him when exiled to England, using it in his Glastonbury church. One could thus assume that this was the version, or something very similar which Poullain presented to his Frankfurt flock in 1554. Laing more than suggests that this *Liturgia Sacra* might have served as a model for the *Order of Geneva* used by the British in Geneva as opposed to Calvin's own *Genevan Order*. This would tally with the research done by Karl Bauer in his 1927 dissertation on Valerand Poullain and the French exile church and my own comparisons of the *Liturgia Sacra* with the Strasburg and Genevan orders. Both the Genevan Order and Order of Geneva can thus be traced back to the common source of the work of the Strasburg Reformers led by Bucer. These orders may thus equally be called the Strasburg orders. This shows how futile it is for critics to affirm that the Strasburg Anglicans and the Genevans were in matters of order, discipline and theology poles apart. This is, however, the crux of the argument used to discredit the 'Anglicans' at Frankfurt. Such Anglicans fled to Strasburg because of the very same Bucerian theology represented there that had attracted Calvin to the city when exiled from Geneva in 1538.

Laing, perhaps the main authority on this matter in the English-speaking world, merely mentions the changes made between Strasburg and Geneva but does not outline them. Clearly, Calvin left out the absolution against his will because of strong pressure from his church members. He did not want to be thrown out a second time. He changed the rather lengthy Christian testimony leading up to the Apostles' Creed into the brief words 'In the name of the people' and abolished the chanting of the Ten Commandments. It is interesting to note that Calvin changed the names of church officers from the German (Pfarrherr, Kirchendiener, Kirchspielspfleger, Helfer etc.) or French indigenous terms back to their Greek forms. Though the French Church in exile held to a three-fold ministry, ministers, elders and deacons, the Genevans prefered merely elders and deacons. Whereas the Strasburg forms, including the *Liturgia Sacra* firmly stressed the necessity of celebrating Holy Communion with the sick on the same day that the church gathered for the same rite, the later Genevans frowned on this practice. Bauer emphasises how Poullain kept to the Strasburg 'original and normal' (Ursprüngliche und Normale) and did not follow Calvin's 'derived and secondary' (Abgeleitete und Sekundäre).[10]

Right conclusion, wrong argument

There has been a great deal of confusion amongst scholars concerning the identity of the *Liturgia Sacra*, especially in relationship to the various orders which Knox rejected at Frankfurt or were rejected by the majority vote, the *Liturgy of Compromise* and the so-called *Knox Prayer Book* of 1556 printed in Latin. Though I agree wholeheartedly with Laing concerning the similarities between the *Liturgia Sacra* and the Strasburg and Genevan orders, I do not agree with the way he has reached these conclusions. My doubts were first raised on reading H. J. Wotherspoon, who, in his introduction to the *Second Prayer Book of Edward VI and the Liturgy of Compromise* refers to the *Liturgia Sacra* as a draft, based on the Glastonbury order, 'printed privately', and a few copies circulated among the Frankfurt exiles with a view to consideration and adoption, and possibly reappears as 'the Order of Geneva.'[11] So far, so good. But, in his Appendix 'The Rival Orders of Worship at Frankfurt', Wotherspoon mentions merely the full title of the Frankfurt *Liturgia Sacra* with signatories, adding in brackets 'Described by Laing, iv. 145 fn 2'. I thus turned to the reference given, hoping to find the description promised. Laing, however, had also merely listed the full title of the work with signatories but had added no further information concerning the document, let alone quoted from it.

---

[10] *Villerand Poullain*, p. 143. It is difficult to make out what immediate changes Calvin made whilst in Strasburg as his order used there was never printed and the originals are lost.

[11] *The Second Prayer Book of King Edward the Sixth and the Liturgy of Compromise*, p. 19. Witherspoon gives a detailed summary of the problems involved in his Appendix *The Rival Orders of Worship at Frankfurt*, pp. 59-61.

Laing's own footnote here refers to *Troubles at Frankfort* which also gives no description of the *Liturgia Sacra* but refers to a later work allegedly drawn up by the English church themselves. However, on the previous page (p.144) Laing says that 'Strype, in his Ecclesiastical Memorials, has given a short abstract of this Argentine or Strasburg Liturgy'. Laing then claims, giving no evidence whatsoever, that, 'the Liturgy already mentioned (i.e. the Strasburg liturgy) was, with some changes, adopted by the mutual consent of the French and English congregations, and published under the following title *Liturgia Sacra, seu Ritus Ministerij in Ecclesia peregrinorum Francofordiae* etc..' Though nothing yet has been said regarding the actual contents of the *Liturgia Sacra*, Wotherspoon tells us that Laing recognises the *Liturgia Sacra* as the form of service used in Frankfurt mutually by the French and English. He then says, 'Dr Mitchell (Scot. Ref., p.127 editor's note) expressed his "strong conviction that the words and matter of Knox's Latin Prayer-Book of 1556 were derived directly from the *Liturgia Sacra* of Pollanus." On this point he entertained "no doubt whatsoever."'[12] However, Knox authorship of the 1556 Latin Prayer Book has not been established, though at a later period it came to bear his name. It is also mere guess work to presume, as does Laing, that the 1556 Prayer Book, whose dating is also doubtful, was the order which was rejected at Frankfurt prior to the *Liturgy of Compromise* being drawn up.[13] Furthermore, the entire arrangement of the liturgy is different and many essential features of the *Liturgia Sacra* are missing.[14] Indeed, the Knox book is what it professes to be *The forme of prayers and ministration of the sacraments* and is even less a complete order of service than the *Liturgia Sacra*.

Unsubstantial evidence
The evidence given here is merely Laing's undocumented opinion linking the *Liturgia Sacra* with the Strasburg order and the refer-

---

[12] Ibid, p. 60.
[13] Laing, Vol. IV, p. 146.
[14] See Appendix III for an outline of the *Liturgia Sacra* and the so-called Knox Prayer Book.

ence he gives to the *Troubles at Frankfort* where a decision is mentioned in the English church in July, 1554, two months before the French presented their *Liturgia Sacra* to the Senate. As a result of the July conference, during the following August, copies of a letter were sent to Strasburg, Zürich, Duisburg and Emden explaining that the Frankfurt men had constituted a church and now invited all the British exiles to join them. In this letter, we read 'And for that it was thought the Church could not long continue to good order without Discipline; there was also a brief Form devised; declaring the Necessity, the Causes, and the Order thereof; whereunto all those that were present subscribed.'

Was this the *Liturgia Sacra*? Prof. Arber states in a footnote that these words apply to the so-called *Old Discipline* which is placed on pages 142-149 of his edition and also appended by Wotherspoon to his book as part of the *Liturgy of Compromise* drawn up the following year. This document of a few pages, however, bears little resemblance to the 92 paged *Liturgia Sacra*. Furthermore, the description given in Laing's and Wotherspoon's source, mentioning arguments regarding 'necessity, causes and order' does not tally at all with the contents of the *Old Discipline*. All the signs show that the document is actually a much later British work. Part Two begins by referring to a former order used in the church annexed to the document but which neither Laing, nor Arber, nor Wotherspoon refer to, let alone include (p.147). This 'former order' might have been the *Liturgia Sacra* but the claim under examination is that the *Old Discipline* itself and *Liturgia Sacra* are identical. There is also a reference to the British martyrs in the final prayer of the *Old Discipline* which would rule out a date of composition in 1554. According to Knappen in his *Tudor Puritanism*,[15] there is also possibly a reference to John Jewel in the document (p.144) who arrived in Frankfurt the year after the *Liturgia Sacra* was published. In spite of this, however, Knappen states, 'I have followed Arber in accepting the *Old Discipline* as containing the substance of the original constitution of the Frankfurt church.'

---

[15] P. 120.

Rather than referring to the *Liturgia Sacra*, Knappen surprisingly mentions the *Old Discipline* in one breath with the *Liturgy of Compromise* reprinted by Wotherspoon and Sprott[16] which was composed in the Spring of 1555. Knappen argues that this liturgy was the first 'constitution' used by the British and was drawn up by 'Whittingham's group'.[17] Whittingham and Knox along with Parry and Lever, did indeed form the committee which compiled the *Liturgy of Compromise*. Nevertheless, there is strong evidence that Knox opted out of this responsibility and to affirm that Parry and Lever belonged to 'Whittingham's group' quite contradicts documentary evidence. Furthermore, of the British signatures under the *Liturgia Sacra* John Makebray's is first just as Poullain is placed at the head of the French and Spanish signatories in the usual order of responsibility. Whittingham is placed last – a strong indication that Whittingham did not lead the British. So, too, Makebray is the only British signatory with an M. placed after his name, indicating that he held the office of at least a minister, whereas the rest held no offices. Poullain signed himself Pastor (Pastor Ecclesiae). It was a peculiarity of Pullain's that he called all other ordained co-workers 'Deacons' as he did not believe in a co-pastorship. Makebray, however, according to the author of *Troubles at Frankfort*, did not assist in drawing up the *Liturgy of Compromise*. Makebray's early leadership at Frankfurt is entirely ignored by pro-Knoxian, pro-Presbyterian apologists, presumably because he was a staunch contender against the Knoxian position and such Knoxian polemists would have all believe that the initial church at Frankfurt was anti-Prayer Book and anti-Anglican.

It is obvious that there were far more than five English in Frankfurt in September, 1554. A John Bendall is otherwise nowhere referred to in other lists of early members and the name is entirely absent from the collection of documents in *Troubles at Frankfort*, the *Zürich Letters* and the two volumes of *Original Letters* which cover the affairs at Frankfurt. It may be that this is a pseudonym as

---

[16] Knappen, p. 120.
[17] Ibid, p. 119.

a number of exiles used assumed names to help ward off persecutors. Knox, for instance, took on his mother's maiden name in France, calling himself John Sinclair,[18] Miles Coverdale called himself Michael Anglus[19] and Theodore Basil was the pseudonym of Thomas Becon.[20] As the signatories signed in cursive Latin, John Bendall (*Ioannes Bendallus*) may be a faulty reading of John Bale, a moderate Prayer Book man and one of the earlier English refugees at Frankfurt. Subsequent orders drawn up by the English church, such as those on discipline reproduced in *Troubles at Frankfort*, bear the signatures of all who accept them. Here, however, only a tiny minority of the men who were at Frankfurt in September signed the French order. This rather indicates that it was a matter of personal support rather than official recognition as the English order. Laing points out, too, that this liturgy was republished in the following year but without English subscribers.

Knappen describes the original order of service in the terms recorded in the 'History' prefaced to the *Troubles at Frankfort*. This order differs in places radically from both the *Liturgia Sacra* and the *Liturgy of Compromise* published by Wotherspoon and Sprott, nor does it resemble closely the supposed *Knox Prayer Book*. Furthermore, the version of the *Liturgy of Compromise* presented by Wotherspoon and Sprott as the Frankfurt version cannot possibly be the original form. Though it is introduced as the *Liturgy of Compromise* and *The Order of Common Prayer*, it does not give the Sunday liturgy, makes no mention of much of the worship, including the sermon, and concentrates merely on 'Christ's holy sacraments'.[21] This is all very confusing and hardly helps piece together the actual liturgy of the Frankfurt church. All that can be said is that all these attempts to draw up Reformed orders of service and discipline reflect the theological sentiments of the Strasburg orders, though not at all slavishly so.

---

[18] Ibid, p. 225.
[19] *Original Letters*, Vol. 1, p. 245.
[20] See Heaton's *The Puritan Bible*, p. 175.
[21] See Wotherspoon p. 232 ff.

Actually, the *Liturgia Sacra* is not a set liturgical order at all, nor is it any more than a very rough guide as to how the French church, including possibly a group of English, were worshipping at the time. The occasion of presenting this document to the Senate, according to the testimony of the *Liturgia Sacra* itself, was not the setting up of what came to be called the Church of the Foreigners but an answer to papists' criticism after the church had been established, that they were an Anabaptist sect. Furthermore, the French church worshipped in their mother tongue but, as also in the case of all correspondence with the English and Dutch churches, the Senate demanded that they should be kept informed in Latin of all that they undertook. Thus the *Liturgia Sacra* is merely a rough Latin account of the general proceedings during a French language service. Furthermore, the document makes it quite clear that the congregation is prepared to compromise greatly in their worship in order to live at peace with the Senate.

Differences between the *Liturgia Sacra* and later polemic accounts

Rough and unspecific as this 92 paged document is, it differs radically from what the Knoxians have always claimed was the original Precisian liturgy of the Foreigners at Frankfurt and of which every jot and tittle, they maintain, was followed by Knox in opposition to the Coxian rebels. So, too, the testimony of the author of the 1574 'History' prefaced to the *Troubles at Frankfort*, obviously is not an eye-witness account of the liturgy Whittingham first favoured, but reveals a later interpretation. The Knoxian claims were, and still are, that in this original liturgy standing only was practised in prayer and at communion; that no responses were made by the congregation; that one set liturgy was always binding; that witnesses or godparents were not present at baptisms; that church officers were democratically elected; that no compromises were to be made in worship, that no litany was used and that the public reading of Scripture was forbidden.

On page 8 of the *Liturgia Sacra*, dealing with the Absolution we read 'Ac toto hoc tempore populus magna cum reverentia vel astat, vel procumbit in genua, ut ut animus cuiusque tulerit.' i.e. All the time the people stand or kneel with great reverence according as it suits each. Thus the congregation had a sensible solution to the problem of how one should show reverence. Knox forbade kneeling outright, believing that it was a papal 'diabolical invention'[22] and that the disciples had stood during the Lord's Supper.

At the beginning of the Sunday morning service, the precentor first sings the opening words of the *sursum corda* in French (Leve le cueur)[23] and is then joined by the congregation. As an alternative, the Decalogue in verse form is suggested. In the Glastonbury service, the Decalogue was split into two parts with a psalm and prayer attached to the second half. In the Frankfurt liturgy, the Decalogue is to be sung in its entirety at the beginning of the service, when the Leve le cueur is not used, thus shortening the worship by a psalm and a prayer. However, the singing is also non-compulsory (p.6) each member of the congregation having the freedom to sing or remain silent. A minister then sings from the pulpit the words 'Our help cometh from the Lord who has created heaven and earth,' after which he admonishes the congregation to repeat the General Confession together. Here the Latin and German versions refer to 'singing' but this could also be understood as 'chanting'.

Though the 'History' in *Troubles at Frankfort* and Knox's subsequent defenders claim that the earliest Frankfurt forms rejected the Litany, this is not supported by either the Bucer-Poullain liturgies nor the *Liturgy of Compromise*.[24] Bucer, in his *Censura* showed the Anglicans the importance of the Litany's suffrages for the Reformation. The *Liturgy of Compromise*, like the *Liturgia Sacra*, includes the absolution frowned on by the Knoxians and adds the very responses that the tiny Knoxian-minority would not accept. The facts thus show that instead of defending the liturgies accepted by the Frankfurt church majority, Knox rejected them and this rejection caused all the trouble at Frankfurt.

Concerning the public reading of Scripture, during the sermon, the preacher is advised by the *Liturgia Sacra* to read only as much

---

[22] *Letter to Mrs. Lock*, 6 April, 1559.
[23] Original spelling.
[24] Op. cit. p. 234.

as he intends to expound (p. 8). At the monthly communion service, the minister opens in prayer after which the congregation sing the Apostles' Creed (pp. 12; 17) but the minister himself may decide whether to read passages from Scripture or announce a psalm to be sung whilst the elements are being distributed (p. 22). Poullain and his elders argue that they would prefer to read publicly through the entire Scriptures passage by passage, and not merely the texts to be expounded so that the congregation could become familiar with the entire Word of God (p. 61). It could thus be that the stricture to limit oneself to the texts preached on was the decision of the Senate and not the church, though this agrees with later Precisian practice.

On page 31 of the liturgy it is stressed that the minister is free to use whatever liturgical forms he wishes and that the Spirit is not bound to one set form. One must give due regard to the time and situation and allow the Spirit to move as He wills. None should be limited in their freedom. Constant re-occurring phrases in the document are 'as he sees fit', or 'as he feels moved'. In other words, the worshippers recognised no such thing as a set service and it was up to the minister to be led fittingly by the Spirit.

The collection is not taken during a break in the worship as in the Glastonbury liturgy but the congregation are told that the congregation will be able to place their offerings in receptacles at the door when leaving the building. This was also obviously to speed up the service as the English and Dutch were waiting to take their turns.

During the baptismal service (which Knox refused to conduct), the *Liturgia Sacra* specifically states that witnesses and godparents must be present (p. 32). The necessity of godparents at a time when parents were dying for their faith is defended in a special section entitled *Admonito Ad Lectorem Pro Liturgia* (p. 65). In keeping with the early church and Anglican teaching baptism is referred to as a seal of '*fidei ac renovationis per Christum*', that is, 'faith and renewal' and it is also here described as 'renasci' or regeneration (p. 34). During the service the minister may read a passage of Scripture if he so wishes (p. 42).

The passage referring to the election of Elders, *De Electione Seniorum* in the *Liturgia Sacra*, does not allow for a 'democratic' vote. If new elders are to be elected, (the total was 12 in all) these are chosen by the already existing ministers and eldership and then presented to the congregation as their suggestions. However, twice as many candidates are presented as there are vacancies. Voting by secret ballot ensues. Those under consideration are expected to agree as they have pledged themselves to follow the voice of the church. The congregation is then asked if they are in agreement with the vote and the elders chosen and they are then expected to agree by remaining silent. The new elders are then ordained by the existing elders by the laying on of hands (p. 53 ff).

Here, there is a departure from the Glastonbury order as in England, the ministers were elected by open and oral voting whereas in Frankfurt, the vote was secret and written. According to Baur, who follows F. Cl. Ebrard in his *Die französisch-reformierte Gemeinde in Frankfurt a. M., 1554-1904*, (p. 56), only six elders were actually voted for in 1554 and seven in 1555.[25]

The *Liturgia Sacra* is a liturgy of compromise for two reasons. First, the worshippers were not of one mind concerning public worship and secondly, in the section *Ad Lectorem Candidum: Pro Liturgia Admonitio*, which is the longest section in the book, the authors emphasise that the refugees are offering the Senate a cut-down liturgy in order to avoid breaking the peace. The authors air their frustration at the pressure put on them to worship in Latin, arguing that as they are French-speaking, their worship should be in French. Thus an exact comparison of the *Liturgia Sacra* with the *Liturgy of Compromise*, and Strasburg-Geneva orders cannot be made but the general purport is the same. In spite of its vague nature and lack of detail, the *Liturgia Sacra* is of great importance in the Knoxian-Coxian debate as it is obviously closer to the Coxian point of view than the Knoxian, though traditionally both Presbyterians and Independents argue that it coincided with Knox's own personal demands.

The Glastonbury order remained the French Church's norm

Bauer demonstrates that Poullain did not establish a new church in

---

[25] See Bauer, p. 202.

Frankfurt but, as he had moved *en bloc* with his Glastonbury church to Frankfurt, he remained their pastor and kept more or less to the order of worship he had used at Glastonbury. Indeed, one of the first signs of trouble in Poullain's church was that he continued his Glastonbury practice of having each new member recite the church order off by heart. Newcomers soon made him demand a mere signature of agreement. When a number of newcomers objected to kneeling at the General Confession, individual freedom was allowed and the Lutherans immediately protested that the Reformed had stiff knees. Also, it was declared that vestments were a matter of indifference and each was free to think as he wished on the matter. Instead of the Apostle's Creed being sung by the whole congregation, it was now merely recited by the pastor alone. Unlike, the English who had a plurality of pastors, Poullain would not tolerate a co-pastor and when he received an assistant, probably through Calvin's influence, he angered the Genevan by calling him merely 'my deacon'. Also, unlike the English who did not change anything without full consultation with the Senate, Poullain often angered them by unilateral changes in his liturgy. Indeed, rather than the English drawing criticism from the Senate because of their Anglican ways in contrast to the French-speaking church, as argued by such as Lloyd-Jones, it was Poullain who practised a more radical confrontation and the opposition he gained from such as arch-Lutherans Brenz and Westphal, and even Geneva, tended to spill over to the Anglicans.

Bauer also points out the differences between the Glastonbury order and that of Strasburg during the many revisions Poullain undertook which were mainly in the Strasburg direction. For instance, voting had been direct by the raising of hands in Glastonbury but was changed to the former Strasburg method of a secret vote by using stones put into an urn. Each voter passed his hand over the open voting urns provided for different candidates to preserve anonymity, but only dropped the stone into one. Indeed, Doumergue argues that Poullain was not able to set up a Strasburg order in Frankfurt until 1555.[26]

Poullain, however, had a far more difficult time with the Frankfurt Senate than the English had and he was continually revising

---

[26] Bauer, p. 183.

his liturgy to suit the Precisian newcomers in his own church and the Melancthonians outside. The city's preachers even insisted on taking part in the Walloon church's voting. Once Poullain, to keep the peace, even signed the Augsburg Confession, though he made marginal notes of dissent here and there.[27] Poullain had also a quite vicious temper which made him go from one extreme to another at times in ardent discussion with the Senate, though he never really departed from the Reformed path. The Dutch in the city were very critical of Poullain and the Lutherans accused him of being an Anabaptist. We are given a hint of the reason for this otherwise unfounded accusation in a letter dated from Frankfurt, written 20 April, 1554 in which Anne Hooper tells Bullinger:

> The day after the opening of the church of the white virgins to us, when master Valerandus Pollanus, the husband of my relative, and the chief pastor of the church, preached a sermon, and baptised his young son in the Rhine.[28]

As Anne Hooper, the wife of Bishop Hooper the martyr, is listed later as a member of the English Church, it could be that we have an indication here that the Belgians and English worshipped together at least during April with Poullain as their pastor. There is little information from these days which cannot be argued one way or another. If Poullain preached in the Weißkirche and then baptised his son in the Rhine, the question is, why did he go down to the Rhine when Frankfurt is situated on both sides of the Maine? It is thus suggested that Mrs Hooper, who wrote in French, had either written le Rhin, instead of le Mein or her letter has been wrongly transcribed.[29]

The Senate received denunciations against Poullain from Amsterdam and the Northern principalities of Germany. At times, however, much of the re-structuring of the refugee's liturgies had nothing whatsoever to do with doctrines, as is made out by so many later

---

[27] Bauer, p. 194.
[28] *Original Letters*, Vol. 1, p. 111.
[29] Bauer gives the appropriate passage in French, p. 185.

English-speaking writers but merely because of practical reasons. The Weißkirche was used by nuns, the French, the English and the Dutch. Often, in the early days, the Protestants worshipped together but gradually they wished to worship apart. So that they could all hold their services on a Sunday, the Senate asked the congregations to cut down their orders of worship drastically to shorten the services as the next congregation would be waiting to enter the church. Even so, the Weißkirche was in constant use from 6:00 am Sunday morning to late at night. Similarly, the use or non-use of leavened bread in the refugee churches points to the ruling of the Senate, which was far from consistent, rather than to the doctrines of the refugees who often compromised on small matters to keep the peace.

Dalton has preserved for us a record of the weekly services. Once the Dutch had found their own church building in the Katherinenkirche, Sundays in the Weißkirche still saw a great deal of activity which caused friction at times. The English worshipped from 6-8 am; the French service was from 9-11 am, followed by an hour's catechizing and a further service at 2:00 pm. This was followed by a church business meeting. The English then took over from 4-6. The two churches held mid-week services on Tuesdays and Thursdays.[30]

The evidence suggests at least two refugee churches present in Frankfurt during 1554

The *Ratsprotokolle* and *Burgermeisterbücher* show clearly that at times some English worshipped with the French-speaking exiles and at other times they worshipped with the Dutch so there were obviously at least two different congregations meeting at the White Ladies Chapel (Weißkirche) as early as the spring of 1554. The French-speaking pastor, Valerand Poullain, a native of present day Belgium, had sought asylum, according to the Frankfurt records, on Tuesday, 13 March, 1554 and had applied for a church building on Thursday 15 March, but as the council meeting was so poorly attended, they tabled the motion until the following Tuesday. Those in favour of Poullain's motion, however, (probably the two Glauburgs)

---

[30] Dalton, p. 466.

persuaded the Senate to meet on Sunday, 18 March, when permission to meet in the Weißkirche was given. A month later, we find French, Dutch and English worshipping in the same building. On Tuesday, 3 August, 1554, the minutes of the Senate record that 'all the English' had sent a petition to the Conraten (members of the Senate or Council) Humbracht, John von Glauburg and Adolf von Glauburg, requesting citizenship. The city records are always confusing in mixing up the various nationalities of the exiles, however, it does seem that both congregations brought out written statements of belief in September, 1554. The records of Thursday, 13 September, state that both the French and English churches were accused of being Anabaptist and in order to avoid such criticism, they issued Confessions of Faith. The Lord Mayor's minutes speak of the English 'Predicanten' i.e. preachers producing a printed Confession and the Senate minutes refers specifically to Valerand Poullain 'and the other English' producing a Confession. This is not conclusive evidence for two different confessions but it points in that direction. What happened to the English confession is a matter for further research.

As the Frankfurt English congregation were, at the time of the signing of the French Order, striving to call a plurality of pastors to lead them, and also expecting the Zürich and Strasburg congregations to join them making a total of at least a hundred members, it would have been rather unusual for a mere five men to hope that the vast majority of the oncoming members would accept a form without question which a mere handful had signed. C. S. Carter gives grounds for assuming that this order was indeed the first, very temporary, order of the very earliest English Frankfurt exiles who worshipped with the French but as they grew in numbers during the following days and weeks and before sending out the invitation to exiles in other cities they received permission from the Senate 'to settle their own order of service, provided their ceremonies were not repugnant to the French, and accordingly they elected to use the Second Prayer Book of King Edward, after making considerable alterations to it.' If this were the case, and it is backed by several Elizabethan and Jacobean historians as will be shown below,[31] then the whole pro-Knox argument that Knox found the English worshipping according to the Genevan Order at Frankfurt and pro-Prayer Book men were non-existent must be seen to be the myth it is.

The records show that several forms of worship had been tried out

Indeed, it is obvious from the records that discussions over forms of worship had occurred within the fellowship from the summer of 1554 and several forms were tried out before adopting a greatly modified Prayer Book order. Arber states firmly that, at this early stage, 'discussions were rife among them as to the use of the Prayer Book.'[32] Echoing many former commentators, Arber says that it was a Prayer Book man, James Haddon, who was first invited to pastor the church, but on his refusal, John Knox was invited to represent the 'Calvinist majority' and Thomas Lever to represent the 'Anglican Minority'.[33] The evidence however, given below, does not indicate that there was such a sharp division at this time, and certainly not in the proportions Arber gives. Indeed, Arber is obviously reading into the facts his strange idea that Anglicans such as Haddon, Becon, Bale, Lever, Grindal, Jewel and the rest were not Calvinists because they were Anglican. Those who invited Knox, such as Bale, who appears to have taken the initiative, were 'Anglican Calvinists' and Knox himself was known only as an Anglican minister at the time. The call to Lever has not been preserved, but that to Knox gives no indication whatsoever that he was expected to take one of two party lines. If the five signatures on the Calvinistic French order reflect the alleged 'Calvinist majority, they must have been greatly outnumbered by the 'Anglican minority'! Nor does this speculation help to determine why, if the majority were not 'Anglicans', did they invite an Anglican, i.e. a presumed non-Calvinist and an anti-Puritan, to pastor them and only when he refused did they invite two pastors representing two different branches of the

---

[31] See Chapter XIII: The Continental Exiles, in Carter's book *The English Church and the Reformation*.
[32] *The Trouble at Frankfort*, p. xiii.
[33] Ibid, xiii.

Reformation which no one has proved were represented to any degree at Frankfurt at all! Indeed, the whole debate is burdened by the quite unfounded idea that during 1554-55 the Reformed Church of England men were not Calvinists and that the Knoxians were. This idea also takes it for granted that Calvinism is not a doctrinal matter but one of church order and discipline only. Nor do such writers as Lloyd-Jones prove helpful in arguing that 'Puritans' were synonymous with 'Presbyterians' and 'Separatists' as, when Presbyterianism developed in the next century, many of its leaders such as Arminius and Grotius could not be called 'Calvinist' by a long way. Indeed, George Carleton at the Synod of Dort told his Presbyterian colleagues straight that had they had Episcopalian discipline, Arminianism would not have been rampant in Holland. Sadly, it was from Holland that this error infiltrated England through Dutch Presbyterianism and the Anabaptists. It was thus no wonder that the Presbyterian delegates at Dort told their Episcopalian English brethren, they looked upon the Reformed Church of England as the most Reformed Church of all yet they were prevented from taking on her orders because of the chaotic political situation on the Continent.[34]

The English Congregation was Reformed to a man

The church's call to Knox, signed on 24 September, i.e. in the same month, bears twenty-one signatories which does not even then give the sum total of members of the English congregation according to other authorities. Finally, if the Genevan-Strasburg Liturgy had been adopted by the English church in September, 1554, the question arises, which order had they been using since the early summer? A further problem would be why Knox, on his arrival in Frankfurt in November, refused to celebrate communion according to this order. The argument of most of the critics of the Anglicans in their back-projection of 17th century controversies onto 16th century Frankfurt, maintain that from the supposed constitution of the church in June,

---

[34] See Toplady on *The State of Calvinism under James I*, Works, p. 244 and *A joint attestation of several Bishops and learned Divines of the Church of England, avowing that her Doctrine was confirmed, and her Discipline was not impeached, by the Synod of Dort*, given in full in Morris Fuller's, The Life of Bishop Davenant, pp. 99-109.

1554 to the arrival of the Strasburg party in March, 1555, one church order had been used throughout. This theory will be shown to be untenable.

Thomas Fuller provides a list of twenty-eight men who, he claims, were at Frankfurt at the founding of the church and before the influx of the exiles who came from Aarau, Zürich and Strasburg. If Fuller's list is in order of 'rank' which was usual at the time, we find that he places John Bale at the head, followed by Sutton, then Makebray, Whittingham and Cole. Wood finds a place in the middle of the list. Arber speaks of Calvinists as if they could not possibly be Prayer Book men. The characters and beliefs of the men on this list show that it is quite impossible to link the Calvinists solely with those who rejected the Prayer Book and the Non-Calvinists solely with those who accepted the Prayer Book as Arber (though he is far from a lone voice) does. This is confirmed by Horton Davies' findings which show irrevocably that both sides, if there ever were the sides that later commentators have suggested, were of Calvinistic-Puritan persuasion.[35] Actually, this artificial Anglican-Puritan division can be traced back, amongst other factors, to the anti-Puritan activities of Arminian Peter Heylin[36] in his *History of the Reformation* in which he, according to J.B. Marsden 'never ceased to attribute much of the discontent that followed to the Genevan exile.'[37] Marsden, in his fine work *The Early Puritans*, shows how both parties in the Frankfurt controversy were Puritan to a man and grew together rather than apart. Marsden comments:

> The relative strength of the two infant parties, the episcopal and presbyterian, was not immediately changed. What

---

[35] See his excellent overview of the situation in *The Worship of the English Puritans*, Soli Deo Gloria, 1997.

[36] Heylin also strove to denigrate the standard of Calvinism shown by the British delegates at the Synod of Dort and his Arminian false propaganda is sadly taken nowadays by critics of episcopalianism to deny that they contended for the doctrines of grace.

[37] *The Early Puritans*, p. 19. It is interesting to note that Heylin, along with John Goodwin, is the source for the libel that the English delegates at Dort were not doctrines of grace men.

was gained was an equal advantage to both sides, - on both sides an increase of mutual confidence and christian love.[38]

A brief look at the pioneer members

According to Fuller, the constituting Frankfurt congregation was composed of John Bale, Edmund Sutton, John Makebraie (Makebray), William Whittingham, Thomas Cole, William Williams, George Chidley, William Hammon (Hammond), Thomas Steward, Thomas Wood, John Stanton (Staunton), William Walton, Jasper Swift, John Geofrie, John Graie (Gray), Migell (Michael) Gill, John Samford, John Wood, Thomas Sorby (Sowerby/Serbis?), Anthonie Carier, Hugh Alford, George Whetnall, Thomas Whetnall, Edward Sutton, John Fox, Laurence Kent, William Kethe and John Hollingham.

Arber gives no evidence whatsoever to show that Sutton did not believe in the doctrines of grace commonly called Calvinism. The fact that he remained in fellowship with Whitehead and other pronounced 'Calvinists' rather suggests that he was one in faith with them. Furthermore, by the time the Frankfurt church sent out the General Letter of 2 August, asking all the English exiles to join them, Arber says that there was a 'vigorous Minority of Prayer Book men' amongst them. This was before Whitehead and Lever (both Calvinists and moderate Prayer Book men) and their parties arrived and some time before Knox joined the church.[39]

S. C. Carpenter calls Bale along with the later Frankfurt exile Thomas Becon, 'intense reformers'. He was certainly a Calvinist and he also campaigned throughout his time in Germany and Switzerland for the use of the Prayer Book. It appears that Bale even took the initiative in inviting Knox to the Frankfurt pastorate. However, Bale only knew Knox as a moderate Prayer Book man and most certainly expected the Scotsman to continue with the same order of worship that he had used throughout his duties as Edward VI's chaplain. Perhaps Bale was not aware, however, that Knox had introduced his own personal orders of worship during his itin-

---

[38] Ibid, p. 19. Marsden's first chapter deals most positively with the English exiles, seeing them all as fine examples of 'early Puritans'.

[39] *Troubles at Frankfort*, p. xiii.

erant preaching in England. Nevertheless, even if Bale did know of this, he would probably have looked upon it as 'a thing of indifference' as few, if any, of the English were as particular as Knox regarding forms and orders. Yet, it was obviously a shock to Bale when Knox opted out of the majority vote concerning the modified use of the Prayer Book and when he joined the Basle church, he objected to the Knoxians who were striving to take over there as they had striven at Frankfurt.[40]

John Makebray stayed on at Frankfurt after the Knoxians left and eventually became pastor after Whitehead. He was obviously more a Prayer Book man than a French Order man as when Thomas Cole, under Whitehead's pastorate protested at the use of godparents in a letter written in 1574, he relates how Makebray had taken on the role of godfather at Frankfurt according to the Prayer Book order, though there was heated discussion in the church regarding godparents.[41] Here, it is interesting to note that though Cole is very critical of the Prayer Book teaching regarding godparents as opposed to the French Order which he says was once used at Frankfurt and which dispenses with such 'beautifying of men's traditions', David Laing relates how Knox chose Whittingham as godfather to Nathaniel, his son, when the child was baptised on 23 May, 1557 in Geneva.[42] The use of godparents was a stone of stumbling to many Precisians[43] but the Genevan Order used by Knox in Geneva and later in Scotland ruled that the child be presented for baptism by the father and godfather, there being no mention of the mother or a godmother.[44] However, *the Liturgy of Compromise* which was drawn up by the Frankfurt church in February, 1555, which was accepted by the majority, contains the words under the heading *Public Baptism*, 'Then shall the Minister demand of the godfathers and godmothers these questions following . . . ' So, too, the French

[40] Patrick Collinson, *Archbishop Grindal*, p. 73
[41] *Troubles at Frankfort*, pp. 94-95.
[42] *The Works of John Knox*, Vol. I, p. xvii.
[43] See Neal's *History of the Puritans*, Vol. I, p. 158 for 'Puritan' thoughts on godparents.
[44] Ibid, Vol. IV, pp. 186-187. The Book of Common Prayer rules that for male children two godfathers and one godmother must be present and for female children two godmothers and one godfather.

Liturgia Sacra prescribes godparents so Cole must be referring to yet another order or simply mistaken.

Thomas Steward was most likely a moderate Prayer Book man as he left Frankfurt very early to fellowship with the Strasburg brethren and was certainly there in November 1554 when he signed a letter from Strasburg to the Frankfurt church expressing the desire to stick as close to the Prayer Book as possible under the altered circumstances of exile.

John Graie (Gray) was one of the few founding members left at Frankfurt at the death of Mary, but the very fact that he stayed on when the 'Knoxians' are supposed to have left, indicates that he was of the moderate Prayer Book party and opposed to Knox's innovations. Otherwise, Gray played no major part in the controversies from which the church suffered, his signature being merely found under the invitation to Knox at the beginning of the period of exile and under the letter of reconciliation at the end. Like Beesley, mentioned below, he appears to have played no outstanding part in the Elizabethan Settlement.

John Fox also signed the letter inviting Knox to the pastorate. He was perhaps less of a Prayer Book man than Bale but he accepted the Anglican Church order as being superior to the Genevan, though he had the same antipathy towards clerical gowns as did exiles Becon, Lever and Sampson. These 'Anglicans' were staunch Calvinists but moderate Prayer Book men, with Becon and Lever being more strict in their adherence than Sampson. Thomas Cole, a prominent pioneer member of the Frankfurt church became Archdeacon and Prebendary in the Church of England and was likewise a modified Prayer Book man though he objected to godparents. Even Thomas Wood, whom Patrick Collinson describes as 'an extreme puritan'[45] remained in the Church of England, Prayer Book and all! Sorby was one of first and last members of the Frankfurt church. He alone puts to flight the idea that the original members were anti-Anglican 'Calvinists' who left in 1555 to set up a schismatic church in Geneva. As late as September, 1557, we find Sorby writing with David Whitehead from Frankfurt to Henry Bullinger,

---

[45] Patrick Collinson, *Archbishop Grindal*, p. 236.

whom Marsden calls 'the sponsor of the English Reformation',[46] thanking him for his support of the Reformation. These men were probably the most well-known of the early Puritan Anglican exiles, yet they were not the only members by far who adhered to the Prayer Book, with a few alterations to suit the customs of the host-country. Furthermore, Fuller's list is not complete. Of the lesser-known original members of Frankfurt, not listed by Fuller, Richard Beesley (also Beasley), a modified Prayer Book man, must be mentioned as he was present at the founding of the church[47] and remained in fellowship there until the commencement of Elizabeth's reign. Beesley supported such as Whitehead, Nowell, Sorby and Sutton in the New Discipline debate at Frankfurt, arguing that in church government 'We see not, by the Scriptures, that any authority is given to any One above others; but rather the contrary.'[48] From the beliefs attested to by Beesley's signature, it is obvious that he must be regarded as a Puritan. This again puts to flight the commonly held idea that all who remained at Frankfurt were 'Anglicans' and therefore not 'Puritans'.

On 3 December, 1554 George Whetnall, Thomas Whetnall, John Knox, John Bale, William Whittingham, Edmund Sutton, Thomas Wood, William Williams, John Stanton, John Samford, John Fox, William Kethe, John Makebraie, William Walton, Migell Gill, Laurence Kent, and John Hollingham all testified to their wish to use the Book of Common Prayer 'with as little alteration as is possible.' In this letter, the Prayer Book is referred to as 'a most worthy Confession'. As former names listed in letters from Frankfurt are omitted in this list of signatories, it could be that they were no longer at Frankfurt. Given the fact that not all of the original members are mentioned by the author of *Troubles at Frankfort* and Fuller, they do not appear to have numbered more than thirty-two or so of whom two thirds were definitely Prayer Book men of sorts. Thus, in December, 1554, representatives of the various factions in the church professed a desire to use the English Prayer Book and wrote on

---

[46] *The Early Puritans*, p. 17.
[47] See *The Troubles at Frankfort*, p. 225.
[48] See 'The Second New Discipline' in *The Troubles at Frankfort*, p. 150 ff.

behalf of the full church body. Noteworthy here is that John Knox also placed his name under this letter, thus affirming that he was basically a Prayer Book man when he invited the Strasburg exiles to join the church at Frankfurt. Yet, when the Strasburg men joined the church at Frankfurt, Knox totally changed his attitude and could not have been more condemnatory of the Prayer Book if it had been a popish missal.

Though Fuller lists John Bale and John Fox as being present at Frankfurt[49] before the Whitehead, Lever and Cox parties joined, it is doubtful whether Bale was in Frankfurt in June and Fox only left England in July and spent some time in Antwerp before proceeding to Frankfurt. When Fox arrived at Frankfurt, he stayed with Anthony Gilby whom Loades describes as 'A prominent member of that party' i.e. those who were prepared to go a long way in compromising with the authorities. However, Fuller does not list Gilby as an original member of the Frankfurt church. This may mean that Gilby also arrived after the founding of the church but might equally mean that Fuller had no information about him at this time. Oddly enough, Loades calls the initial agreement of the church with the authorities 'radical' whereas it was moderately enforced conformity to the Senate's will. It is extremely doubtful that Fox would have agreed to a total neglect of the Prayer Book, though he was certainly against vestments other than a plain gown. Of Fox Loades says, 'he never accepted Genevan ideas of church government, or abandoned the 'national' church position which is normally associated with the Prayer Book party of Cox.'[50] When Bale and Fox left Frankfurt, they did not join the exiles at Geneva but helped to establish a church at Basle.

It is often pointed out that Fox left Frankfurt out of protest against the former Strasburg party which is hard to believe as Fox was on the very best terms with Cox and Grindal and also Lever and Jewel and continued to be so. His complaints re Knox's politics and the Precisians tactics are well-known but there is no record of his criticising the older leaders of the other exiles. Furthermore, Fox all along professed full agreement with Cranmer on the question of

---

[49] *The Church History of Britain*, VIII Book, p. 726 (26 in separate book).
[50] *The Oxford Martyrs*, pp. 262-263.

the Lord's Supper which led him, whilst in Germany, to translate Cranmer's answer to Gardiner on the subject. The church historian, however, could find no publisher for the work on the Continent owing to the Eucharist controversy going on in Germany and Switzerland.[51]

Writing from Frankfurt to Peter Martyr, Fox blamed young hotheads for his dissatisfaction and said of them, 'I have discovered what otherwise I could not have believed, how much bitterness is to be found amongst those whom continual acquaintance with the sacred volume ought to render gentle, and incline to all kindness. As far as in me lies, I persuade parties to concord.' One anecdote of Fox's dealings with such young rebels is preserved in the RTS collection: Fox was told by a youngster who seemed proud of his own ignorance that when studying the old authors, he could conceive no reason why men should so greatly admire them. Fox replied that it was 'No marvel indeed, for if you could conceive the reason, you would admire them yourself.'[52]

It is known that during Knox's stay at Frankfurt, Fox suggested that Martyr should settle down there as lecturer to the English congregation, believing this would induce more of the English to settle there.[53] As Peter Martyr was on the closest of terms possible with the so-called Coxians, this does not indicate that Fox was antagonistic to them. Fox's statement, however that the youngsters had been causing bother all the winter of 1554-55, was at least one of the reasons why he signed a letter of dissatisfaction before leaving Frankfurt for Basle. This is an unexplored venue in the history of the Maryan exiles and this writer has not been able to follow up the matter from the documents at hand. However, by the Spring of 1555, many new refugees had joined the Frankfurt congregation and thus added a third party to that of the original members and the Strasburg and Zürich contingents.

---

[51] *The Writings of John Fox*, etc., RTS, pp. v-vi.
[52] Ibid, p. xxiv.
[53] Ibid, pp. vi-vii.

The Liturgia Sacra, 1554

Chapter Four:
The Struggle for an Acceptable
Form of Worship and Church Order

Objections to the public reading of God's word

It would appear astonishing that Reformed Englishmen would bow
to a ruling which forbade the public reading of Scripture in church
worship. Stranger still is the obvious fact that a faction in the church
found this praiseworthy. Indeed the more radical Precisian clergy
protested against the reading of the epistles and gospels until well
into Elizabeth's reign. One can only speculate on their reasons. It
appears that they could not accept this method of hearing the entire
Word of God throughout the year, thinking that the reading of the
Word had become 'ceremonialised'. They did, however, insist on
the text for exposition being read out before preaching on it, feeling that where God's word was read publicly, it must be expounded.
Thomas Fuller, striving to maintain a balanced position, refused to
believe that the public reading of the Word was prohibited, arguing
that though such a reading was not mentioned *expressis verbis*, this
did not mean that it was not the custom. However, David Whitehead of the Frankfurt church wrote to tell Calvin that the faction
under John Knox, did indeed suppress the reading of the Word in
public worship.[1] Writing on behalf of this alleged 'puritan' side,
Edward Arber, in his explanatory notes to the documents behind
the troubles at Frankfurt, states:

---

[1] *Original Letters*, Vol. II. Parker Society, Letter CCCLVIII, pp. 755-763.

It will be noticed that in the above Calvinistic Scheme of Public Worship, the Public Reading of the Scriptures has no place. This confirms the statement, at page 89, of the later Anglican Congregation in that same Church of the White Ladies at Frankfurt, that these Calvinists exclaimed against the Public Reading of the Word of GOD 'as an irksome and unprofitable Form.'[2]

Arber's reference to 'page 89' of *Troubles at Frankfort* shows once again how careless the use of terms has become in more modern times. The 'Anglican' letter to which Arber refers, as opposed to those of 'the Calvinistic Scheme', was a defence of the Frankfurt church from false criticism after Arber's so-called Calvinists, under Knox, had left and was penned principally at the instigation of David Whitehead who was a known Nonconformist, an ardent Calvinist, and the democratically elected pastor of the Frankfurt church. Whitehead alone shows how wrong it is to force the black or white party-spirited thinking of the Great Rebellion onto church life of a century before. The evils of that period were great enough without back projecting them on to the most fertile period of Reformation in the history of the British church.

Actually, the original order of worship of the church, in as far as it can be reconstructed, was not as anti-Scriptural as the forms Knox later strove to use but which were nevertheless rejected by the church. Horton Davies, in fact, finds that the first order of service at Frankfurt started with an Exhortation using scriptural sentences. This was fully in keeping with the order set up by the Edwardian Prayer Book. This was followed by a confession of sins, a metrical Psalm, a prayer for the Holy Spirit, a Scripture reading and sermon, a general prayer followed by the Lord's Prayer, the recitation of the Apostles Creed and the singing of a further metrical Psalm. As in the Edwardian Prayer Book, the service ended in the Blessing.[3] Fuller's version of the order given in his *The Church*

---

[2] *Troubles at Frankfort*, 1907 edition, p. 25.
[3] *The Worship of the English Puritans*, p. 117.

History of Britain, VIII Book, p. 727 (27 of separate issue) omits the Scriptural sentences and the reading before the sermon but expresses a belief that some form of Scripture reading was used, nevertheless. The author of *Troubles at Frankfort* in his history of the church does not mention Scriptural readings at all but as he is careful to explain merely the *differences* between the Frankfurt order and the Edwardian Prayer Book, it could be concluded that what he does not mention, was acceptable. However, though Knox and Whittingham always insisted that they adhered to the letter of the original Frankfurt order which had been drawn up for all time, in their interpretation of it, besides the use of the litany, they omitted the Scriptural exhortations and the public reading of Epistles and Gospels, yet read out the Scriptures to be expounded before the sermon. That this was the original agreement is most doubtful as Horton Davies' research and that of this author shows. Neither the French forms, nor the Genevan forms of Calvin neglected public Scriptural exhortations and even if they had done so, the Frankfurt church was not as bound by them as later commentators have presumed. The author of *Troubles at Frankfort* clearly states in his history:

> When the Church was in this sort granted; they consulted among themselves, what Order of Service they should use: for they were not so strictly bound, as was told them, to the Ceremonies of the French, by the Magistrates; but that if the one allowed of the other, it was sufficient.[4]

Furthermore, the *Liturgia Sacra*, which Whittingham signed, contains not only Scriptural exhortations but allows for the public reading of Scripture without exposition. It seems therefore most likely that the idea that a once and for all time church order was drawn up to which the so-called Puritans kept yet which the so-called Anglicans broke is but a back projection of later polemics. It is to be noted here that Knox's Genevan *Forme of Prayers* published in 1556 diverges from those of his fellow Puritans and Pres-

---

[4] See the section: *The Calvinistic Order of Public Worship*, p. 25.

byterians who nearly all, apart from Knox, open their services with Scriptural exhortations. Knox also differs from Calvin's Genevan Order by omitting the Scriptural sentences at the baptism rite. All of the so-called Puritan Liturgies, listed by Horton Davies in Appendix A of his *The Worship of the English Puritans*, including Calvin's and Knox's forms, omit the reading of the Epistles and Gospels which was an integral part of the Reformed Church of England's worship.[5] However, in most of the other Genevan versions used by the English in Elizabethan England and in Holland, the service was opened by the reading of an appropriate Bible chapter.

The facts reveal that the Edwardian Book of Common Prayer emphasised and proscribed the public reading of God's Word more than any other Reformed order of worship. By this means, worshippers hear almost the entire Word of God from Genesis to Revelation during the ecclesiastical year. However, the liturgy that Knox adopted after leaving Frankfurt had no prescribed readings at all apart from the sermon text. He thus departed radically from the view of Poullain and the English, including Whittingham, who had supported him in drawing up the *Liturgia Sacra*, to which Knoxian writers have always maintained their hero adhered.

The Frankfurt church looks for a pastor and church officers
Once they had reached agreement that the first church of English exiles should be constituted at Frankfurt, the members decided to set themselves up as a communications, co-ordination and evangelistic centre for all the exiles on the Continent. They thus sent out a general letter, dated 2 August, 1554, to Strasburg, Zürich, Duisburg, Wesel and Emden, inviting all the English Reformers scattered throughout the Continent and not yet formed into churches to join them in one large church in a great and influential city which offered them protective security and, to a large extent, freedom of worship scarcely found elsewhere.[6] They also planned to set up a university in Frankfurt and applied for lecturers.

---

[5] See Appendix
[6] See ibid, p. 26 ff. for copy of letter.

Meanwhile, John Bale, formerly Bishop of Ossory in Ireland, had been compelled to flee to Frankfurt with his family in 1554. Though the church looked to Bale for leadership, he felt his poor health and premature old-age would prevent him fulfilling such duties and would also interfere with his calling to complete his great work on the history of the church and the martyrs.[7] At this time John Knox, an Anglican minister, though a Scotsman, and former Chaplain to King Edward, had fled to Geneva after the King's decease, and worked on political reform with Christopher Goodman there. On 24 September, 1554, finding that Knox was leaving Geneva,[8] Bale led the church in inviting Knox to become one of three pastors of the church.[9] Thomas Lever, then at Zürich, was also invited, as also James Haddon of Strasburg. It is significant that these three men were all ordained ministers of the Church of England and at least two of them, Lever and Haddon, were Prayer Book men, more or less. It is no daring stretch of the imagination to presume that this choice thus reflected the high percentage of pro-Prayer Book men in the congregation. James Haddon refused the call but Lever and Knox accepted. Apparently no substitute for Haddon was found, possibly because the church had ordained Whitehead as their pastor shortly before Knox's and Lever's arrival. Knox initially hesitated to accept the offer and there was some delay in his journeying to Frankfurt. He finally accepted the call through Calvin's intervention. It was this decision which in God's providence caused the controversy which would split the Frankfort church from November 1554 to March 1556.

The invitations sent out to Lever and Haddon have not been preserved but the author of *Troubles at Frankfort* has saved the invitation to Knox from oblivion, so we may presume that the other invitations were similar. The Frankfurt congregation wrote:

---

[7] See Archbishop Parker to Matt. Flacius Illyricus, Letter XXXVI *Zurich Letters*, Second Series, p. 77, for details of Bale's earlier works and Parker's efforts to trace them.

[8] Lindsay claims that Knox was preparing a treatise on the right of subjects to rebel. Hastings Robinson suggests this was Knox's Genevan associate, Goodman. The two men obviously worked together.

[9] *Letter from Frankfort*, 4 Sept., 1554.

WE HAVE RECEIVED Letters from our brethren of Strasburg; but not in such sort and ample wise as we looked for. Whereupon we assembled together, in the HOLY GHOST, we hope, and have, with one voice and consent, chosen you so particularly to be one of the Ministers of our Congregation here, to preach unto us the most lively Word of GOD, according to the gift that GOD hath given you: forasmuch as we have here, through the merciful goodness of GOD, a Church to be congregated together in the name of CHRIST, and be all of one body, and also being of one nation, tongue, and country. And, at this present, having need of such a one as you; we do desire you, and also require you in the name of GOD, not to deny us, nor to refuse these our requests: but that you will aid, help, and assist, us with your presence, in this our good and godly enterprise; which we have taken in hand to the glory of GOD, and the profit of his Congregation, and the poor sheep Of CHRIST dispersed abroad, who (with your and like presences) would come hither, and be of One Fold; where as now they wander abroad as lost sheep, without any guide.

We mistrust not, but that you will joyfully accept this Calling. Fare ye well! From Frankfort, this 24th of September (1554).

Your loving Brethren,

JOHN BALE   WILLIAM HAMMON
JOHN GRAY   EDMUND SUTTON
THOMAS STEWARD   MICHAEL GILL
JOHN MAKEBRAIE   THOMAS WOOD
JOHN SAMFORD   WILLIAM WHITTINGHAM
JOHN STANTON   JOHN WOOD
THOMAS COLE   WILLIAM WALTON
THOMAS SORBY   WILLIAM WILLIAMS
JASPER SWIFT   ANTHONY CARIAR
GEORGE CHIDLEY   JOHN GEOFFREY
HUGH ALFORD

The difference between pastor and minister in the church was that the former conducted the ordinances and took care of visiting and counselling whereas the latter took care of the preaching.

David Whitehead becomes the first pastor of the Frankfurt church

There was no speedy reply from Knox and the Frankfurt congregation were eager to start a regular church ministry. Then, in October, 1554, David Whitehead joined the Frankfurt church with a number of fellow exiles who were also moderate Prayer Book men. Whitehead, was immediately asked to take charge of the congregation in lieu of the pastors already invited. Whitehead accepted the call and commenced teaching from the Epistle to the Romans, carrying out full pastoral duties. Again, there is no record of Whitehead's call but it is noteworthy that the supposedly anti-Anglican majority again elected a moderate Prayer Book man as pastor. It is uncertain whether Whitehead's call was a permanent one or merely until the other invited pastors came. Whether Whitehead kept his pastoral office, because of Haddon's refusal is also a matter of speculation, though when new officers were elected and re-elected five months later, i.e. in March, 1555, Whitehead was re-elected as pastor. Whitehead was a close friend of Cranmer's and a Nonconformist and had refused the Archbishopric of Armagh. Yet he preferred to use the English Prayer Book, though he, too, was open to changes which were necessary because of being a church in exile. Whitehead sincerely believed that brethren in Christ should not split church unity by dogmatically sticking to externals. Sadly, the Reformer was sequestered from his English church in 1564 for dogmatically sticking to his broad views of tolerance! Pro Knox commentators tend to argue that, immediately on his arrival, Knox carried on the status quo of Whitehead's pioneer work. They fail to note the very obvious, indeed glaring, fact that Knox broke with Whitehead and the earlier compiler of *Troubles at Frankfort* looks on Whitehead as representing a church order fully opposed to Knox's. Indeed, Whitehead became one of Knox's strongest critics, seeing in him a danger to the work of the Reformation.

The answer of the Zürich brethren

The brethren at Zürich replied that they would earnestly consider the request but would prefer to use the Second Book of Common Prayer and not the political and ecumenical compromise which they had heard the Frankfurt exiles were using.[10] They were supported by Bullinger in this matter who was anxious to introduce the Reformer Thomas Lever to the Continental Reformers such as Calvin[11] and also send him from Zürich to help lead the Frankfurt church.[12] Lever was an anti-vestiarian but a moderate Prayer Book man and well grounded in the doctrines of grace and experimental religion. The Zürich brethren asked Richard Chambers to take their letter and bring back any reply that might be made. Chambers was a most independent man and seems to have had something of a wandering spirit. He used this in God's service as wherever he went, he collected money for the exiles and thus was able to relieve many struggling brethren. Sadly, Chambers too had his troubles at Frankfurt some three years later when the church rebuked him for not using money that he had collected for certain poor. They also demanded of Chambers that he gave the church a full account of the money he collected and how it was spent. Chambers was in membership at Frankfurt, they argued, so the money he collected should be distributed according to the democratic decision of the church. Chambers argued that as the Frankfurt church had never officially commissioned him to collect funds on their behalf, and as he never made any promises to Frankfurt concerning financial aid, he felt himself free to alleviate want wherever and whenever he felt it was necessary.[13]

The letter which Chambers took back to Zürich from the Frankfurt brethren, dated 15 November, states that they are in full agree-

---

[10] *Troubles at Frankfort*, reply dated 13 October, 1554, pp. 32-33.

[11] See *Original Letters*, CCCLII, CCCXXVI. See also Lever's letters to Bullinger in Vol. I. especially LXXXI.

[12] It is difficult to determine whether Lever was eventually *called* by the Frankfurt church or *sent* there by the Zürich brethren.

[13] See Chambers letters of 20 and 30 June, 1557, *Troubles at Frankfort*, pp. 216-17.

ment with him and with the wishes of the men he represents. Concerning the Anglican order, the Frankfurt brethren say:

> As touching the effect of the Book, we desire the execution thereof as much as you, so far as God's Word doth commend it: but as for the unprofitable Ceremonies, as well by his consent (Chambers') as by ours, are not to be used. And although they were tolerable, as some are not; yet, being in a strange common-wealth, we could not be suffered to put them in use: and better it were, they should never be practised; than they should be the subversion of our Church, which should fall in great hazard by using them.[14]

It should come then as no surprise that when Knox and his few followers broke with this arrangement and left Frankfurt, Chambers, who had been instrumental in uniting the Frankfurt men with their Zürich and Strasburg brethren, stayed at Frankfurt with the majority.[15]

---

[14] P. 37.
[15] Chambers moved to Geneva at the end of the Maryan exile but for other reasons which will be mentioned as the story proceeds.

IOANNES CNOXVS.

From Theod. Beze Icones, etc., M.D.LXXX.

John Knox

Chapter Five:
Knox Arrives at Frankfurt

Prayer Book men head the signatories in inviting Knox to Frankfurt

The extant Frankfurt letter inviting Knox, with Bale's, Sutton's and Makebray's signature uppermost, is of great importance in the controversy as modern defenders of Knox argued that as he was there before the 'Anglican' faction, he had a greater right than they to determine the church's policy. The letter, however, reveals that a substantial and influential group of Prayer Book men were there before Knox. Whitehead and his party were also enrolled as members before Knox and Whitehead believed strongly that Knox's opinions were not in keeping with Reformed piety and order. Furthermore, Thomas Lever who arrived at Frankfurt about the same time as Knox, was very similar to Whitehead in his Nonconformist views, and he, too, preferred the Book of Common Prayer to the various Reformed alternatives in use on the Continent. As yet, it must be emphasised, the Frankfurt congregation still apparently believed that Knox was a Prayer Book man as he was an Anglican minister appointed by royal patronage.[1]

---

[1] This writer must leave the matter of Knox's ordination open as he has not been able to find evidence to prove or disprove that Knox had a Reformed Church of England ordination, not that it mattered much at the time.

Knox's refusal to celebrate the Lord's Supper with the English brethren

When Knox eventually arrived at Frankfurt, he refused point blank to celebrate the Lord's Supper with the brethren on the rather 'churchy' grounds that he had no order to go by and that he was not 'suffered to minister the Sacrament according to his conscience.' This was a strange utterance as nobody had forbidden him to celebrate the Lord's Supper either according to the French or English forms or by simply adhering to the Word of God. This is illustrative of Knox's whole position. He was a liturgical man through and through and could not think of celebrating the ordinances according to the plain words of Scripture or an order which he thought had a few oddities in it. Roman Catholics were to tease Knox for professing to be a bibliocrat though his rites bore little outward resemblance to the Scriptural situation. He criticised others most strongly for faithfully worshipping Christ in the Eucharist according to their understanding of the Word and insisted that they followed his way or none at all. Thus Knox refused to take up the pastorate offered him and suggested that he might stay on as a preacher. One cannot help believing that Knox refused to administer the Lord's Supper as a means of disciplining the congregation and forcing them to comply fully with his ways. This had been Calvin's method who withheld the bread and wine from communicants when he wished to humble them. When he banned the whole city of Geneva from the Lord's Table, this proved too much for the otherwise patient Genevans and they exiled their own senior pastor for three years (1538-1541). However, during Calvin's absence, a number of church members refused to take communion with their brethren on various grounds and the church was split for a number of years.

The Frankfurt congregation thus requested Knox to stay and preach until disagreements as to the pastoral office and church order were solved. However, because of Knox's stubborn refusal to adopt one of a number of compromises offered to him by the Church, the brethren remained without due celebration of the ordinances for several months. This forced the members to go to the Lutherans to have their children baptised, a fact which brought yet more strife to the church. As the members could not accept the semi-popish Lutheran doctrine of consubstantiation, they were not able to fellowship around the Lord's Table either inside or outside of their own church building!

Knox then complicated the matter by refusing further suggestions to promote unity such as using the Geneva Order in the form drawn up by Calvin. It is also quite certain that Knox never had anything approaching a majority backing in his refusal to accept any of the Reformed Orders used hitherto. In spite of these facts, commentators of yesteryear such as Neal and those of modern times such as Martyn Lloyd-Jones, have perpetuated the myth of a Reformed pastor being supported by a faithful people, who worshipped according to the Geneva Order but was plagued by a popish minority of 'cruel' Coxians who loved 'an abundance of ceremonies'. The Genevan Order was never implemented at Frankfurt, solely on account of John Knox's resistance. The so-called Coxians could not have protested at its use because they were not even there. As matters turned out, they agreed wholeheartedly to use the French Order, which was similar to Geneva's.

Thus the argument that Knox accepted a previously drawn up order and carried on this 'church tradition' of four months standing and protected it against the onslaught of the 'Coxians', as per critics such as Lloyd-Jones, is a myth indeed. Horton Davies shows how the Frankfurt church first decided to draw up a permanent order of worship after Knox's arrival and Knox refused point blank to accept their suggestions.[2] Surprised at Knox's stance, the congregation, supported by John Fox, said that he was quite welcome to use Calvin's Genevan Order as they were no stickers to forms. Again, Knox refused the church's compromise on the self-contradictory grounds that the form was not generally used in all the English churches in exile. This would have been an argument for the Second Prayer Book which was universally accepted.

One of Knox's major criticisms of Anglican customs with which he disagreed was that they were 'Aaronotic'. This emphasis on

---

[2] *The Worship of the English Puritans*, p. 30.

Old Testament ritualism, he believed, was typical of the 'English face' of the Reformation. If, however, the wearing of gowns were Aaronotic to the Knoxians, and not a mere traditional development of ordinary clothing, and if they condemned Old Testament influ- ence on New Testament behaviour, then such a condemnation proves to be a sword which cuts both ways and wounds the judge more than those he condemns. The Genevan vestments, which many English Episcopalians looked on in protest as 'Turkish Robes', became the proscribed form during Knox's Scottish Reformation. Furthermore Knox's own views of what is allowed in Christian conduct and what not is strictly Old Testament and his view of church discipline was strictly based on case law, which is clearly shown in Scripture to be but shadows of things to come. Indeed, in such works as *The Appellation of John Knox from the cruel and most injust sentence pronounced against him by the false bishops and clergy of Scotland* he not only lays down the Christian pattern of conduct as adhering to the letter of case law but he proscribes the death penalty for those who would rather be ruled by Christ than Moses. On the other hand, the English Reformation always emphasised that Christian practice was based on a pan-Scriptural understanding of divine revelation. This was eventually formulated in the Canons of 1571, compiled at the height of the Church's strug- gle with the Old Testament-minded Precisians, which specified that nothing was to be taught in the Church which was not in keeping both with the Old Testament and the New. Contrary to this, Knox's views of church discipline, in general, in which he strove to found a Christian church on the basis of the Jewish dispensation were en- tirely Old Testament, yet interpreted in such an extreme way that one would be hard put to find an Old Testament saint who would have agreed with him. Lang sums up Knox's general attitude to Scripture via his attitude to celebrating the Lord's Supper:

> To us it may seem that the sudden denunciation of a Christian ceremony, as sheer 'idolatry', equivalent to the worship of serpents, bulls, or of a foreign Baal in ancient

Israel – was a step calculated to confuse the real issues and to provoke a religious war of massacre. Knox, we know, regarded extermination of idolaters as a counsel of perfection, though in the Christian scriptures not one word could be found to justify his position. He relied on texts about massacring Amalekites and about Elijah's slaughter of the prophets of Baal. The mass was idolatry, was Baal worship: and Baal worshippers, if recalcitrant, must die.[3]

These ideas, Lang defines justly as 'extreme unchristian' and it is the old problem of the mote and the beam. Knox saw in his Don Quixote vision of the Anglican' 'things indifferent' and 'inessentials' i.e. in their 'externals' a devilish devotion to Jewery and Baalism. He thus made giants out of harmless, even useful windmills. His conscience, however, was never apparently troubled by his adhering not only to external displays of Judaism but accepting their most legalistic practices as a gospel authority for him to root out 'heresy' and purge Scotland, when he came to power there, of 'pagan' elements, so producing his ideal state. Knox never ceased to use the political and secular arm to bring his views of Conformity to bear on Scottish citizens. He knew little of Christian liberty and freedom of conscience so loved by Nonconformists and even Separatists. Thus Knox's evangelistic policy sadly became, as one frank biographer puts it, 'convert or exterminate.' This policy stood in stark contrast to that of Fox, Jewel, Grindal, Becon, Lever, Cox and Whitehead, indeed, if one were to give Knox a rating for Christian tolerance when faced with Nonconformity in comparison with all the Frankfurt divines, the Scotsman would be at the bottom of the list. It is a tribute to the tolerance of McCrie, an eminent Free Kirk man, that his hero would never have viewed his biographer with the same leniency. However, Knox's Scotland was blessed with a Government who did not agree with their religious leader that idolaters must 'die the death'.

---

[3] *John Knox and the Reformation*, p. 64.

Kneeling in worship anathema to Knox

Apparently, Knox's reason for thinking the English celebration of
the Lord's Supper was devilish (yes, his word) was that worshippers knelt whilst receiving the bread and wine and whilst in prayer
to the Almighty. Nobody, however, one would think, by any stretch
of the imagination, would believe that kneeling in worship before
God was tantamount to worshipping the elements. Knox believed
it was, but his belief, as in most of the cases where he disagreed
with the English Prayer Book, was based on a misunderstanding of
the Biblical narrative, the events leading up to the Reformation
and the Reformation faith of the English Reformers. It was sheer
ignorance that fired Knox's antagonism to the Reformers' respect
for God's holiness shown by kneeling before Him. An example of
the former is that Knox insisted that the apostles sat at table, in
good 16th century style when the first Lord's Supper was celebrated
and thus he could only administer the sacraments to people who
sat. Here Knox would not budge an inch and he was prepared to
denounce anyone as a papist who did not agree with him. However, unlike the original celebration of the Lord's Supper, Knox, as
Ninian Winzet was quick to point out, did not mind a *plurality* of
officials *standing* and *moving about* in order to administer communion. So too, alleged Winzet, Knox broke the original order of
the Lord's Supper by having those who were not shepherds of the
flock and not even ordained ministers distribute the bread and wine.
If Knox wished to be thoroughly Reformed, added Winzet, he should
hold the Lord's Supper in the evening and not early in the morning! Nor did Knox have qualms about decorating a table on four
legs with fine linen and other decorative elements probably quite
unknown to the original Lord's Supper worshippers. Indeed, though
Knox tells his readers in *The Book of Discipline* that the celebration 'is then most rightly ministered when it approacheth most nigh
to Christ's own action',[4] the ceremony he proscribes differs not only
quite radically from that of the Anglican service and Dissenters of
the age but would strike both Anglicans and Dissenters, and not

---

[4] II. Of Sacraments.

merely a critical Winzet, as being quite different to the original historical celebration.[5] After describing the customs of all the Reformed churches, E. Stähelin concludes that 'In no church, however, is the imitation of the ancient form of the communion so close as in the Church of England.'[6]

Knox not only set up a new tradition but he proscribed that those who diverged from it be punished by death. Those Dissenters, whether Anglican or otherwise, who believed this was 'Popery without its mask' surely had both Scripture and history on their side! Knox came very near to Calvin's high view of the sacrament in viewing it as signs whereby belief is elevated to that which they signify and in this way it communicates the benefits rather than the mere remembrance of Christ's work. Here, surprisingly enough, Knox would have found an ally in Hooper who quickly changed his former Zwinglian views of the Eucharist and urged that the sacraments 'are not only signs whereby something is signified, but also they are such signs as do exhibit and give the grace that they signify indeed.'[7] Many, if not most, of the Anglicans whom he opposed, however, were more Zwinglian in their view of the Lord's Supper. Some, such as Humphrey, Sampson, Becon and apparently Bale, too, radically so. Such an observation led E.C.S. Gibson to state that the 1552-53 Article XXIX (Article XXVIII in the 1563 and 1571 version) was specifically drawn up so as to be acceptable to those who held 'that the Presence was merely figurative'.[8] This fact illustrates the great weakness in Knox's intolerant attitude to diversity of opinion and conviction. For him, those who knelt at communion were papist, even if their view of the benefits of the rite were more 'low church', less sacramental, and thus by Knox's normal logic, less papist, than his own. Perhaps, after all, the most

---

[5] See *The Book of Discipline*, II Of Sacraments.

[6] Lord's Supper, *Schall-Herzog Encyclopaedia of Religious Knowledge*.

[7] *The Later Writings of John Hooper*, Parker Society, p. 45. See Hardwick's *A History of the Articles of Religion*, The XLII Articles of 1553 for a discussion of Hooper's contribution to the drawing up of the Articles.

[8] *The Thirty-Nine Articles of the Church of England*, p. 645. Gibson was admitting a position taken by the Article which was contrary to his own.

acceptable and tolerant interpretation of a Scriptural understanding of the ordinance is that proscribed by Queen Elizabeth:

> Christ was the Word that spake it:
> He took the bread and brake it:
> And what the Word did make it,
> That I believe and take it.[9]

Cranmer and history versus Knox and his new traditions

Scholars, such as Cranmer, told Knox in vain that the apostles reclined whilst eating. Knox, who made sitting at the Lord's Table a doctrine and sign of salvation, stuck to his opinion claiming that he would give place to no angel or any man who professed the contrary. He had established a tradition and would not give it up though it broke the unity of the Reformation. Cranmer called Knox's attitude '*gloriosus*' in the sense of 'boastful' or 'arrogant' and, according to Knox's definitive biographer Andrew Lang, claimed that Knox's understanding of Scripture and his own view of himself were subversive to the work of the gospel.[10] Be this as it may, Knox had no reason to quibble over the Prayer Book's admonition to kneel as the so-called Black Rubric, probably included to pacify Knox and Hooper, explained that the kneeling had nothing to do with adoration of the elements but respect before God. As Whitgift said in his debate with Cartwright, who tended to out Knoxianise Knox, whether one sits or stands has nothing to do with adoration as one can adore a thing sitting as well as kneeling or standing, in fact, in any body position whatsoever![11] Indeed, it is odd that Knox should think that kneeling on receiving the ordinance was in any way popish as the Roman Catholic method had been to receive the

---

[9] Taken from Daniel's *The Prayer Book*, p. 391. See *Select Poetry: Chiefly Devotional of the Reign of Queen Elizabeth*, Edward Farr, Ed., 2 vols, Parker Society for Elizabeth's rendering in verse of Psalm 14.

[10] See Lang's most honest and frank sections *Knox and Kneeling* and *Cranmer on Knox*, in his *John Knox and the Reformation*, pp. 32-35.

[11] See Dawley's *John Whitgift and the Reformation*, p. 136. Also, Elton's *Reform and Reformation: England 1509-1558*, p. 365.

ordinance standing and when the host was carried about to be worshipped, those worshippers prostrated themselves.

The Knox party, past or present, has always sought to tone down the opposition Cranmer showed to Knox, especially on the matter of kneeling whilst receiving the Lord's Supper. They invariably claim that Cranmer, if given the opportunity, would have come over to Knox's view. We thus read so often, the rather lame argument that 'Cranmer, Bishop of Canterbury, had drawn up a Book of Prayer a hundred times more perfect than this that we now have.'[12] However tempting the idea of a Prayer Book one hundred times better than the Second Book of Common Prayer, may be, known records from Cranmer's pen hardly point in that direction. In a State Paper concerning the revising of the Prayer Book, Cranmer was quite explicit concerning the subject of kneeling and rejected those who wished to abandon the practice as being thoroughly un-Biblical in their reasoning, writing:

> After my right humble commendations unto your good Lordships.
>
> Where I understand by your Lordships' letters that the King's Majesty his pleasure is that the Book of Common Service should be diligently perused, and therein the printers' errors to be amended. I shall travail therein to the uttermost of my power - albeit I had need first to have had the book written which was past by Act of Parliament, and sealed with the great seal, which remaineth in the hands of Mr. Spilman, clerk of the Parliament, who is not in London, nor I cannot learn where he is. Nevertheless, I have gotten the copy which Mr. Spilman delivered to the printers to print by, which I think shall serve well enough. And where I understand further by your Lordships' letters that some be offended with kneeling at the time of the receiving

---

[12] See, for instance *Troubles at Frankfort*, p. 75. It appears that the author is using Hooper as his source but as, judging by the context, the author misunderstood Hooper regarding Bullinger, he may have misunderstood him regarding Cranmer, too. See also Neal, Vol. I., pp. 81-82.

of the Sacrament, and would that I (calling to me the Bishop
of London, and some other learned men as Mr. Peter Martyr or such like), should *with them expend, and weigh the
said prescription of kneeling, whether it be fit to remain as
a commandment, or to be left out of the book. I shall ac-
complish the King's Majesty his commandment herein: -
albeit I trust that we with just balance right weighed this at
the making of the book, and not only we, but a great many
Bishops and others of the best learned within this realm
appointed for that purpose.* And now the book being read
and approved by the whole State of the Realm, in the High
Court of Parliament, with the King's Majesty his royal as-
sent – that this should be now altered again without Parliament – of what importance this matter is, I refer to your
Lordships' to consider. I know your Lordships' wisdom to
be such that I trust ye will not be moved with these glorious
and unquiet spirits which can like nothing but that is after
their own fancy; and cease not to make trouble when things
be most quiet and in good order. If such men should be heard
– although the book were made every year anew, yet it should
not lack faults in their opinion. 'But', say they, 'it is not
commanded in the Scripture to kneel, and whatsoever is not
commanded in the Scripture is against the Scripture, and
utterly unlawful and ungodly.' But this saying is the chief
foundation of the Anabaptists and of divers other sects. This
saying is a subversion of all order as well in religion as in
common policy. If this saying be true take away the whole
Book of Service; for what should men travail to set in order
in the form of service, if no order can be got but that is
already prescribed in Scripture! And because I will not trouble your Lordships with reciting of many Scriptures or proof
in this matter, whosoever teacheth any such doctrine (if your
Lordships will give me leave) I will set my foot by his, to be
tried by fire, that his doctrine is untrue; and not only untrue;
but also seditious and perilous to be heard of any subjects,
as a thing breaking their bridle of obedience and loosing
from the bond of all Princes' laws.

My good Lordships, I pray you to consider that there be two prayers which go before the receiving of the Sacrament, and two immediately follow – all which time the people praying and giving thanks do kneel. And what inconvenience there is that it may not be thus ordered, I know not. If the kneeling of the people should be discontinued for the time of the receiving of the Sacrament, so that at the receipt thereof they should rise up and stand or sit, and then immediately kneel down again – it should rather import a contemtuous than a reverent receiving of the Sacrament. 'But is not expressly contained in the Scripture' (say they) 'that Christ ministered the Sacrament to his apostles kneeling.' Nor they find it not expressly in Scripture that he ministered it standing or sitting. But if we will follow the plain words of Scripture we should rather receive it lying down on the ground – as the custom of the world at that time almost everywhere, and as the Tartars and Turks use yet at this day, to eat their meat lying upon the ground. And the words of the Evangelist import the same, which be ἀσακειμαι and αναπιπτο, which signify, properly, to lie down upon the floor or ground, and not to sit upon a form or stool. And the same speech use the Evangelists where they show that Christ fed five thousand with five loaves, where it is plainly expressed that they sat down upon the ground and not upon stools.

I beseech your Lordships take in good part this my long babbling, which I write as of myself only. The Bishop of London is not yet come, and your Lordships require answer with speed, and therefore am I constrained to make some answer to your Lordships afore his coming. And thus I pray God long to preserve your Lordships, and to increase the same in all prosperity and godliness.

At Lambeth, this 7th of October, 1552,

Your Lordships' to command,

T. Cant.[13]

---

[13] Taken from Blunt's *The Reformation of the Church of England*, Vol. II., pp. 103-105.

Witty Ninian Winzet, whom Knox never strove to refute, though
he attacked lesser critics vigorously, was quick to point out that
Knox was more popish than the pope and his ideas of Scripture
norms amounted to superstition having no real basis whatsoever in
the Word of God.[14] Winzet lists case after case, over forty in all,
where Knox leaves the 'Reformed' path. This causes Hugh Watt to
claim that though Winzet was a papist, it would have taken little to
have made him a leading Reformer.[15]

The Knoxian view of history
Just as Knox's over-scrupulosity in his selective and peculiar treatment of Scripture angered many, so his apparent carelessness in
historical assessment angered even more. He stubbornly refused to
see any distinguish between the first and second Edwardian Prayer
Book and accused the latter for containing the teaching of the former.
For instance, he accused his fellow Anglican exiles of accepting
full papal vestments, though he saw they never wore them and the
Second Prayer Book actually banned them. When he worshiped
with the Frankfurt Anglicans, he believed that they were only waiting for him to look the other way and then they would quickly set
up altars decorated with candles and crosses. When babies were
born, he lived in the fixed conviction that his English brethren would
baptise the child according to Roman rites. This made him ban
everything that he thought was a superfluous ceremony in his own
practice of baptism, including exhortations from Scripture which
the Reformers had insisted upon placing in their order for baptism.
This not only warped and plagued his suspicious imagination but
controlled his reports of Frankfurt practice in his letters to others.
It was not so much that Knox was guilty of intentional false witness. He did not question the validity of what he was saying but
was possessed by a fixed idea that was eating into his character,
destroying his witness and perverting his objective understanding
of the truth which was practised by the 'Anglicans' before his eyes.
His own wrath had consumed him.

---

[14] See Hugh Watt's *John Knox in Controversy*, pp. 26-47.
[15] *John Knox in Controversy*, p. 47.

Nonconformist Whitehead had quite a time, striving to convince Calvin that Knox and his party had given a totally false picture of what the Anglican exiles believed. Leaving all euphemisms aside, Whitehead tells Calvin that he has been told a pack of lies. It is thus no surprise and yet to be welcomed, that Andrew Lang, always striving to be objective and truthful in depicting the man whom he so much admired, comes to the point at the start of his work by explaining that in politics and history, Knox sailed as near the wind as he could. Lang warns his readers that they must get behind the Traditions[16] regarding Knox, especially those tales told in Knox's own 'History'. Presumably Lang is referring to *The History of the Reformation in Scotland with which are included Knox's confession and the Book of Discipline*, here. Concerning this work, Lang, echoing several other commentators, tells us that Knox 'needs such careful watching,' and that 'it is difficult to determine the amount of truth it may contain.' Time and time again, we find Lang pointing out that Knox's dating does not fit the events recorded and that sequences of events are 'dislocated', and statistics blown up by several hundred percent.[17] The height of Lang's many criticisms on Knox's subtle use of 'disinformation' to gain his own ends is reached in his chapter 'Knox's Intrigues, and His Account of them', where the author reveals deceit after deceit on the part of Knox and concludes 'Knox uses his ink like the cuttle-fish to conceal the facts'.[18] On reading such accounts from secondary literature as in the original documents, the words of Butler's biting satire in Hudibras come to mind:

> For saints may do the same things by
> The spirit, in sincerity,
> Which other men are tempted to,
> And at the devil's instance do!

---

[16] Lang uses a capital T to show what authority such Traditions have in modern opinion-building.

[17] See, for instance, *John Knox and the Reformation*, pp. x-xi, 88, 93, 275 and passim.

[18] *John Knox and the Reformation*, p. 145.

Lang also complains that 'Knox ran so very far ahead of the Genevan pontiffs of his age in violence,' and says of his language, 'His favourite adjectives are 'bloody', 'beastly', 'rotten' and 'stinking'.[19] This latter use of brutal, biased and totally exaggerated language must have come as a shock to the Frankfurt church as whenever they disagreed with Knox to the slightest extent, the Scotsman bombarded them with abuse as if they had called Knox's mother a harlot or something possibly worse!

Lang's animadversions against Knox's unreliability as a historian were not peculiar to this biographer alone but commented on at length by other biographers such as Lord Percy who often disagreed with Lang concerning Knox but agree with him on this specific issue. Starting with the comment, 'I hope I have been frank in admitting the dishonesties with which Knox has been charged from 1559 onwards,' Percy spends a good part of the Preface to his biography of Knox dealing openly and honestly with this topic.

Furthermore, unknown to most of the church members at this time was a fact that was to make the congregation rethink concerning Knox as a worthy candidate for the Frankfurt pastorate. Whilst working with Goodman in Geneva, Knox had written a work entitled *A faithful Admonition made by John Knox unto the Professors of God's Truth in England*. In this work, he taught that it is God's commandment that idolators be put to death and 'If Mary and her Councillors had been sent to Hell before these days, her cruelty should not have so manifestly appeared to the world.' He also maintained that the Emperor is no less enemy to Christ than Nero.[20] The latter was particularly harsh and most undiplomatic as Charles V had just given the English exiles freedom of religion and worship in his cities. This work, however, was not printed in Geneva, probably because its extreme position would certainly not have suited Calvin, but it was printed and published in Kalykow, Poland on 20 July, 1554. This would explain why Knox's extreme views took some time in circulating amongst the Frankfurt brethren.

---

[19] Ibid, pp. x.-xi.
[20] See *Knox's Account of his Banishment from Frankfort, in March 1555*, in *Troubles At Frankfort*, pp. 67-68.

Though John Knox claimed to make the Scriptures his regulating principle for faith, worship and church discipline, with hindsight, it is not difficult to see that he often had great difficulty in keeping to his own norm. Thus Kenneth Koole's review of Knox's *First Blast of the Trumpet* ends on a most objective and unbiased note when the author says:

> Those who read John Knox with approval today ought to keep in mind that Knox permitted his doctrine of Christian citizenship to be determined by the social evils and wickedness of his day, understandable as that may be, rather than basing his doctrine solely on the teaching of the apostles, who, while they bore testimony against evil rulers with a boldness matching that of Knox, yet never sounded one note encouraging revolution against God-ordained government. Any blast that does not take into account the clear notes of Romans 13:1-4 and of I Peter 2:13-20 has not been composed by listening to the Spirit of the Lord.[21]

---

[21] *The Standard Bearer*, Knox Edition, The First Blast of the Trumpet Against the Monstrous Regiment of Women: A Brief Review, October 15, 2000, p. 43.

Archbishop Edmund Grindal

Chapter Six:
Grindal and Chambers Prepare the Way for the Strasburg Brethren

The reply from Strasburg

Meanwhile, after receiving the letter of invitation from Frankfurt, the Strasburg brethren were showing great interest in leaving their city and joining the Frankfurt brethren, in spite of the fact that Strasburg had enjoyed the ministry of Bucer and Calvin, and now Peter Martyr was lecturing there. The brethren, not knowing of Frankfurt's further plans, pointed out that they would need a pastor and suggested that John Bale, now at Frankfurt, would be ideal as a shepherd. They also recommended Bale's close friend John Ponet (Poynet), formerly Bishop of Winchester[1], Richard Cox, the former Chancellor of Oxford University and John Scory who had been Bishop of Chichester during Edward's reign. These were all eminent Reformers. They decided to send a delegation to Frankfurt under the leadership of Edmund Grindal to prepare the way for their brethren's journey and reception as lodgings had to be found and permission from the secular authorities sought. Strasburg also wished to keep the unity of testimony amongst the exiles by adhering as far as the Continental situation allowed to the Prayer Book reforms of such as Cranmer, Latimer, Cox and Ridley. The main argument of the Strasburg exiles was that doing away totally with the Book of Common Prayer was tantamount to joining the papist

---

[1] John Ponet died in Strasburg on 2 April, 1556.

condemnation of the Reformers as many of those who had helped to author the Reformed work were now awaiting martyrdom.[2] Pointing out that Strasburg was mid-way between ultra Prayer Book of Zürich and the politico-ecumenical compromise of Frankfurt, Strype gives his opinion that theologically as well as geographically, Strasburg was in between and 'made a motion, that they might have the *substance and effect of the Common Prayer-book, though such ceremonies, and things, which the Countrie could not bear, might well be omitted.'*[3] This was, however, exactly what the Frankfurt church had promised the Zürich brethren and probably the reason why Chambers speeded back to Zürich and then travelled to Strasburg at once to inform the brethren there that they would receive a warm reception from brethren who believed as they did and would thus accept them on mutual terms.

On 28 November, 1554, Edmund Grindal visited Frankfurt, accompanied by Richard Chambers, bringing with them a letter from the Strasburg Christians. Knox had just arrived and was already in the midst of controversy. The purport of the Strasburg brethren's letter read out by Grindal, was that they accepted the invitation to join the church but, like Whitehead, Lever, Bale and the majority of the members already constituted at Frankfurt, they wished to use some kind of modified English Prayer Book during their worship. The letter, in full, reads:

> WHEN WE DO consider what inward comfort it were for the faithful people of England (now dispersed for the Gospel, and wandering abroad in Strange countries as sheep without a Pastor) to be gathered, together into one Congregation that with one mouth, one mind, and one Spirit, they might glorify GOD: we have, at all times, and do presently think it our duties, not only in heart to wish that thing; but also to labour, by all means, so much as in us lieth, to bring

---

[2] A copy of the Strasburg reply to Frankfurt is found on page 10 of Strype's *Grindal* biography.

[3] Italics are Strype's. See *The Church History of Britain*, p. 729.

the Same to pass. And having now perfect intelligence of the good minds which the Magistrates of Frankfort bear towards you and others (of) our scattered countrymen; and also understanding of a free grant of a Church unto us, wherein we may together serve GOD; and not doubting of their further friendship in permitting us frankly to use our Religion according to that godly Order set forth and received in England: we both give GOD thanks for so great a benefit; and also think it not fit to refuse so friendly an offer, or to let slip so good an occasion.

Therefore, neither doubting of their good furtherance hereunto; nor yet distrusting your good conformity and ready desires in reducing the English Church, now begun there, to its former perfection of the last (Order) had in England, so far as possibly can be attained; lest by much altering of the Same, we should seem to condemn the chief Authors thereof (who, as they now suffer; so are they most ready to confirm that fact with the price of their blood); and should also both give Occasion to our adversaries to accuse our doctrine of imperfection and us of mutability; and the godly to doubt in that Truth wherein before they were persuaded; and to hinder their coming hither, which before they had purposed.

For the avoiding of these, and the obtaining of the others, moved hereunto in conscience and provoked by your gentle letters; we have thought it expedient to send over unto you, our beloved brethren, the bringers hereof, to travail with the Magistrates and you concerning the premises; whose wisdom, learning, and godly zeal, as they be known unto you, so their doings in this shall fully take place (be confirmed) by us. And if they obtain that which we trust will not be denied at no hands; then we intend, GOD willing! to be with you the 1st of February [1555] next, there to help to set in Order and establish that Church accordingly: and so long all together to remain with you as shall be necessary, or until just Occasion shall call some of us away.

And we doubt not but that our brethren of Zürich, Emden, Duisburg, etc. will do the same accordingly; as we have prayed them by our Letters: trusting that you, by yours, will make like request. Fare ye well! From Strasburg, this 23rd of November.

Your loving friends,

JAMES HADDON	JOHN PEDDAR
CHRISTOPHER GOODMAN	
EDWIN SANDYS	THOMAS EATEN
HUMPHREY ALCOCKSON	
EDMUND GRINDAL	MICHAEL REYMUGER
THOMAS LAKIN	JOHN HUNTINGTON
AUGUSTINE BRADBRIDGE	
THOMAS CRAFTON	GUIDO EATEN
ARTHUR SAUL	JOHN GEOFFREY

Strangely enough, this event is characterised by enemies of the English Episcopalian Reformation as the beginning of the end of Puritanism at Frankfurt. Needless to say, Grindal was one of the greatest Reforming Puritans England ever had and he showed a tolerance for other orders and towards Nonconformists, separatists and radicals, unknown north of the border. Though altars and crosses and other popish regalia were totally removed from his own bishoprics and archbishoprics, in 1569, Grindal, then Bishop of London, wrote a tragic-funny story to Sir William Cecil, informing him of English Puritans who travelled to Dunbar, Scotland at the height of Knoxian reforms and arrived there on Good Friday where: 'They saw certain persons go bare-footed and bare legged to the church, to creep to the cross. If it be so, the church of Scotland will not be pure enough for our men.'[4] John Strype fills in the details of this story by telling his readers that the visitors to Scotland were English Precisians who were unhappy with the Reformed order of

---

[4] *The Remains of Archbishop Grindal*, Parker Society, 1843, pp. 295-296.

the Church of England. Grindal thus sent the men to Scotland with introductory letters to church dignitaries there, asking for the men to be employed in the ministry so as to serve Scotland and become accustomed to the Scottish Reformation which they had heard was exemplary. The men quickly returned entirely disheartened with what they had experienced but Grindal told them that as they found Scotland in such a terrible state spiritually, it had been their duty to stay there and evangelise the Scottish churches rather than return to English comfort which gave them warmer physical and spiritual climes.[5]

Most pro-Knoxian commentators relate that Knox fell out with Grindal at once and indeed, we know from Grindal's letters that he saw Knox as the biggest disturber of the Frankfurt church's peace which was only restored when Knox quickly left. The efforts made by Neal and others to depict Grindal as a man who went back on his word, are not reconcilable with Grindal's biography and works. Professor Dawley, in his *John Whitgift and the Reformation*, says of Whitgift's predecessor:

> Grindal was one of the moderate party of former exiles, and like Jewel, Sandys, and Cox, sympathetic with the Precisians in the early vestiarian phase of the Puritan controversy. He never seems to have understood the developments that changed the Puritan program into one challenging the entire structure of the establishment. Kindly and gentle, always willing to think the best of the nonconformists, his chief interest was in the improvement of the education of the clergy and their consequent ability rightly to proclaim the Word of God. When he devised articles in consultation with Whitgift[6] for the Convocation of 1575-6 their major stress was in this direction.[7]

---

[5] Strype's *Grindal*, pp. 121-122.
[6] It would surprise many a modern Presbyter and Dissenter to learn how low church Whitgift was. It is tragically amusing to see mocked-up pictures of Whitgift in critical works depicting the Reformed Archbishop in full papal regalia, though he had nothing whatsoever to do with such ornaments.
[7] See *John Whitgift and the Reformation*, p. 148.

In the light of the above quoted letter from Strasburg and the defence of Grindal's fine Reformed credentials given, Neal's most biased interpretation must be rejected. In his *History of the Puritans*, he makes the totally ungrounded accusation concerning the Strasburg brethren that they had written a letter in which 'they exhort them (the Frankfurt brethren) in the most pressing language to a full conformity.'[8] Such a 'full conformity' was never on the Strasburg agenda, though it would have hardly questioned their Reformed credentials if it had been. On the other hand, what are we to make of Neal's quote from the 'Knoxian' party of 10 February, 1556, that 'the late service book of King Edward being now set aside by Parliament according to law, it was in no sense the established worship of the church of England, and consequently they were under no obligation to use it.'[9] This would seem very much like arguing that the Knoxians rejected the Prayer Book because popish Mary had done so! Never the one for consistency, Knox forced his own order of service through in Scotland without taking note of the fact that the political powers refused to ratify it.

Efforts made to place Nonconformist Chambers in the opposite camp to the Puritans cannot be taken seriously. Edward Arber writes enigmatically, 'Richard Chambers is a perfect mystery. He was undoubtedly a good man: yet one finds it hard to believe it.'[10] Yet he bears testimony of how highly Chambers was thought of by both the supposedly 'Anglican' camp and that of Whittingham, i.e. that of the Knoxians without Knox. Indeed, Chambers used his own fortune to support the English exiles and after the Elizabethan Settlement, became closely connected with Thomas Cartwright and the radicals around him. He protested strongly against his brethren who conducted the Lord's Supper or baptism without preaching a sermon. Such services were 'polluted', he argued.[11] Collinson, in mentioning this, places Chambers rightly in the radical Calvinist camp and sees him as more a Presbyterian than an Episcopalian.

---

[8] Vol. I, p. 78.
[9] Ibid, p. 80.
[10] *Troubles at Frankfort*, p. xxi.
[11] Collinson, *The Elizabethan Puritan Movement*, p. 358.

It is interesting to note that Christopher Goodman, who had been with Knox in Geneva, signed the letter from Strasburg. Goodman was a good friend of Knox's and had worked closely with him on works recommending political revolt. Of these works, Collinson says, 'These writings, published in Geneva, were so subversive as to be counter-productive, at least in England.'[12] Even Goodman, however, felt it was better to keep to the Edwardian Prayer Book with local modifications rather than create an entirely new order of worship. When Knox left Geneva for Frankfurt, Goodman did not accompany him but joined the Prayer Book men at Strasburg, though he moved to Geneva later when church rivalry grew less and Geneva became reconciled with Frankfurt. There, he co-pastored with Knox. It is an irony of history that those who look upon the Strasburg signatories as High Church Conformists and non-Calvinists must also place Christopher Goodman in that camp, though he was one of the greatest radicals and Calvinists in exile and the man who always stood closest to Knox until he repented of their joint radicalism several years later. Here is a clear attempt to alter history for polemic effect without taking any notice whatsoever of the historical facts

The three wishes of the Strasburg brethren
Knox, assisted by Whittingham, who became something of an adjutant to Knox at Frankfurt, strove to draw Grindal into a debate concerning what could be considered the 'substance' of the Prayer Book, but Grindal diplomatically said that he, as a formal delegate, had been given strict orders by the Strasburg brethren to stick to his agenda. His commission was to ask three questions. The first was regarding what parts of the Prayer Book were to be admitted. This actually went further than Knox's question which centred on what was to be retained. The Strasburg men preferred the more open and lenient form of asking what could be admitted in the first place. The Frankfurt Christians answered that they would admit all

---

[12] *Archbishop Grindal*, p. 79. Collinson adds Ponet and Gilby to the list of those who wrote on popular resistance to tyranny.

that could 'stand with God's Word'. The second question was whether the Frankfurt brethren had any chance of becoming an independent church, presumably meaning one independent of the French church and secular control. The answer to this was less encouraging. The Frankfurt Christians confessed that this was a matter for the Imperial Council which was sitting at Augsburg.[13] This meant that the English church at Frankfurt had no separate legal rights and its presence in Frankfurt was thus merely a matter of imperial toleration. Used to Convocation and the church courts, the more 'Anglican' of the brethren did not like the idea of a church directly governed by the magistrates. This matter did not appear to bother the 'Knoxians' yet was to cause the Anglican and reformed churches in Germany great suffering in the following months.

The Peace of Augsburg of 1555 brought no peace to the Anglican refugees as Clauses 15, 16 and 17 stressed that the clearly marked boundaries of Lutheranism and Romanism should be kept closed to those of other churches and peace could only be maintained by no one side poaching on the side of the other. Thus Germany's territories were split into either Lutheran or papist with nothing left over for the various Swiss or Anglican forms of worship and doctrinal beliefs. As J. M. Thompson says in his *Lectures on Foreign History 1494-1789*, it was as if Germany was now covered with 'Trespassers Will Be Prosecuted' signs. This made the Anglican Church's situation at Frankfurt and Wesel very precarious as Clause 17 specifically branded such congregations as being outside the Peace Treaty and is another of the many reasons why there was a swift turnover in the congregation and men such as Whittingham, Fox and Bale looked for openings in less perilous areas. The Peace of Augsburg, however, hit back at the Lutherans, too, because it proscribed that if a Protestant head of State became a Roman Catholic, his territories would automatically follow him. If, however, a papist ruler became Lutheran, he had to forfeit his

---

[13] The Council broke up on 25 September, 1555 without a decision being made as to the Frankfurt church. This coincided with the supposed Anglican-Puritan split in the church. It is very likely that some internal strife in the church was because of their lack of independence.

State.[14] The Calvinists could not summon up any display of unity until 1609 when they formed the Evangelical Union under Elector Frederick of the Palatine. The Lutherans, however, refused to unite with them finding that the idea 'would neither be agreeable to God nor profitable to the Church.' This fact explains why, during the rest of 1555 and later, many English exiles of Reformed Anglican views, moved to Switzerland because of a degree of greater freedom offered there. This had nothing to do with a supposed Coxian-Knoxian controversy as Christians of all persuasions fled.

Actually, the Peace of Augsburg brought lasting relief to the Protestant churches in a way never intended by Charles V. The Emperor had left his brother, Ferdinand I, in charge of the proceedings at Augsburg, but, when he found that he could neither wipe out Protestantism by war, nor bring peace between the Lutheran and Reformed churches, Charles gave Germany and the imperial crown to his brother implying, 'You have got us into this mess, now you can take full responsibility of this divided country.' Charles then retired in 1556 to San Juste in Spain with the predominantly papist countries still showing him some form of allegiance. This move not only weakened the entire Romish system but led to the break-up of what was hitherto called the Roman Empire, German Nation.

The third question from Strasburg was what guarantee could be given them concerning rights to live freely in Frankfurt. They were told that the freedom of the city had been given to all English exiles, so they would have no problem on that account. The Frankfurt Christians then wrote a reply to the Strasburg brethren, outlining their conditions for accepting new members and expressing the conviction that they were in basic agreement with the Strasburg men. As it was customary in writing such letters for the person mainly responsible for its compilation to place his signature first, we can presume that George Whetnall took care of the wording rather than Knox, who still had not established himself in the church, indeed, had refused to lead it. The Frankfurt reply in full was:

---

[14] See the Chapter X, The Thirty Years' War in *Lectures on Foreign History*, esp. pp. 154 ff.

Grace, Mercy, and Peace, etc.

AS IT WAS ever most true, so at this present we feel most sensibly, that wheresoever GOD layeth the foundation to build his glory, there he continueth till he bring the Same to a present work. All thanks and praise be to him therefore, that hath moved your hearts so as, in no point, ye seem to forslow your diligence to the furtherance of the same. And as the work is of most excellence; so the adversaries cease not most craftily to undermine it or at the least (through false reports, and defacing of the work begun) to stay the labourers which should travail in the finishing thereof. But Truth ever cleareth itself: and as the sun consumeth the clouds; so misreports, by trial, are confounded.

Our brethren sent from you can certify you at length touching the particulars of your Letter: to whom we have in all things agreed which seemed expedient for the state of this Congregation.

As for certain Ceremonies which the Order of the country will not bear, we necessarily omit; with as little alteration as is possible, which in your Letters ye require: so that no adversary is so impudent that dare either blame our doctrine of imperfection, or us of mutability; except he be altogether wilfully ignorant, rather seeking how to find faults than to amend them. Neither do we dissent from them which lie at the ransom of their blood, for the doctrine whereof they have made a most worthy Confession.

And yet we think not that any godly man will stand to the death in the defence of Ceremonies; which, as the Book specifieth, upon just causes, may be altered and changed.

And if the not full using of the Book cause the godly to doubt in that Truth wherein before they were persuaded; and to stay their coming hither, according as they proposed: either it signifieth that they were very slenderly taught, which, for breach of a Ceremony will refuse such a Singular benefit; or else that you have heard them misreported by some false brethren, who, to hinder this worthy enterprise, spare not to sow, in every place, store of such poor reasons.

Last of all, it remaineth that ye write that, the 1st of February next, you will come to help to set in order and establish this Church accordingly; which thing, as we most wish for your company's sake, and for that ye might see our godly Orders here observed: so we put you out of doubt, that for to appoint a journey for the establishing, of Ceremonies should be more to your charges than any general profit; except ye were determined to remain with us longer than two months as ye write to our countrymen at Duisburg and Emden: which Letter, notwithstanding are now stayed; and, as appeareth, we (are) never the neare(r).

We refer the rest to our brethren Master CHAMBERS and Master GRINDAL; who, by their diligent inquisition, have learned so far of our state as we wrote unto you in our former Letters, that is, That we have a Church freely granted to preach GOD'S Word purely, to minister the Sacraments sincerely, and to execute Discipline truly. And as touching our Book, we will practise it so far as God's Word doth assure it, and the state of this country permits. Faire ye well! At Frankfort, this 3rd of December (1554).

GEORGE WHETNALL	THOMAS WOOD
JOHN MAKEBRAIE	JOHN KNOX
WILLIAM WILLIAMS	WILIAM WALTON
THOMAS WHETNALL	JOHN STANTON
MICHAEL GILL	JOHN BALE
JOHN SAMFORD	LAURENCE KENT
WILLIAM WHITTINGHAM	JOHN FOX
JOHN HOLLINGHAM	EDMUND SUTTON
WILLIAM KETHE	

It is important to note that even Knox signed this letter. With hindsight this seems an odd move on Knox's part as he later turned radically from the letter's sentiments. Obviously, he was going through a period of uncertainty at the time and was still unsure of his position. He first came down heavily against the Prayer Book and Anglican Reformed piety on the first Sunday after the Strasburg Reformed men arrived when he denounced them and their position from the pulpit.

Meanwhile, Grindal and Chambers had returned to Strasburg and presented the Frankfurt letter to the exiles who had sought asylum there. The more often the Strasburg Christians read this letter, the more they found words and phrases in it which seemed ambiguous, leaving them in something of a dilemma. On the surface, the letter obviously underscored their request for a modified version of the Prayer Book which the Frankfurt brethren still called 'our Book'. Yet the idea that parts of it may be contrary to the Word of God had not been presented in the letter carried by Chambers and Grindal. This opened up a new dimension in the debate. A further point was that as the Frankfurt magistrates had as yet come up with suggestions and requests rather than commands and absolute strictures, one of the major points that the Strasburg brethren had made was that the Frankfurt men should approach the magistrates with the wishes of the wider church and find out exactly what was allowed by them and what not. The Strasburg men were genuinely puzzled by the status of the church and wished to know exactly what freedom they had. This was not specified in the letter. Puzzling, too, were the strong words that the letter used against those who would seek to use the Book of Common Prayer in its entirety, as the Strasburg brethren had sent Chambers and Grindal to argue the very opposite.

Finally, the letter contained ambiguous words which revealed a grave misunderstanding not to mention a lack of tact, yet they gave the Strasburg brethren hope that a union might be attained. The Frankfurt brethren had written, 'so we put you out of doubt, that for to appoint a journey for the establishing of Ceremonies should be more to your charge than any general profit; except ye were determined to remain with us longer than two months.' The simple explanation here might be that the Frankfurt church were willing to draw up a new order with the Strasburg men if they had a guarantee that they would remain in fellowship for a longer period. Again, however, the Frankfurt brethren showed suspicion and distrust concerning the Strasburg men's acceptance of their honest plea for a Prayer Book order to suit the Frankfurt situation. Furthermore, the Strasburg exiles had made it quite obvious that they wished to settle down in Frankfurt, so why the warning concerning the two months? Knowing the fine reputation that these Strasburg ambassadors to Frankfurt had, the suggestion that they might have been less than honest in their statements was bad taste indeed but there is nothing more apparently deceitful than fine, honest words when the hearers are over-cautious and over-sensitive. Sadly such thinking often breaks the unity of Christian fellowship.

Knox's and Whittingham's deceptive action.
It was during this period that Knox acted in a most dishonest way. This can only be seen as a desperate effort to have his own way and justify his now almost superstitious view of an Anglican church order. Knox, assisted by Whittingham, sent Calvin what they called a Latin Plat[15] of the English Prayer Book, and told the Reformer that they were ashamed to tell Calvin all that was in the book and they had omitted parts out of pity for those who believed such things. This garbled, Latinised compendium, (Arber calls it a 'scoffing analysis'), he assured Calvin, was about to become the Frankfurt church's order of service. In sending Calvin this mocked up version Knox and Whittingham not only presented a most prejudiced view of the Prayer Book, they omitted to tell Calvin that they themselves had rejected the various orders suggested by the church and John Fox, including Calvin's own form of worship. As Wotherspoon points out, it is also significant that Calvin is told nothing of the willingness of Chambers and Grindal, as representing its supporters to be content with its "substance and effects" and to omit ceremonies and other things "which the country could not bear"'.[16]

---

[15] Short for 'platform'. The word was used for a summary or abstract.
[16] Wotherspoon, p. 26.

There was no sense whatsoever in the move apart from sheer spite. It was now clear, however, that Knox wished to present his brethren at Frankfurt to Calvin as papists unmasked. The Scottish equivalent of Don Quixote of La Mancha now saw Grindal, Bale, Fox and Lever and all those who represented the mainstream English Reformation as ogres to be fought and vanquished with whatever weapon he thought might be useful.

Obviously quite unaware of what was really going on at Frankfurt, Calvin replied:

> To the godly and learned men, Master JOHN KNOX and Master WILLIAM WHITTINGHAM, his faithful brethren, at Frankfort, etc
>
> THIS THING TRULY grieveth me very much, and it is a great shame, that contention should arise among brethren banished and driven out of their, country for one Faith, and for that Cause which only ought to have holden you bound together as it were with a holy band, in this your Dispersion. For what might you do better in this dolorous and miserable plague, than, being pulled violently from your country, to procure yourselves a Church, which should receive and nourish you, being joined together in minds and language, in her motherly lap. But now for some men to strike, as touching the Form of prayer and for Ceremonies. as though ye were at rest and prosperity; and to suffer that to be an impediment that ye cannot join into one body of the Church, as I think, it is too much out of season.
>
> Yet, notwithstanding, I allow their constancy, which strive for a just cause; being forced, against their wills, unto contention. I do worthily condemn frowardness; which doth hinder and stay the holy carefulness of reforming the Church.
>
> And as I behave myself gentle and tractable in mean things, as external Ceremonies: so do I not always judge it profitable to give place to their foolish stoutness, which will forsake nothing of their old wonted custom.

In the Liturgy of England I see that there were many tolerable foolish things. By these words I mean, that there was not that purity which was to be desired. These vices, thought they could not, at the first day, be amended; yet, seeing there was no manifest impiety (in them), they were, for a season, to be tolerated. Therefore, it was lawful to begin of such Rudiments, or Abecedaries; but so that it behoved the learned, grave, and godly, Ministers of Christ to enterprise farther; and to set forth something more filed from rust, and purer. If godly Religion had flourished till this day in England; there ought to have been a thing better corrected, and many things clean taken away.

Now, when these principles be overthrown, a Church must be set up in another place; where ye may freely make an Order again, which shall be apparent to be most commodious to the use and edification of the Church. I cannot tell what they mean which so greatly delight in the leavings of Popish dregs. They love the things whereunto they are accustomed. First of all, this is a thing both trifling and childish. Furthermore, this new Order far differeth from a Change.

Therefore, as I would not have you fierce over them whose infirmity will not suffer (them) to ascend an higher step; so would I advertise others, that they please not themselves too much in their foolishness; also that, by their frowardness, they do not let (hinder) the course of the holy Building. Last of all, lest that foolish vain glory steal them away. For what cause have they to contend, except it be for that they are ashamed to give place to better things. But I speak in vain to them; which, perchance, esteem me not so well as they will vouchsafe to admit the counsel that cometh from such an Author. If they fear the evil rumour in England, as though they had fallen from that Religion which was the cause of their banishment; they are far deceived. For this true and sincere Religion will rather compel them, that there remain, faithfully to consider into what deep gulf they have fallen. For their downfall shall more grieviously wound them, when they perceive your going forward beyond (the) mid-course, from the which they are turned.

Fare ye well, beloved Brethren! and faithful servants of CHRIST!

The Lord defend and govern you

From Geneva, this 20th of January, anno 1555.
Yours,

JOHN CALVIN.

This seemingly rather supercilious attitude to the work of the great English Reformers and Calvin's own view of his own importance must be seen against the background that he himself was under suspicion of thwarting the work of the Reformation by many Presbyterian and Episcopalian men, not to mention the growing band of Anabaptists. He was accused by Pierre Caroli of opening the way to Arianism and dismayed his fellow Reformers in refusing to accept the teaching of the Apostles', Nicaean and Athanasian Creeds which took pride of place in the confessions of the Reformed Churches elsewhere. The Bernese Reformers, as a body, were very suspicious of Calvin's Reformed credentials. Furthermore, it was widely believed that Calvin secretly accepted the dogma of purgatory and his teaching on justification and repentance were far below Luther's, not to mention Wycliffe's, Tyndale's, Jewel's and that of a good number of other English Reformers. Also his demand for minute adherence to every jot and tittle of his own forms of worship stood in stark contrast to the freedom of expression treasured by the Anglican exiles. Furthermore, he had quarrelled with all the leading Reformers on the matter of the Lord's Supper, producing a formula which appeared to many (who obviously misunderstood Calvin here) to be but an empty ritual, void of true worship and an empirical meeting with the Lord. Even nowadays, after theological and doctrinal analysts over the centuries have examined every word of Calvin's writings on the ordinance, few appear to agree as to what the Genevan Eucharist involves.

Regarding externals, whereas Calvin was very strict in his ideas of clerical dress, the Anglican exiles who came to govern the Church of England never reached his dogmatism. Even ninety years later during the time of the notorious Archbishop Laud with his ideas of absolute uniformity, one could find bishops administrating the ordinances in normal 'street dress'. On his northern journey with Charles I, Laud even discovered that bishops had no scruples in conducting a 'Royal' service and even administering the Lord's Supper to the King, without donning their clerical garb. The exiles from Strasburg especially will have noticed that in that region of Germany where Calvin formerly pastored, he stood very much in the shade of Strasburg's own son, Bucer and of his successor Martyr. Nor did the Anglican Reformers wish to adopt Calvin's way of merging secular with ecclesiastical powers. Indeed, Calvin's own stubbornness played a large part in hindering the tiny land of Switzerland from a union of Reformed faith and order between the various states, whereas the bishoprics and archbishoprics of England had proclaimed their unity in Reformation doctrines and order in their country throughout the time of Edward VI and did so until the Laudians and the Great Rebellion put an end to it. During this period, too, the Continental Reformed churches were accepted as brethren and Englishmen abroad urged to worship and share the Lord's Supper with them.

Partly because of language problems, partly because of an inability to stand criticism and partly because of political differences, it is not an exaggeration to say that Calvin rarely understood his opponents.[17] The letter above would be a typical example of this but for one feature – it is obviously a very poor and very selective

---

[17] Apart from Calvin's works, mostly available today on cheap CDs or to be downloaded free of charge, Francois Wendel's *Calvin*, Thomas Lawson's *Calvin His Life and Times* and Imbart de la Tour's *Calvin et l'institution chrétienne* (German version *Calvin – Der Mensch – Die Kirche – Die Zeit*) will give some idea of development and stagnation in Calvin's faith and witness.

translation and thus does not really show Calvin's view of the matter. Nor does it flatter the compiler's objectivity. Calvin is quoted by the author of *Troubles in Frankfort* as saying that the English Prayer Book contained 'tolerable foolish things'. However, the Latin original[18] reads, '*In Anglicana Liturgia, qualem describitis, multas video fuisse tolerabiles ineptias*' which, according to Prof. Hume Brown, quoted by Laing,[19] should be translated as, 'In the Anglican Liturgy, *as you describe it,*[20] I see many trifles that can be put up with.' In other words, Calvin is not committing himself to an objective criticism of the Prayer Book as such, but referring merely to the 'scoffing analysis' sent to him in Latin by Knox and Whittingham. This leads Laing to agree with Dyer in his *Life of Calvin*, who says: 'Some of the expressions are twisted to a meaning more favourable to the Frankfurt Congregation than the original warrants.' Here, Laing and Dyer are obviously referring to the Knoxians in the congregation.[21]

One could also translate Calvin's '*tolerabiles ineptias*' to mean 'little things which do not cause offence'. Indeed, it would appear that Knox's main occupation in Germany was to spend, or rather waste, his energies combating 'little things which do not cause offence'. Calvin, however, clearly explains in his letter that one should not go to such 'Precisionist' extremes and believes that one should be 'gentle and tractable in mean things' or, 'easy and flexible'. Now Knox almost always quoted from the Prayer Book in its 'unreformed' first edition and not the 1552 edition. This was the edition, judging by the 'plat' he sent to Calvin, which he would have Calvin believe represented the views of his Frankfurt opponents. Now Hooper, in a sermon before Edward VI on 5 March 1550, described the First Prayer Book in exactly the same terms as Calvin and argued for a revision. Hooper was not alone by far in suggesting such alterations and these were completed in 1552. It

---

[18] Laing reproduces the entire letter in Latin taken from the Amsterdam 1667 folio in *The Works of John Knox*, Vol. IV, pp. 51-53.
[19] *John Knox and the Reformation*, p. 58.
[20] Italics mine.
[21] *The Works of John Knox*, Vol. IV, p. 51.

was this Second Prayer Book, alias The Reformed Prayer Book, which was the edition favoured by the 'Coxians'. It is very likely that Knox's 'plat' brought to Calvin's mind Hooper's sermon and he used Hooper's term.[22] This would again indicate that Calvin was neither in possession of the 1552 Prayer Book which banned the popish Eucharist vestments, certain former ceremonies and condemned the papacy in the Litany, nor did he know of it. He thus took Knox at his word that such 'tolerable things to be borne with for the weak's sake awhile'[23] still needed revision. However, the Knoxians took Calvin's letter to mean that Calvin was fully on their side and against the so-called Anglicans. Indeed, Calvin's letter, according to the report penned twenty years later, 'so wrought in the hearts of many; that they were not before so stout to maintain all the parts of the Book of England, as afterwards they were bent against it.'[24]

On reading this introduction to the Chapter entitled *The Truce of February 6th*, it would appear that the writer is saying that now agreement reigned. However, none of the congregation, as far as we know, had pressed for a full use of the Prayer Book, nor had the large number of Anglican exiles who were at that very hour loading their wagons with their earthly goods, yet moved to Frankfurt. If the Frankfurt congregation is to be split between Knoxians and the Coxians, any imagined controversy was thus amongst the Knoxians as the Coxians had not arrived and it was uncertain if and when they would. Knox's and Whittingham's battle with the 'Anglicans' had merely been sabre rattling to ward off any feared future attempts to enforce full use of the Prayer Book in Frankfurt. Even Knox and Whittingham[25] did not agree for long on this matter, and it soon turned out that, instead of whispering peace to the

---

[22] See Blunt, *Reformation of the Church of England*, Vol. II, pp. 97- 98.

[23] So Hooper. *Early Writings of John Hooper*, Parker Society, p. 479.

[24] *Troubles at Frankfort*, p. 52.

[25] Whittingham continued in the Reformed Church of England ministry until his death which indicates some conformity to the Prayer Book and subscription to the Anglican Articles, whereas, Knox, who had subscribed in Edward's reign, now detested the Anglican Confessions and forms of worship.

congregation, Knox's and Whittingham's unilateral action caused strife and disharmony. The over-biased compiler relates how hot the debate was between 'one party which sought Sincerity' i.e. the Knox-Whittingham 'Puritan' party, and 'the stirrers of contention and unquietness,' alias the 'Anglicans'.[26]

The Knox-Whittingham extremely critical 'plat' version of the Edwardian Prayer Book sent to Calvin may be compared to the version sent to Henry Bullinger by Robert Horn who was first at Frankfurt and then moved on to Aarau. Sadly, this correspondence is undated but must have occurred shortly after the restitution of the Protestant Monarchy. Horn's description is sober and respectful and reflects the true Reformed state of the Edwardian Church. Bullinger, in reply says he personally does not like the linen surplice as it reminds him of Judaism but asks teasingly 'Why did they not retain the ephod, according to the Lord's institution?' Bullinger is far from being an anti-vestiarian himself and adds, 'I wish, however, that the habit in which the minister performs divine service should be decent, according to the fashion of the country, and have nothing light or fantastic about it.' Bullinger states that though the early Christians used the sign of the cross, he personally did not because 'the abuse of the cross is so implanted in all, as that it does not seem possible any longer to adopt that sign among the common people without superstition.' Bullinger approves of the Anglican manner of catechising and confirming, though he admits that these have 'received no direction from the apostles.' Private baptism by women or midwives, Bullinger rejects as also private celebration of the Lord's Supper.

In all these points, Bullinger was close to, if not exactly in union with the Frankfurt Anglicans and the correspondence between Horn, other Frankfurt Anglicans and Bullinger show how such matters may be discussed objectively amongst brothers without the scorn, sarcasm and condemnatory tone used by Knox and Whittingham.[27]

---

[26] *Troubles at Frankfort*, pp. 52-53.
[27] See 'Bishop Horn to Henry Bullinger' and 'Bullinger's Remarks upon the Preceding', (undated), in *Zürich Letters*, pp. 354-358.

Another story of how things happened

Martyn Lloyd-Jones in his book *The Puritans*, goes to great lengths to tell another tale. Leaving Fox, Gilby, Lever and Cole fully aside, he relates that Knox and Whittingham 'did something which is typically and characteristically Puritan.' They 'drew up an Order of Service to replace that of the Common Prayer Book which they disliked.' This work, Lloyd-Jones argues, was the product of Knox's moderation and it was accepted by the congregation. It is noteworthy here that Lloyd-Jones omits to mention that it was Lever's moderation that initiated this order and that Prayer Book men also worked on the project. On the contrary, Lloyd-Jones goes on to say, copying Knox's style, 'militant, ungentlemanly, abominable, intransigent and rude' Richard Cox came and put a stop to it.

Now this story cannot be accepted for a number of most solid reasons. First, Lloyd-Jones affirms that the order used before the Cox party arrived was the very same as that used by Knox at Geneva in 1556. This order was first published on 10 February of that year under the title *The Forme of Prayers and Ministration of the Sacraments, etc., used in the English Congregation at Geneva: and approved by the famous and godly learned man, Iohn Caluyn.* Since then, it has always been called the 1556 order but never the 1554-5 order. Furthermore, as Knox was very keen to have his order advertised and used amongst all the exiles, it is rather odd that the Genevans did not add a phrase like 'as formerly used in Frankfurt' and not merely 'as used in Geneva'. Furthermore, it was Lever's suggestion that Calvin supported and not Knox's, thus doing away with Lloyd-Jones' criticism that it was the 'Anglican' party who refused the compromise. It was Knox who refused to use Calvin's order at Frankfurt and the Anglican party who pressed for a very similar order which eventually became Knox's.

Furthermore, the author of this section of *Troubles at Frankfort* whether Wood or Whittingham, or someone else, was an obvious eye-witnesses of the scene and it would have been a triumph for his party to report that the new order, initiated by Lever and compiled by Knox, Fox, Whittingham, Gilby and Cole was generally accepted. However, what happened was that Fox, Whittingham,

Gilby and Cole again presented the Genevan Order to the Church. That order was rejected as many thought it 'new-fangled' and 'singular.'[28] Nor is Lloyd-Jones correct in saying the Geneva Order replaced the Book of Common Prayer in the Frankfurt worship as the congregation had, as yet, never used the Prayer Book but a mixture of the French and English orders, modified by political restrictions. The author of *The Truce of February 6th* in *Troubles at Frankfort*, blames the Anglicans for this non-acceptance[29] but a previous report under the title *Lever's proposed Order is rejected* records:

> At length, it was agreed that the Order of Geneva which then was printed in English and some copies there among them, should take place, as an Order most godly, and farthest off from superstition.
>
> But Master Knox, being spoken unto, as well to put that Order in practice as to minister the Communion, refused to do either the one or the other; affirming that, for many considerations, he could not consent that the same Order should be practised till the Learned Men of Strasburg, Zürich, Emden etc., were privy. Neither yet would he minister the Communion by the Book of England; for there were things in it placed, as he said, 'only by warrant of Man's authority, and no ground in God's Word for the same; and had also a long time very superstitiously in the Mass been wicked abused'.
>
> But if he might not be suffered to minister the Sacraments according to his conscience; he then requested that some other might minister the Sacraments; and he would only preach.[30]

That Lloyd-Jones' theory cannot possibly be fact is witnessed by the author of *Troubles at Frankfort* who writes that in February of 1555 the congregation made yet one more attempt to reach a

---

[28] See pp. 43 and 52.
[29] P. 52.
[30] P. 42.

compromise. This time, Lever was appointed as an active member of the committee alongside Parry,[31] Knox and Whittingham. This was a well-balanced committee as these four men represented all the different parties in the congregation. Lever and Parry, especially were known for their flexibility in external matters. Obviously both sides made a valiant effort to create unity in the congregation but they merely managed to agree on a provisional order of worship which was to last two months only.[32] It is interesting to note that though Knox was elected as a member of the committee, he affirmed that he would first 'discharge his conscience' and then if the other members of the committee would not agree with him, he would resign from it rather than work with his brethren. We are not told how agreement was reached and what part Knox played or did not play in it.[33] Nevertheless, there was much rejoicing in the congregation at this part success. Now, for the first time in months, the brethren gathered around the Lord's Table together. The compiler does not relate who administrated the ordinance. If it were Knox and not Lever, one would have thought that the pro-Knox compiler would have declared this as one up for his hero. As Lever was the initiator of the compromise, it may be presumed that Lever administrated. It would have been good to hear that both men served at the Lord's Table together, however, the *Liturgy of Compromise* states that only one pastor was present in the church at the administration.

Lloyd-Jones makes no attempt to document his self-contradictory misunderstandings of the liturgical situation at Frankfurt in his coverage of the events. A possible source for his view might be Janet G. Macgregor's *The Scottish Presbyterian Polity* written in 1926 in which the authoress states: 'The Book of Geneva is precisely stated by Knox to be one of the forms of congregational organisation drawn

---

[31] A Leonard Parry is listed on page 202 of *Troubles at Frankfort* as being a member in 1557, but this must have been Henry Parry who informed the Senate of Knox's severe criticism of the Emperor in whose city Knox had been given asylum.

[32] See *The Truce of February 6th*, pp. 52-53.

[33] P. 53.

up at Frankfurt during the controversies there is the years 1554 to 1555.' We note here that Macgregor, unlike Lloyd-Jones, refers to a plurality of orders and not to a single one. However, Macgregor gives Vol. iv. p. 30 of Laing's edition of Knox's works as evidence. This passage, from *Troubles at Frankfort* is obviously not written by Knox, as Laing explains in his Foreword, adding 'the internal evidence in favour of Whittingham being the author is all but conclusive.' Furthermore, the passage argues firmly that the Genevan Order was rejected by the congregation without it ever being used and Lever, Parry, Whittingham and Knox were asked to draw up a more favourable one. Moreover, the passage to which Macgregor refers states clearly that when Glauburg visited the Frankfurt church to ask them to use the French Order, it was Cox, not Knox, who took the initiative in recommending the order and Knox is not even mentioned as having anything to do with the decision. We are only told that Cox confessed to the assembled congregation, 'I have read the French Order, and do think it to be good and godly in all points' and he it was who advised the congregation to 'obey the Magistrates' commandments.' Thereupon, the author of *Troubles at Frankfort* writes, 'Whereupon the whole congregation gave consent'. So as, before the Magistrate departed the Church; Doctor Cox, Lever, and Whittingham, made report unto him accordingly.' Indeed, though the author of these records is obviously pro-Knox, he gives him no part whatsoever in this matter which later writers attribute solely to Knox.[34]

Actually, the order drawn up immediately before the arrival of the so called Coxians was basically the same order as the church majority had aimed for all along, in spite of Knox's frequent protests. It was a compromise, consisting of 'some part taken forth of the English Book; and other things put to, as the state of that church required'[35] and included the litany. This left Knox, who had said he would leave everything to the others if differences ensued, now complaining, that the agreement was not specific enough. Indeed,

---

[34] See also *Troubles at Frankfort*, p. 59.
[35] P. 53.

time and time again, we find Knox backing out of controversy when his opinion would have been valued, only to complain when things went wrong. Lloyd-Jones puts this down to Knox's humility and humble nature. One would have expected that one who was humble enough not to open his mouth in a committee, would be humble enough to keep it shut when he disagreed with the committee's findings after resolutions had been passed.

Now Knox, began to suspect, quite rightly, that Lever viewed the responses of the congregation as being within the committee's agreement not to use anything in the service which would be offensive to the host city. His fears went further and he began to suspect that as the Senate was now so tolerant, Lever might be able to bring in the whole Prayer Book, with all the papal paraphernalia in its train. This, of course, had never been Lever's intention at all, though this very negative thought had caused Knox sleepless nights all along.

It would appear obvious that the new provisional order, which became known officially as *The Liturgy of Compromise*[36], had been worked out to last until the expected large influx of English exiles arrived from Strasburg and Zürich. This party had originally intended joining the Frankfurt church in February but because of the troubles there, they had postponed their journey, hoping for a more peaceful opportunity to join their brethren. This fact is very important in accessing the troubles at Frankfurt as the bulk of pro-Knoxian commentators argue that peace reigned all along at Frankfurt until the Coxians came. Actually, the Strasburg exiles, who were all more or less Nonconformist brethren, had been greatly alarmed, through their correspondence with fellow-exiles and with Calvin, to find that Lever and his friends had been gravely misrepresented by Knox and Whittingham. As it now appeared that preacher Knox was willing to work with, if not under, pastor Lever, they hoped that their joining the church would be well received by both former factions. The Strasburg men thus left for Frankfurt on 13 March with their

---

[36] See G. W. Sprott's (ed) *The Liturgy of Compromise*, Church Service Society, 1905.

families and personal effects. It is, however, very clear that they looked upon Richard Cox, the former Chancellor of Oxford University, as the ideal arbitrator in any future strife because of his reputation as a sound Reformer, a fierce contender against Rome and because of his great learning. From the point of view of the Strasburg men at least, their journey to Frankfurt was a mission of peace to calm the troubled seas of Frankfurt and help unite the work of the Reformation amongst the exiles. They had not reckoned with the fact that Knox was increasingly separating himself from the body of the church and had worked himself into a position where he felt that he could no longer divert from his own path. When the Strasburg group arrived, Knox made it quite clear that he looked on the more learned, more experienced, peace-loving Cox as an unwanted rival and said things against him which cannot be claimed to have been from Christian motives, but rather, as Fox described Knox's temper, they derived from Knox's 'coler'.[37]

---

[37] Fox's letter has not been preserved but Knox's brief reply is extant in which he says, 'My rude vehemencie and inconsidered affirmations, which may appear rather to procead from coler than of zeal and reason, I do not excuse.' Laing, *The Works of John Knox*, Vol. V, p. 5.

Henry Bullinger

Martin Bucer

Chapter Seven:
The Strasburg Christians Join Frankfurt

The character of Richard Cox

By Sunday, 17 March, 1555, the Strasburg exiles including Cox, Grindal and Becon had joined the church. The invitation they followed had been sent to them before the decision to call Knox as pastor, so, however much Knox protested at their coming, they were joining the people who had stretched out the right hand of fellowship to them. The Strasburg men had grown to look to Richard Cox as their leader. Cox was one of the first and foremost of the English Reformers. He had served as tutor to Edward VI, as Royal Almoner, a member of the Privy Council, Dean of Christ Church, Chancellor of Oxford University and Commissioner for the Reform of the Lord's Supper. When Cox took over Oxford, he soon started reforming the university and John Stumpius wrote to Henry Bullinger on 28 February, 1550 to tell him that Cox was 'cutting off' the 'rotten members of Antichrist'.[1] Cox was greatly loved by the Italian and Swiss Reformers such as Peter Martyr and Henry Bullinger because of his views on the Eucharist but especially because of his friendliness shown to persecuted Continental Reformers who sought asylum in England during Edward's reign. One such exile whom Cox took care of was John Ab Ulmis who wrote to Bullinger from Oxford in

---

[1] *Original Letters*, Parker Society, Vol. 2, p. 465.

1548 to tell him of the great strides that had been made in reforming the country. The first name he mentions in this connection is Cox of whom he says: 'Cox, the king's tutor, a man of noble disposition, and of great influence, and possessed of great acuteness and weight of character, entertains and expresses most excellent and correct notions respecting every article of the Christian faith.'[2] Ab Ulmis writes often and long concerning Cox and the blessings the Continentals have obtained through his witness, teaching and generous patronage. So, too, when John Burcher, writing in 1551 to Henry Bullinger, listed the main men of the Reformation, he mentioned Cox, Hooper and Cranmer first.[3] Indeed, Cox is often mentioned in one breath with Hooper though the Knoxians referred to them as if they represented opposite poles. Cox was not only imprisoned during Henry's reign for his faith but was one of the very first to be arrested by Mary. His Reformed credentials are thus second to none. However, Cox was convinced that the golden age of the Reformation had been under Edward VI and that Elizabeth sadly failed to keep up the same momentum. He was a man who looked for a continuing Reformation.

The earlier compiler of *Troubles at Frankfort*, and generations of writers who have built on his account, give the impression that Cox and his party had come straight from England as raw recruits to an old, well established church of vintage exiles, and began to throw their weight about. The facts, however, show that though the Frankfurt exiles and those of Strasburg had arrived in Germany at roughly the same time, Cox and Grindal had been in Germany since May of 1554 at the latest, i.e. before the majority of the Frankfurt exiles had arrived. Cox, like Grindal, took on no formal office in the church, one of his main tasks being to organise the university. For this, with the church's backing, he chose Robert Horn from Zürich as Hebrew Reader, John Mullings, also from Zürich, as Greek Reader and Bartholomew Traheron, the Duke of Suffolk's former tutor, as Lecturer in Divinity. All the Strasburg men came deter-

---

[2] Ibid, p. 384.
[3] Ibid, p. 680.

mined to uphold God's Word, denounce popery, and live in unison with their brethren. Traheron is of special note here as he was a Calvinist of the Calvinists and a staunch Supralapsarian, and had been persecuted severely under Henry VIII. Nevertheless, he challenged Knox and Whittingham at Frankfurt and supported Whitehead in his pastorate and also wrote to Calvin complaining of the Knoxians. Traheron's letter to Bullinger dated, 3 June, 1553 is extant in which the Reformer says:

> You do not approve of Calvin, when he states that God not only foresaw the fall of the first man, and in him the ruin of his posterity, but that he also at his own pleasure arranged it. And unless we allow this, we shall certainly take away both the providence and wisdom of God altogether.[4]

Traheron referred to Calvin as his 'loving friend' and told Bullinger on another occasion concerning himself and the English Reformers:

> But the greater number among us, of whom I owe myself to be one, embrace the opinion of John Calvin as being perspicuous, and most agreeable to holy Scripture. And we truly thank God, that that excellent treatise of the very learned and excellent John Calvin against Pighius and one Georgius Siculus should have come forth at the very time when the question began to be agitated among us. For we confess that he has thrown much light upon the subject, or rather so handled it, as that we have never before seen any thing more learned or more plain.[5]

So much for the modern lame duck theory that Traheron and his friends were merely 'Anglicans' and thus not 'Calvinists'!

---

[4] Ibid, Vol. I, p. 327.
[5] Ibid, p. 325. The work referred to is *De Aeterna Dei Praedestinatione*.

Grindal, the all round man of God

Here, too, it will be profitable to take a deeper look at Edmund Grindal of the Strasburg group as it would appear impossible for anyone to identify him with a 'High Church' anti-Reformed party or doubt his reforming, evangelical fervour. Strype says of Grindal, 'Before he came to be taken notice of in the church, he made a figure in the university, as one of the ripest wits and learnedest men in Cambridge.'[6] Grindal first became well-known in 1549 when he spoke before the King in a university dispute where he pointed out the unbiblical and superstitious nature of the papist substitute for the Lord's Supper. He then quickly became Lady Margaret preacher and president of his college and was appointed as Bishop Ridley's chaplain in 1550. Ridley told Sir John Cheke, 'Now the man master Grindal, unto whom I would give this prebend, doth move me much; for he is a man known to be both of virtue, honesty, discretion, wisdom and learning.'[7] During this period, Grindal was licensed to preach throughout the diocese and was well-received by the public. He also, with David Whitehead whom he was to join in Frankfurt, disputed with the Romanists on the meaning of 'This is my body.'

In December 1551 Grindal joined John Knox as one of Edward's chaplains and the year after he became Prebendary of Westminster. Being chaplain to Edward was no sinecure position but entailed travelling throughout the entire country, preaching the gospel. Grindal was promised a northern bishopric to replace papist Tunstall[8] but the King died on 6 July, 1553. Grindal fled to Strasburg and diligently studied German so that he could do itinerant preaching. This work took him to Wasselheim, Spires and Frankfurt. His chief employment was, however, collecting records of the Reformation and the sufferings of the martyrs which he gave to Fox for incorpo-

---

[6] *The Life and Acts of Archbishop Grindal*, 1710, p. 5.

[7] Biographical Notice of Archbishop Grindal, p. iii, *The Remains of Archbishop Grindal*, Parker Society 1843. The version of this letter taken from Burnet (Letter II) reads rather differently but with the same sentiments. See *The Works of Nicholas Ridley*, Parker Society, p. 331.

[8] Tunstall's old diocese of Durham was to be split up into several bishoprics.

ration into his *Acts and Monuments*. Grindal's correspondence with
Fox is preserved in the Parker Society records and in Strype's biography of the Archbishop. This correspondence shows that Grindal
was virtually a main author of the work commonly attributed only
to Fox, the latter merely compiling the material he received from
Grindal and translating it into Latin. Fox also gained much material from John Bale and the records show that Thomas Sampson
also assisted Grindal, as did Becon and Coverdale. These men all
met at Frankfurt.[9] This great work must also be seen as a most
positive aspect of the fellowship at Frankfurt. Sadly the preoccu-
pation with the church's 'troubles' has quite disguised the fact that
much good gospel work was done there. Also whilst in Germany,
Grindal gathered together works of Bucer for publication.

When Grindal returned to England, he joined the leaders who
were busy re-reforming the country and the more he climbed the
ecclesiastical ladder, the more powers he was able to use to cleanse
the churches of papist paganism. With reference to Romanism,
Grindal quickly received the nickname Grind-All and his injunctions to the clergy and the laity in his diocese prove this name to be
applicable. His 1571, Injunctions for the entire Archbishopric of
York is typical of the cleansing of the North which he set in motion:

> That the churchwardens and minister shall see that
> antiphoners, mass books, grailes, portesses, processionals,
> manuales, legendaries, and all other books of late belong-
> ing to their church or chapel, which served for the supersti-
> tious Latin service, be utterly defaced, rent, and abolished.
> And that all vestments, albes, tunicles, stoles, phantons,
> pixes, paxes, handbells, sacring-bells, censers,
> chrismatories, crosses, candlesticks, holy-water-stocks, or
> fat images, and all other relics and monuments of supersti-

---

[9] Fox's name has been traditionally associated with many works which were
merely translated by him or compiled. However, without this piece of industry
on Fox's part, many of these works would have been lost.

tion and idolatry, be utterly defaced, broken and destroyed; and if they cannot come by any of the same, they shall present to the ordinary what they cannot come by, and in whose custody the same is, to the intent further order may be taken for the defacing thereof.[10]

What would Grindal have thought of today's Nonconformity and Dissent with its robed, mixed choirs, baptismal gowns, handbell bands, banner and candle processions, festivals, 'revivals', bazaars, raffles, Christmas decorations, Schofield Bible notes, chorus book graduales and even Sung Eucharists and what the American Baptist churches call 'Musicals'?

The Knoxians give the Strasburg brethren a cold reception

The author of *Troubles at Frankfort* shows what a cold reception Cox and his party received from Knox and the few hardliners who supported him. He wrote concerning the new arrivals 'At which time, Doctor Cox, and others with him, came to Frankfort out of England; who began to break that Order which was agreed upon.'[11] Needless to say, Cox neither broke any order that had been agreed upon nor had he and his party come directly out of England. Furthermore, there were men in his party such as Goodman who had been intimate friends with Knox and would become such again. Actually, Cox led a fine bunch of Nonconformists[12] and Puritans that were to be greatly used of God in the future and to make names for themselves as preachers, pastors, teachers and authors of sound expository literature.

On 17 March, when the first Sunday service after the arrival of the Strasburg party came round, they automatically according to the author of *Troubles at Frankfort*, 'answered aloud after the Minister' during the service. In other words, they did what they had been

---

[10] *Injunctions for the Clergy and Laity*, 1571, *The Remains of Edmund Grindal*, Parker Society.

[11] *Troubles at Frankfort*, p. 54.

[12] The author uses the term 'Nonconformist' in the Anglican sense of the word. The term 'Nonconformist' as a synonym for Dissenter originated in post-Cromwellian times.

used to doing in Strasburg where lay-participation in the service had not been forbidden. They also did what was common practice amongst all the Reformed churches. This much criticised incident has been blamed wholly on the Coxians by a number of writers, though it appears that Cox had nothing, at least directly, to do with it. The three separate accounts given in *Troubles at Frankfort* must be compared to find out what actually happened as they are contradictory and together they exonerate Cox (if the term may be used where no evil was done) rather than condemn him. We read:

> And the Sunday following (17 March) one of his (Cox's) company, without the consent and knowledge of the Congregation, got up suddenly into the pulpit, read the Litany; and Dr. Cox with his company answered aloud.[13]

The question now is, who was this 'one of Cox's company' who was 'answered aloud' by the congregation. It is very strange that the recorder mentions no names, although he is otherwise very quick to name those whom he feels are 'on the other side'. If we turn to Whittingham's account in a letter to a friend, we find he, too, preserves the anonymity of the person but says critically, 'A stranger (was) craftily brought in to preach, who had been at Mass and had also subscribed to blasphemous Articles.'[14]

Knox, in *Knox's Account of his banishment*, does not name the speaker but he calls him 'a Minister' which was the word for a preacher (not pastor) amongst the exiles and the title Knox gave himself after refusing to take on the office of a pastor. Knox writes, 'Master LEVER brought in one to preach, who had been at Mass in England, and had subscribed to blasphemous Articles: who read the litany in the pulpit, the people answering.' Here, Knox is totally ignoring that both the French and the British churches had accepted a majority vote in favour of using the litany. This action he saw as the 'subtle undermining of Master Lever: who ought of the same to

---

[13] Ibid, p. 54.
[14] *Troubles at Frankfort*, p. 73. Undated letter but entitled 'Whittingham's Letter of April.'

have been Patron and Defender, as he was chosen by them Minister and Pastor.' This explanation is most revealing. It was not a member of Cox's party who asked the stranger to enter the pulpit but the pastor of the church himself. Further on in his account, Knox says that Lever was backed by others in the church. It can thus hardly be considered a crime for the pastor of a church, supported by members, to invite a visiting preacher to enter the pulpit. Particularly when that pastor had been formerly invited to shepherd the church by a majority vote. We gain here, however, another instance of Knox's extraordinary behaviour. He had withdrawn himself from the pastoral work of the church, refusing to administer the ordinances during this period, but staying on as a minister or preacher. Yet he had protested at the use of alternative forms which would have enabled the congregation to continue celebrating the Lord's Supper under Lever. He had given his fellow-committee members Lever, Whittingham and Parry a free hand to do without him yet, instead of backing his pastor and the majority decisions of the church as a faithful member and preacher, he reserved the right not only to isolate himself from the general fellowship but sit above the church and complain of her actions and even judge her. Indeed, Knox did his level best to split the church by calling rival meetings in his private home. Though Knox's statement shows that what Knox thought was a disturbance came from the Frankfurt church itself, he still does not name the 'bother-causer' whom the author of *Troubles at Frankfort* says was of Cox's party.

Prof. Heron, probably relying on Neal's unreliable dating, puts the event a week later than Whittingham and states that Lever (obviously officiating as pastor-in-charge), asked John Jewel to read the Litany. As this was Lever's idea, it was responded to by many of the 'old' congregation as also the newcomers. Now here we see why the author of *Troubles at Frankfort* had been so reluctant to name Jewel. This nigh blameless man of God was one of the greatest protagonists of the English Reformation and comparable with Peter Martyr for his refutation of Roman novelties and myths. Fellow exile Laurence Humphrey, Jewel's first biographer, calls his subject, 'the first and fairest primrose in this late spring of the church.'[15] When Jewel's magnum opus against Rome *Apologia Ecclesiae Anglicanae* reached Peter Martyr's hands in 1562, he wrote telling of how well it had been received by the Continental Reformers. He further told Jewel that the Reformation had received a setback on the Continent, 'But now you have, by this your most elegant and learned Apology, raised such an hope in the minds of all good and learned men, that they generally promise themselves, that whilst you live, the Reformed religion shall never want an advocate against its enemies.'[16]

Furthermore, Jewel was not a member of Cox's party but had indeed just arrived from England and had made straight for Frankfurt. He thus neither represented the Frankfurt group nor the Strasburg group. In other words, far from the Cox party causing a disturbance, these men had nothing to do with the action as neither Lever nor Jewel were of their party. Jewel's sole reason for journeying to Frankfurt was because he had been informed that the largest number of exiles were settled there. Erasmus Middleton, whose chronology is sound, states that Jewel did occupy the pulpit, but for a far different reason than that given in *Troubles at Frankfort*. Thus, if the 'Minister' on that occasion were John Jewel, only a most prejudiced and ill-informed mind could associate him with the 'popish plot' that Knox, Whittingham and their recorder imagined was afoot.

Jewel, called by Spurgeon 'a Father of the English Church', had been in Christ quite as long as Knox so it seems most strange that Knox would hold Jewel's popish past against him. If Knox were born in 1505[17], he was Jewel's senior by seventeen years and was serving in the popish church and adoring the mass some twenty-two or three years before Jewel was ordained into the Edwardian Reformed Church of England in 1552. In other words, Jewel hardly knew the Roman hierarchy from inside, whereas Knox, like many more of the exiles, had sworn allegiance to that superstitious system, had taught it and spread it for years but had happily repented

---

[15] *Fathers of the English Church*, Vol. VII, p. xxiii.
[16] The full letter is printed in *Biographia Evangelica*, Vol. 2, p. 132.
[17] There are various reports concerning Knox's year of birth which span ten years.

of it and joined the Reformation. It appears, however, and this is one of the many paradoxical features in Knox's character, that though Knox constantly denounced the popish sacramental ordination of ministers, he never challenged his own Roman past in this respect and always considered that his popish ordination was valid in his case only. Thus Dale Kuiper, in his John Knox, *Reformer and Preacher*, concludes:

> Knox was ordained into the priesthood shortly before 1540. He employed himself in giving private instruction to the sons of prominent Scottish families, rather than engaging in parochial duties. It is generally thought that Knox never renounced his priestly vows but considered his original ordination to suffice even as he took up the cause of the Reformation in Scotland.[18]

Rather than having an ordination that marked him out as a sacrificing priest, Jewel had been ordained according to Cranmer's new Ordinal of 1550 which showed much of Bucer's influence on the English Reformer. Cranmer had struck out references to the priestly offering of sacrifices and emphasised the roles of pastor and teacher. Furthermore, members older than Knox such as Bale had been serving Christ for very many years before Knox left off worshipping the Mass in middle life. Bale never criticised a believer for having previously adored the Mass but humbly said 'Yea, I ask God mercy a thousand times, I have been one of them myself.'[19] This was also Grindal's answer when holier than thou Precisians asked him if he had ever worshipped the Mass—as if they had never done so themselves. Neither Jewel, Bale nor Grindal took on Knox's 'holier than thou' attitude. Many of the English Reformers celebrated mass until the time of the Edwardian Prayer Books and the mass was openly celebrated in Scotland for a number of years after it was abolished in England.

---

[18] *The Standard Bearer*, Knox Number, October 15, 2000 Vol. 77, No. 2., p. 27.
[19] John Bale – His Writings, p. 14, from *Writings of John Fox, Bale and Coverdale*, RTS.

Furthermore, a number of the exiles such as Thomas Becon and Robert Wisdom, had, in their early youth, been enraptured by the more revolutionary side of the Reformation and joined hands with the Reformers more out of youthful zeal than spiritual persuasion. When the first flush of youthful rebellion wore off, they then recanted and returned to Rome, as Becon and Wisdom did in 1544. However, such men stood firm against Rome in later years as mature Christians and suffered much for Christ's sake. Becon spent seven months under the most terrible prison conditions before fleeing to Germany.

Cranmer himself first fully rejected transubstantiation in 1549 and even Ridley was not completely convinced until Edward himself taught him a better way, shortly before the Second English Prayer Book was authored. Indeed, the bulk of the Reformation in Britain had only occurred from between 1547 and 1552 and, regarding the Lord's Supper, England had certainly not lagged behind the Continent. In 1548, Peter Martyr pointed out to Bucer that transubstantiation was abolished in England, but in Bucer's Strasburg where Calvin[20] and Bucer himself had preached for so long, the mass was 'universally received'.[21] Knox's mentor Hooper was very slow to condemn those Reformers who had yet taken the mass as Hooper told Henry Bullinger in 1546.[22] Be this as it may, it is obvious that the blame that perpetuity has given Cox for initiating this alleged breech between the original Frankfurt party and the newcomers from Strasburg is groundless as Jewel, a newcomer to both parties had been invited to preach by Pastor Lever of Frankfurt, a move which was supported by founder members of the church.

But this, the author of *Troubles at Frankfort* will not admit. It was Cox who was behind all and the 'Seniors',[23] of the congregation, he tells us, had to admonish him for this breach of the peace. But again, this statement cannot be taken too seriously. Who were

[20] Calvin was pastor in Strasburg from 1438-41 whilst banned from Geneva.
[21] *Original Letters*, Parker Society, Vol. II, p. 471.
[22] *Original Letters*, Parker Society, Vol. I, pp. 38-39.
[23] P. 54.

the 'Seniors'? If age is meant, then Bale was probably the most senior, and had been in Christ since 1529, yet he signed a letter of complaint against the Knoxians sent by the church to Calvin. If church officers are meant, which seems more probable as 'Senior' became the Frankfurt term for 'elder', then surely the pastor, Thomas Lever, must be counted here and he had initiated the situation and was thus obviously in favour of having Jewel preach and lead the worship. Whitehead, who had also been ordained in the Frankfurt church as pastor was still a preacher and regained the pastorate after Knox left for Scotland via Switzerland and France. This brave Nonconformist was one of the earliest members of the Frankfurt church but became Knox's most hefty critic and a sturdy supporter of Lever's position. Nor can Parry, who was looked upon as a Prayer Book man have 'admonished' Cox, especially as it was his own pastor who had asked Jewel to preach and not Cox who had no office in the church and never took one. We can hardly include Knox as one of the 'Seniors' as he blamed Lever repeatedly for breaking up the congregation and not Cox. Makebray was also a moderate Prayer Book man. Gilby might have had reservations but he was a very close friend of Grindal's and other so-called 'Coxians' and he preferred, like Fox, to stay out of controversy. He was to pastor the Genevan church with Goodman in 1556 and thus draw a number of exiles there who wished for unity between the two parties of Puritans. Gilby eventually became Vicar of Ashby de la Zouch, a most sought after preferment, and, though he remained a Nonconformist, he was placed under Grindal's protection. We know that Edwin Sandys of the Strasburg party used all his powers of persuasion to have Jewel speak from the pulpit. Two of the leading members of the Church, Chambers and Sampson who were not of the Strasburg party and eventually joined the church at Geneva, not only welcomed Jewel but urged him to enter the pulpit on the Sunday after his arrival, accepting his offer to confess he was wrong to swear allegiance to Mary.[24] Whittingham, Williams, Wood[25] and

---

[24] See 'Biographical Memoir' in *The Works of John Jewel*, The Fourth Portion, Parker Society, Cambridge, 1850. See also Humphrey's *Life of Jewel* prefaced to Vol. VII of *Fathers of the English Church* which also contains Jewel's main works.
[25] Jewel does not specify whether this is Thomas or John.

Goodman were known critics of Jewel, but they do not appear to
have been office bearers. Goodman, indeed, was one of the Strasburg
party and thus one would have not expected him to have protested at
Jewel. However, a letter probably written some time in 1557 from
Jewel to Whittingham and Goodman which also mentions Williams
and Wood, has been preserved. In it Jewel refers to the troubles at
Frankfurt and trusts that peace now reigns concerning the matter.
He writes:

> To my dearest brothers in Christ, M. Whittingham and
> M. Goodman, at Geneva, much health in Christ.
>
> If that most unhappy circumstance of the Frankfort con-
> tention has at all clouded or diminished our mutual friend-
> ship and union, all this, I trust, has long since been either
> extinguished by christian principle, or at least laid to rest
> by lapse of time. As to both of you indeed I have no doubt
> of it; but for myself I may even promise it. But, since si-
> lence often rather conceals than extinguishes disagreements,
> I have thought it the part of christian piety to stir up our
> ancient kindliness by writing; that, should there still re-
> main any traces of former vexation, they might be alto-
> gether blotted out of recollection. I have hitherto deferred
> this, not through any swelling of temper, which long ago I
> had quite done with, or disregard of brotherly love, or pride,
> but because I was in hopes sometime or other to talk over
> the matter with you personally: but now, when our com-
> mon friend and brother was returning to you, I was unwill-
> ing to let the opportunity slip, Wherefore brethren, if in
> that matter, which I cannot even now condemn, I have at
> all injured both or either of you, or, carried away with zeal
> and the heat of contention, have applied to you any unbe-
> coming word, I beg and beseech you to forgive me this
> wrong, and to bury it in everlasting oblivion; that 'not in
> word only and in tongue, but in deed and in truth, we may
> love one another, and may with one mind and one mouth
> glorify God even the Father of our Lord Jesus Christ.' I

was going to write severally to M. Williams and M. Wood on this subject; but a head-ache does not now allow me to do this: I pray you therefore to request them to consider what is written to you two as written also to them. Farewell, my brethren, and pray God for me.

Zurich, from the house of Peter Martyr, June 1.
Yours in Christ,

Jo. Jewel.[26]

We can safely conclude from all this that if some 'Seniors' did protest, they must have been very few and did not include the majority of office-bearers. Furthermore, we have the testimony of Humphreys, who even outdid Whittingham and Goodman as a critic of the Church of England at times, who emphasises that the Frankfurt church was entirely behind Jewel. Thus the account given in *Troubles at Frankfort* is highly misleading. It is typical of the compiler of the 1554-5 account at Frankfurt that when he strives to draw up arguments against the Coxians, though dogmatic in his condemnation, names and exact objective facts suddenly fail him.

Perhaps the most telling truth against Knox's statement that Jewel had been to a mass is the fact that not only are there no records of such an act but Jewel denounced those who partook of the mass up to the day the notorious document was placed before him by the Commissioners of Heretical Pravity who told him to sign it or expect the worst possible consequences if he did not. He had also been told that day that Bonner wanted him executed. Thus Jewel signed the document (whatever it was) as a last stalling before fleeing immediately afterwards, assisted by Latimer's servant Augustine Bernher. Thus Jewel, after placing his signature where the Commissioners demanded it, had no opportunity to partake of the mass subsequently, even if he had wished to, a desire which he never had! He fled the country immediately and arrived at Frankfurt on Wednesday, 13 March, 1555.

---

[26] *The Works of John Jewel*, Parker Society, Vol. VI, p. 1193.

Knox condemns the Strasburg Christians as ungodly and proud
On that same afternoon, it was Knox's turn to preach. He had been doing a series on Genesis and now read out the story of Noah. Departing entirely from his subject, and from the consensus of the congregation, he announced that 'ungodly' 'proud' people had come into the church who had broken 'godly' agreements and wished to impose 'superstitious, unpure, and unperfect things on the church.' He could say all this after attending one service in which none of the Strasburg group had taken part and four days after they had arrived! Knox bemoaned the 'fact' that the newcomers had a want of discipline, giving as his pet but anachronistic reason that Hooper had been condemned by Cranmer and Ridley for wishing to be ordained without a cope and other 'popish' regalia. Knox was careful not to tell the audience that Cranmer and Ridley very soon came round to Hooper's way of thinking and scrapped popish vestments in the Second Prayer Book[27]. Thus Martin Micronius, pastor of the Dutch church in London, could tell Bullinger that 'on the 15 May (1550) he (Hooper) gained the victory.'[28] Nor did he tell his hearers that Hooper defended the 1552 Prayer Book alongside Latimer, Cranmer and Ridley. He was also careful not to tell the church that he was giving false evidence against the Coxians as many of them, if not all, were either anti-vestiarians or thought habits and gowns 'things of indifference'. Indeed, Hooper angered several of the Coxians one Lent by putting on his head a square cap, though, as Fox says in his *Acts and Monuments*, his head was round, and he even donned a scarlet robe! Nor did Knox tell his congregation that the Continental Reformers such as Martyr and Bucer had advised

---

[27] Knox seems to have confused the meaning of Rochet here with the alb and cope. He was not alone in this as the Rochet was really a plain black, woollen gown but the word often was used of gowns in general. Hooper was not an anti-gown man but he objected to what he called 'Aaronic robes'. Coverdale, Hooper and Latimer and even Ridley in time wore the rochet. See the Parker Society letters for Hooper's correspondence on this topic. It is interesting to note that the term 'vestment' is often used to describe Anglican gowns to emphasise their supposedly popish origin, whereas the English Reformers whether pro or anti-gownsmen, referred to gowns as 'habits', i.e. 'clothing'.
[28] *Original Letters*, Vol. 2, p. 560.

Hooper not to make a mountain out of a mole hill, fearing that his action 'cannot be approved by good and pious men.' They advised him to take 1 Timothy 4:4 as a rule, 'Every creature of God is good, and nothing is to be rejected, if it be received with thanksgiving; for it is sanctified with the word of God and with prayer.'[29] Knox was therefore abusing his calling as a preacher and using the pulpit to split the church and spread monstrous, untruthful gossip.

Knox also attacked the accepting of several benefices and privileges by Anglicans, forgetting, perhaps, that he had held several posts simultaneously in England himself and was patronised by both a duke and a king and that many sound men had served two parishes on very tiny wages because of the dearth in Reformed ministers after the executions instigated by Henry, Wolsey and More. Knox indeed had been awarded a sinecure post with an annuity of forty pounds, payable quarterly, though he refused to take on benefices for which the money was originally intended.[30] This money was paid out by a special augmentation office but Knox also received a salary from the public exchequer for his chaplaincy to King Edward. In other words, Knox was criticising many brethren who had existed on salaries of less than a quarter of Knox's English emoluments. Such men had served several parishes daily, yet Knox had merely carried out most sporadic itinerant work. Others had given up their honorary positions on joining the Reformation but Knox took them up after joining the Reformed movement. Archbishops Parker, Grindal and Whitgift were enormously successful in finding ministers for churches but the practical problems involved in a one church, one pastor system were very obvious. Whitgift summed up these problems in a nutshell by exclaiming, 'What man of reason will think that eight pounds yearly is able to maintain a learned Divine? When as every scull[31] in a kitchen, and groom of a stable, is better provided for.'[32] Indeed, Knox was far less success-

---

[29] See correspondence of Utenhovius, Stumphius, Martyr, Bucer, Micronius, Bullinger and Hooper on this topic for a full coverage. *Original Letters*, Vols I and II.
[30] See Middleton's *John Knox*, Vol. 2. p. 138.
[31] Servant who works in the scullery, washing dishes etc..
[32] See Dawley's *John Whitgift and the Reformation*, p. 204.

ful in solving these problems in Scotland than the English Archbishops in their own country and, according to Dr Hay Fleming, in 1596, 'there were above four hundred parishes, not reckoning Argyll and the Isles, which still lacked ministers.'[33] The method the Scottish church chose to combat this lack of pastoral ministry was to encourage patronising which brought with it so many abuses that eventually the stalwart Marrow Men such as the Erskines and Boston felt they could only reform the Scottish ecclesiastical system from outside. The Evangelicals of the Church of England such as James Hervey were entirely in sympathy with these Scotsmen who wished to introduce into Scotland the real Marrow of Divinity.

Knox's sermon was thus merely an abusive, ill-founded attack on all the newcomers none of whom at the time, and very few afterwards, deserved it in any way. On the contrary, there were those in his tiny party such as himself who had subscribed to the Anglican forms, climbing up the ecclesiastical ladder even to the rank of King's chaplain and had been given a licence to serve the Church in all England. The only exception was Whittingham who had possibly been ordained, or would be ordained, into the Genevan church but lacked Anglican orders. This did not trouble the Coxians in the least and they helped Whittingham become a Dean in the Anglican church, the same rank as Cox had enjoyed, without challenging his ordination. Whittingham must have had few 'Knoxian' qualms as he took up the call.

Knox had signed his allegiance to the Anglican Articles in 1553 and had introduced the 1552 Prayer Book at his church in Berwick before fleeing for the Continent. Knox's Scottish churches continued to use the Second Prayer Book after his return to his native country and it was not until 1660 that Knox tells us that the 'Genevan Book' was 'used in some of our Kirks.'[34] In 1662, the General Assembly proscribed the use of the Genevan Order solely for administration of the sacraments and the solemnization of marriages and births. The liturgy remained that of Edward's. It was not until De-

---

[33] See Lang's *John Knox and the Reformation*, p. 175.
[34] *Works* ii., p. 186.

cember 1564 that the Assembly allowed the general use of a modified Genevan Order in Scotland, the modifications being not of Knoxian origin.[35] Macgregor shows that this was modified on principles taken from, amongst others, Edward's Reformed Church. Indeed, one can safely say that the kind of Presbyterianism later writers such as Lloyd-Jones seek to thrust anachronistically onto Knox did not develop until the very end of the 16th century when Knox had been dead for twenty years.

John Rough's testimony is of major importance here. This former co-pastor of Knox's was brought before Bonner in 1557 on a charge that, 'in some places where godly people were assembled he did read the prayers of the Communion Book set forth in the reign of Edward VI. And being asked what his judgement was of the said Book, he confessed, That he did approve the same as agreeing in all points with the word of God.'[36] Rough was martyred at Smithfield on 21 November of that year, his testimony to Bonner being one of the chief reasons. Wotherspoon takes this as further evidence that the Scottish Reformation still looked on the Book of Common Prayer as 'their' book.

Knox's sermon must have fallen mostly on deaf ears as everyone knew that Pastor Lever was an anti-vestment man and that Cox was against candles, crucifixes and the like. Indeed, after Cox's and Lever's protests, they were banned from Elizabeth's chapel.[37] Whittingham's version of this story deviates substantially from that of his fellow-protestors as he maintained that Knox only entered the pulpit to attack the 'Anglicans' and the Prayer Book after, 'many taunting bitter Sermons were made, as they thought, to our defac-

---

[35] See Macgregor's chapter 'Origins of the Ecclesiastical Polity of 1560,' especially pp. 61-62. See also Witherspoon's detailed account of the introduction of the Genevan Order into Scotland in his *The Second Prayer Book etc..*, pp. 52-56.
[36] See Wotherspoon, pp. 35-36.
[37] See *The Lives of the Elizabethan Bishops* by F.O. White, p. 147. White quotes Bishop Parkhurst as saying "Good riddance" when the tidings reached him that the crucifix and candles had been removed from the Queen's chapel. MacCulloch in his *The Later Reformation in England* claims, without giving contemporary evidence, that whenever the crosses and candlesticks were removed, they were replaced.

ing.' As Jewel used the Litany and preached on the morning of the 17 March, and Knox preached his attack on the same afternoon and none of the Strasburg party had arrived before the previous Wednesday, such a series of 'taunting Sermons' was a sheer impossibility.

After Knox's diatribe, there was another brawl. Knox's claim that Jewel was a man of the mass and a subscriber to blasphemous articles had enraged many on both sides. To tone this down, the author of *Troubles at Frankfort* states that Jewel (still unnamed) confessed to popish activities only after being charged with them that Sunday afternoon.

All the sources are united in saying that Jewel entered the pulpit once, which makes a reconstruction of the event easier. That Sunday morning, his first at Frankfurt, Jewel was invited by the pastor to lead the service. He used the opportunity to make a public confession of his signing the document placed before him by the Commissioners for Heretical Pravity.

One early biographer, Nonconformist, Puritan and fellow exile, Laurence Humphrey[38], who remained close to Jewel all his life, continues the story by saying:

> Jewell also, as soon as he came to Frankfort, made an excellent sermon, and in the end of it openly confessed his fall in these words, 'It was my abject and cowardly mind and faint heart, that made my weak hand to commit this wickedness;' which when he had brought forth with a gale of sighs from the bottom of the anguish of his soul, and had made humble supplications for pardon, first to Almighty God, whom he had offended, and afterwards to his church, which he had scandalised, no man was found in that great congregation who was not pricked with compunction, and wounded with compassion, or who embraced him not ever after that sermon, as a most dear brother, nay, as an angel of God. So far was this saint of God from accounting soph-

---

[38] See *Fathers of the English Church*, Vol VII, *Containing Various Tracts and Extracts From the Works of John Jewell, With a Memorial of His Life*, pp.xix-xx.

istry any part of the science of salvation, or justifying any equivocating shifts, which are daily hatched at the school of antichrist.[39]

It was on this occasion that Jewel had recited the words of the Litany, praying for deliverance in England from 'the tyranny of the bishop of Rome and all his detestable enormities.' No man, on hearing these words, Jewel's biographer tells us, was not 'pricked with compunction, and wounded with compassion'. No man? The writer, one of the most radical of the Nonconformists, had not reckoned with Knox.

Thomas Fuller usually keeps closely to the *Troubles in Frankfort* account and shows real sympathy with the Knoxians. Nevertheless, he departs from their account of Jewel's preaching and confession, though he does believe that Jewel signed some sort of subscription. The historian writes under the title of *Mr. Jewel's seasonable and sincere Recovery*. The italics in the quote are Fuller's:

> *Rejoice not over me O mine Enemy, for though I fall, yet shall I rise again,* as here it came to passe: Comming to *Francfort*, he had Dr. *Edwin Sandys*, (afterwards *Arch-Bishop* of *Yorke*,) for his *Board*, and *Bedfellow*, who counselled Mr. *Jewell*, with the joint advice of Mr. *Chambers*, and Mr. *Sampson*, his bosom friends, to make a publicke *Confession* of his sorrow for his former *Subscription*: whereupon on a *Sunday*, after his forenoon *Sermon*, in the *Congregation* of *Francfort*, he bitterly bewailed his *fall*, and heartily requested *pardon* from God and his *People*, whom thereby he had offended. *Wet* were the *eyes* of the Preacher, and those not *drie* of all his *Auditors*: what he fairly requested was freely given: and hence forward all embraced him, as a *Brother* in *Christ*, yea as an *Angell of God*. Yea

---

[39] See *Life of Bishop Jewel* in *Fathers of the English Church*, Vol. VII, pp. xix-xx, also Erasmus Middleton's *Biographia Evangelica*, Vol. 2, p. 110. Middleton emphasises that it was this act that strengthened Jewel's reputation amongst Reformed men.

whosoever seriously considereth the high *Parts* Mr. *Jewell* had in himselfe, and the high *opinions* others had of him, will conclude his *Fall* necessary for his *Humiliation.*[40]

Knox's record of the scene stands in sharp contrast to the above account. He relates, 'Notwithstanding, the Sunday next following (March 17), not consulting with any man that was in Office, to the great grief and trouble of the Congregation, Master LEVER brought in one to preach, who had been at Mass in England, and had subscribed to blasphemous Articles.'[41] Yet one can imagine how many heads nodded in repentant sorrow regarding their own cases on hearing Jewel's confession as the majority of those present, except Cox and a few who had backed Lady Jane Grey as Queen, had not only bowed their knees to Mary but campaigned with all their might to have her made Queen. Even Knox's hero, John Hooper, whom he seems to have known very superficially, was renowned for riding up and down the country, canvassing support for Mary on the grounds that she was the rightful heir to the English throne. Those early Puritans were certainly not Republicans and as Powel M. Dawley says, 'Mary's regime was scarcely more than a measure of the loyalty of Englishmen to the house of Tudor.'[42] Thomas Fuller relates concerning the initial impact of Mary on Oxford:

Ma. John Jewel was chosen to pen the first *Gratulatorie* Letter to the *Queen,* in the *Name* of the University; an office, imposed on him, by his enemies, that either the refusal thereof should make him incurre danger from his foes, or the performance expose him to the displeasure of his friends; Yet he so warily penned the same in such *Generall* terms, that his Adversaries missed their *marke.* Indeed all, as yet were confident, that the *Queen* would maintain the

---

[40] *The Church History of Britain,* VIII. Book., pp. 709-710, (9-10 in separate sections published).

[41] *John Knox's Account of his Banishment from Frankfort,* in March 1555, included in *Troubles at Frankfort,* 1907 edition, p. 63.

[42] *John Whitgift and the Reformation,* p. 45.

Protestant Religion according to her solemne promise, to the Gentry of *Norfolke*, and *Suffolke*, though (she being composed of *Courtship* and *Popery*), this her unperformed promise was the first *Court-holy-water*, which she sprinkled amongst the *People*.[43]

D. M. Loades explains how, though Northumberland found court backing for Lady Jane:

Outside the court, however, men were less impressionable, and Jane's accession was bitterly resented; partly because it was generally held to be unlawful on account of Henry VIII's Will, and partly because it was a manoeuvre blatantly intended to keep Northumberland in power. Religion seems scarcely to have been a factor in determining the popular mood. Certainly the great majority of protestants, as well as the fellow travellers and conservatives, supported Mary's candidature.

In a footnote to this statement, Loades adds: Fox later claimed that Mary had made a promise of limited toleration to induce protestants to support her (VI, 389), but most would probably have backed her anyway, on the grounds of Henry's Will.[44]

Fox is probably thinking of Mary's promise, or rather, lie, to the Suffolk men that if they helped her come to power, she would make no innovations in religion but keep to the Reformed Book of Prayer. This led Strype to say that 'It is notorious to the world that they were Protestants chiefly that placed her in her Kingdom.'[45]

Nor can Jewel be linked in any way with those who would accept no alteration in the Prayer Book, called by Jewel 'The Reformed Book'. No sooner had he returned to England than he stood up at Westminster and challenged any papist to debate with him on the following points:

---

[43] *The Church History of Britain*, VIII. Book., p. 706 (p.6. in separate section.)
[44] *The Oxford Martyrs*, p. 104. Loades is leaning on the findings of A. G. Dickens in his work *The English Reformation*.
[45] *Ecclesiastical Memorials*, Vol. III, part i., p. 17.

1. That it is repugnant to the word of God, and custom of the primitive church, that church service and liturgy should be performed in an unknown tongue. 2. That every church hath power to alter rites and ceremonies for her better edification. 3. The propitiatory sacrifice of the mass for quick and dead hath no warrant in the word of God.[46]

The papist made a feeble attempt to confute Jewel but soon broke off and left him the victor. Similarly, the Council of Trent appointed a Frenchman and an Italian (they had no Romanist in England anywhere near capable) to confute Jewel's great work on the Reformation of the Church of England but they never took up the task.

It is interesting to note that though the author of *Troubles at Frankfort* quotes an abundance of abusive sayings from the minority side, he has no such remarks and insults to pass on from the Cox group. This is a very marked indication of who the troublemakers really were at this time. When we read the records of Fox, Sandys, Grindal, Lever, Humphrey and other exiled saints of the supposed 'Anglican' party, they are full of modesty and pleas for concord. Jewel's earliest biographer, quoted above, emphasises how Jewel strove alongside Peter Martyr to mediate between the Knoxians and the Coxians to find peace and common understanding. Even Cox, who after Frankfurt was attacked the most by the offending party, never stooped to the vocabulary of Knox and his few supporters. Indeed, Cox is merely used as a strawman in the controversy and never took the negative part assigned to him. Though John Fox, as most of the Frankfurt members, sympathised with Knox's anti-vestment views, he nevertheless denounced Knox's politics and verbal outbursts. When Fox left Frankfurt to find peace and freedom to publish, he did not follow Knox to Geneva but settled in Basle where more tolerance reigned. The only time Cox seemed to raise his temper was when he started burning popish books in the university library. However, extreme as this may have

---

[46] *Fathers of the English Church*, Vol. VII. p. xxiii.

been, and it is only rumoured that Cox did this, not proved, Knox would have been fully in sympathy. The Scotsman thought that even the Second Prayer Book was only fit for burning!

One fierce critic at Frankfurt obviously was not moved by Jewel's repentance and on the following Tuesday, 19 March, complained of Jewel having 'subscribed to wicked Articles' and the author of *Troubles at Frankfort* stated that Jewel then 'sorrowfully confessed' this 'even in the pulpit shortly after'. This gives the impression that Jewel only confessed to have sworn allegiance to Mary when he was pressed to do so by the opposition. This view is in total contradiction to the facts which depict Jewel confessing his former weakness on his first Sunday morning at Frankfurt. Perhaps this is why Peter Martyr, on hearing how gentle Jewel was being slandered by some in order to set up a false case, personally invited him to leave the troublemakers and join him at Strasburg and be his permanent guest.

It cannot be emphasised strongly enough that Knox's entire protest against the Litany with Responses had nothing whatsoever to do with a Roman Catholic background but the fact that Knox could not tolerate 'lay' participation in the service. He was certainly not against the Litany as such as he even confessed in his 'Plat'. What he protested violently against were the lay Responses. Indeed, after arguing that Knox agreed with the Anglicans on doctrine, George Sprott claims that the only difference between the two parties was liturgical and that Knox would not have lay participation. Sprott thus sums up the controversy by saying, 'Nothing remained but the responses, and on this rock they split.'[47] Here, as so very often, Knox proved himself to be more High Church than the Anglican Puritans. That to ban 'lay' responses was a permanent High Church Precisianist programme is illustrated by the Savoy Conference at the Restoration where they, under the guise of Puritans, campaigned to have the responses erased from the Book of Common Prayer. It is interesting to note that these same 'Puritans' requested the contin-

---

[47] *Second Prayer Book of Edward VI and the Liturgy of Compromise*, p. 222. See Sprott's discussion in Difference between "the Coxians" and "the Knoxians", pp. 221-223.

ued use of the Litany but not in separate suffrages (short petitions by the congregation) but as one long ministerial prayer. They also protested at the Lord's Prayer and the General Confession in the Communion Service being spoken by any but the officiating minister. The response of the bishops was to strengthen congregational participation in the service. Amongst these Puritan Precisians who wished to alter the Prayer Book in an anti-Reformation direction were John Tillotson and his party of Latitudinarians, besides a number of Erastians and High Churchmen who left Presbyterianism when they realised that it could not be resurrected in England and joined the restored Church of England. When Edward Calamy was deprived of his church in 1662, it was taken over by his former fellow-'Puritan' John Tillotson who now gradually put off his Genevan gown to take up the Archbishop's cope. By welcoming such renegade Presbyterian Laudians and Latitudinarians, the Church of England did itself no service.

The Litany was an order of prayer, petitions, praise and Scriptural exhortation that was particularly loved by the Reformers. It was the first form of worship to be put into the vernacular and contained a special condemnation of Rome. To mark the Litany's importance, it was taken from its mid-week position and placed in the main Sunday worship. Arch-Reformer Bucer looked upon the Precisian and Presbyterian rejection of suffrages as Romanism returned, saying in his advice to Anglicans on the use of the Litany in *De Caeremoniis Ecclesiae Anglicanae*, 'These responses are not the concern of the clergy only, any more than the prayers themselves are, but of the whole people.'

Knox, hitherto opposed to admitting the newcomers as full members, now was compelled to bow to the majority vote and was asked by the church not to act as if he was in authority over them. Here, Knox is most difficult to follow in his personal record of the events which often contrasts markedly with other records. He argues that the church majority were against their Strasburg brethren and tells his readers, 'I only (he alone) made intercession that they (the Coxians) should be admitted; and obtained that which I requested,' He records that he told the Strasburg party that he knew they wished to overthrow his cause, adding 'Howbeit, the matter is so evident,

that ye shall not be able to do it. Wherefore, I fear not your judgement; and therefore do I require that ye might be admitted.' This
would appear as if Knox took the initiative in very grudgingly admitting the Strasburg men to membership on his own authority,
against the wishes of the church, but it is highly improbable that he
had such an authority at the time and it is very obvious that their
pastor Lever and his followers as also Whitehead and his followers
welcomed the Strasburg brethren with open arms. Knox, indeed,
has to contradict himself here by complaining that 'Doctor Cox and
such others' had usurped their new authority at Frankfurt because
of 'their well-doing in England'. In other words, they gained acceptance in the church because of their work hitherto for the Lord, their
fine Christian testimony and their good reputation. It appears here
that Knox had grudgingly to acknowledge the popularity of the
moderate Prayer Book men but to save his own remnant of authority, jumped over his own shadow and bade them welcome after it
became obvious that the majority were on their side. Even though
Knox had suffered defeat after defeat in his dealings with the Frankfurt congregation, he still imagined that he was in control and had
the authority to rule the church single-handed in his self-imposed
office of the church's Superintendent.[48] Amazingly, Knox kept up
this self-deceit even when the congregation asked him not to try and
bully them. This does not mean that all respect for Knox was gone.
He was still followed by half the congregation as a preacher of the
Word but rejected as a troublemaker in his demands to alter the
'English face' and bring in unacceptable and quite unnecessary alterations in discipline, liturgy and church order which many saw as
a step back into Babylonian bondage.

---

[48] See Knox's account in *The Troubles at Frankfort*, pp. 63-66.

The English Monument
Frankfurt 1559

Chapter Eight:
A Welshman looks at an
Englishman and a Scotsman

Dr Martyn Lloyd-Jones takes sides

Even such a respected figure as Dr Martyn Lloyd-Jones joins in the harsh criticism of Cox, though his evidence to support him is even more threadbare than that produced by Neal and McCrie. Indeed, all the new features Lloyd-Jones brings into the debate have no documentary backing whatsoever. He leads his readers into realms of his personal opinions regarding culture, politics and national identity without giving any new insight whatsoever into the troubles at Frankfurt and the more he praises Knox, the more Lloyd-Jones denigrates his idol, turning him into a man who was enchanted by externals and thrilled with altering systems that hitherto had been very effective in the cause of God and truth. Completely ignoring the responsibility of the Frankfurt church to draw up their own Order of Worship, and apparently arguing on the mistaken idea that up to Knox's arrival, the church had used the Book of Common Prayer in its entirety, Lloyd-Jones writes:

> While he was at Frankfort Knox did something which is typical and characteristically Puritan. He and Whittingham, the main translators of the Geneva Bible, drew up an order of service to replace that of the Common Prayer Book which they disliked. Modified mainly because of Knox's moderation, this Order of Service, repudiated

the Book of Common Prayer. He did not say this openly, once more, until confronted by the militant and ungentlemanly opposition of Richard Cox whose behaviour can only be described as quite abominable, intransigent and rude – not the last time Puritans have had to suffer in that way at the hands of Anglicans.[1]

It is interesting to note that though the main body of 'Knoxian' commentators argue that Knox accepted the original order of the church, Lloyd-Jones argues that he brought in a new form. Here, however, Lloyd-Jones departs radically from the account given by Knox, Whittingham and the author of *Troubles in Frankfort* themselves and affirms that it was the quarrel with Cox concerning his non-acceptance of Knox's Geneva Order of Service that led to Knox's preaching against the Prayer Book on the 'next day'. In order to defend his 'first Puritan', Lloyd-Jones has to contradict him! Though Lloyd-Jones says that he has the story from Knox's 'History of these matters', which presumably is either a reference to John Knox's *Account of his Banishment from Frankfort*, in March 1555 or to Knox's *The History of the Reformation of Religion in Scotland*, the Scotsman does not refer to Cox at all in either account but cites the behaviour of the exile church's 'pastor and minister' Lever for bringing 'grief and trouble' to the church which moved Knox to stand up and protest.[2] Then Lloyd-Jones goes on to speak of Cox's alleged 'scandalous' and 'despicable' behaviour, though source evidence for these allegations is totally wanting.[3] Indeed, Lloyd-Jones shows national and denominational intolerance of the worst order.

Lloyd-Jones is obviously reading into past history his well-known low opinions of the Anglican Church of his day which led

---

[1] *The Puritans*, p. 274.

[2] See *John Knox's Account, Troubles at Frankfort*, pp. 62-63. Note that Knox calls Lever 'Minister and Pastor', whereas he describes himself as merely 'Minister', thus suggesting that Knox did not become a co-pastor with Lever but merely one of several preachers.

[3] *The Puritans: Their Origins and Successors*, pp. 274-275.

him to break fellowship with Anglican lovers of doctrinal Puritans in his endeavour to show that one cannot be a true Puritan and remain an Anglican. Lloyd-Jones rubs this opinion in with some most odd anti-English sentiments which came as a great surprise to this author who has lived for almost forty years outside of England and has another nationality. What Lloyd-Jones has to say of the English would be considered racist in other countries. Lloyd-Jones rejects the English 'Coxians' because as Englishmen, he feels they can only 'muddle through', seek compromises, hate definitions and shy away from precise statements.[4] The famous doctor makes much of the fact that the incapable English had to invite a Scotsman to pastor them, forgetting that Knox, was most likely the congregation's second choice (so Arber), but was also, as Haddon, a minister of the Church of England. He also forgets that Knox was to serve in a team of co-equal pastors. However, Lloyd-Jones' criteria for judging Knox to be a Puritan, indeed, the originator of Puritanism, make a mockery of any sensible, historically-grounded definition of the term. In his chapter *John Knox – The Founder of Puritanism*, Lloyd-Jones describes Knox as being able, energetic, shrewd, wise, courageous, moderate, original and vehement. However, it was not so much this as Knox's independence of thought, his cleaving to Scripture and his thoroughness which Lloyd-Jones lists as signs of his 'theoretical or academic Puritan'. Knox's 'applied' Puritanism was that he was against vestments, against kneeling at the Lord's Supper, against baptising the children of those excommunicated, against using wafers instead of a broken loaf, against viewing the Lord's Supper and baptism as conferring grace and against the Prayer Book. One might also add that Lloyd-Jones believes Knox's nationality spoke for him. Knox also, Lloyd-Jones tells us, was ahead of Calvin in his attitude to 'the powers that be' and this marked him out as a true Puritan, as did also the fact that

---

[4] *The Puritans*, p. 277. It is interesting to note here, that Lloyd-Jones, who in emphasising that the English, unlike Knox, always compromised, has just listed many ways in which Knox showed moderation and a willingness to compromise. It would appear that an English compromise is thus different from a Welsh or Scottish one!

he refused a bishopric.[5] It is interesting that Lloyd-Jones looks on personal character and attitude to outward ceremonies alone as the marks of a Puritan, apparently forgetting that the factors which united the second generation of Reformers, called Puritans, was their doctrine, Christian experience and experimental faith. Sadly, almost the entire argument in Lloyd-Jones' book is taken up with defining Puritanism by outward factors of politics, Presbyterianism and a break with the established Reformed Church of England. 'Puritanism' Lloyd-Jones argues, 'must always end in Presbyterianism or Independency'.[6] This is a surprising statement as these groups represent highly divergent opinions regarding a national church and church discipline. Lloyd-Jones appears to forget that Presbyterianism went further than the Anglican Church in its demands for a national church working hand in hand with Parliament. Actually, the Presbyterians and Independents were more bitterly opposed to each other than they were separately opposed to the Anglican Church. Furthermore, as Knox certainly did not believe in a parity of ministers,[7] which appears to be the traditional Presbyterian view, and as Knox was an avowed opponent of Independency in Scotland, one wonders how Lloyd-Jones came by his ideas. This would certainly not only make Knox a non-Puritain but also all the great pioneers of the English Reformation up to the Commonwealth period.

Lloyd-Jones' definition of a Puritan examined
In all fairness to those who quickly requested Knox to leave the Frankfort church in peace, it must be said that they did not believe for a moment that Knox was motivated by Scripture in his denunciation of his fellow-Reformers. This must also be taken into account when analysing Lloyd-Jones' weak claim that Puritanism started with Knox. The evidence he produces would not impress a

---

[5] Ibid. pp. 260-281.
[6] *The Puritans*, p. 255.
[7] He appointed migratory Superintendents who were superior to the local clergy and speaks in the *Book of Discipline* of the function of the 'chief minister' in inducting ministers. Cf. IV. Concerning Ministers and their Lawful Election.

Scouts' Court of Honour, not to mention a court of law, or one might hope, one having any familiarity with his Bible. As a barometer of theological acumen and spiritual life, Lloyd-Jones' arguments are most unconvincing.

Most of the Reformed churches on the Continent, including the Reformed Scandinavian churches and Geneva itself, used wafers. To define Puritanism as wafer-rejecters is hardly meaningful. One must also pose the questions 'When is a popish wafer not a popish wafer?' One also might ask, 'Had the papists used good old Edinburgh baps for their Supper celebration, would these have also been forbidden by Knox, too? The question is valid as it shows that Knox departed from the symbolic factor of the Eucharist and treated the nature and consistence of the bread as having sacral power.

The adulation attached to the popish wafer was partly because of the popish doctrine of transubstantiation and partly because of the crucifix stamped on it. The 'Reformed Church of England wafer' of the First Edwardian Prayer Book, if such a term may be allowed, was thicker than the popish wafer so that it looked more bread-like, it had no offending crucifix stamped upon it and was associated with just about the most Reformed doctrine of the Lord's Supper ever to be practised. However, Dr Lloyd-Jones' criticism does not take into consideration the nature of the case and he is obviously confusing the First Edwardian Prayer Book as Knox often does, with the Second Reformed Prayer Book of 1552-3. His argument is thus plainly and simply not valid at all, whichever way one looks at it, as the Second Prayer Book did not prescribe wafers!

The Lord's Supper obviously reflects the fulfilment of Pascal Feast in which unleavened bread was used. If normal yeast bread were used by Knox, it could be argued, using his criteria, that he was departing from Scriptural evidence for the use of unleavened bread which the First Edwardian Prayer Book introduced in the form of thick, unmarked, unleavened wafers. However, the Second Prayer Book did not confuse the symbolic with the physical, as Knox and the Romanists tended to do, and ruled that the bread should be 'such as is usual to be eaten at the table with other meats', and this was further defined as 'common bread'. In point of fact, whether one used unleavened or leavened bread in the ordinance became a matter of indifference to the Reformers and various kinds of bread were used. However, Knox and Lloyd-Jones will have the symbol to be as exact as possible a replica of the bread used at the original Lord's Supper. Then surely the unleavened wafer would be a 'safer' choice than yeast bread.[8] Perhaps this is why Convocation opted for a re-use of the wafer in 1563. This also brought the Church of England more in line with the Continental Reformed churches.

Ups and downs in the development of the Knoxian view of the Lord's Supper

The Knoxians differed greatly in their attitude to the Lord's Supper in relation to the main-line Reformation. J.C. Philpot, in his review of Anderson's *Knox Tracts*, states that after the 1733 secession of the Marrow Men, the seceeders celebrated the Lord's Supper four times a year and the rest of the church twice a year.[9] In Philpot's days the Scottish church celebrated but once a year, obviously thus keeping to the time-pattern of the Passover.[10]

However, the compilers of the Buke of Discipline of 29 April, 1560 rule that:

> Foure tymes in the yeare we think sufficient to the administratioun of the Lordis Tabill, which we desire to be distincted, that the superstitioun of tymes may be avoided so far as may be.

The book maintains, however that if special guarantees were made and it was obvious that no superstition was involved, it could be celebrated more often. These 'guarantees' were that:

---

[8] See Moeller's *History of the Christian Church*, Vol. III, Reformation to 1648, Evangelical Reforms under Edward VI, The Second Prayer Book, especially p. 209.

[9] Gospel Standard Magazine, April, 1852, p. 135.

[10] Ibid, p. 132.

We think that none ar apt to be admitted to that Mysterie who can not formalie say the Lordis Prayer, the Articles of the Belief, and declare the same of the Law.[11]

This follows the pattern of the English High Church at the time but the main body of English exiles preferred to celebrate (rather than 'administer') communion at least monthly and those who communed were expected to be sound in their faith as well as their familiarity with Reformed articles and what presumably is a mention of the Ten Commandments. Indeed, monthly celebration was the practice of the English church at both Frankfurt and Geneva,[12] and this is laid down in the Genevan Order which was also used in some Scottish churches. It is noteworthy that, in discussing the sacraments, the *Buke of Discipline* mentions the *Book of Common Order* as 'the most perfite that ever yit was used in the Churche,' but, though it follows the Common Order on baptism, it departs concerning the frequency of administrating the Lord's Supper.[13]

The anti-Knox group did not wear vestments
Also most of the Frankfurt opposition to Knox were clearly as anti-vestment as he was. Indeed, the more ultra Nonconformists amongst the Coxians were far more radical than Knox in doing away with 'things of indifference' and superfluous ceremonies, though they disagreed with Knox on what was superfluous. A good number, for instance, would not even admit a black 'Geneva' gown! This writer in his youth has sat under Dr Lloyd-Jones regularly in different places and on different occasions over a period of years but he has never seen 'The Doctor' officiating without his long flowing ceremonial robes. Mention of Geneva here is certainly in place as Calvin's ministers had a most ornate and complicated clerical dress, including gown, bands, cassock and tippet, often called a 'preaching scarf'. This was crowned by a special, symbolic clerical cap. Grindal introduced similar dress in England, purely to appease the Precisian

---

[11] Laing's *Works of John Knox*, Vol. II, pp. 239-242.
[12] Ibid, Vol. IV, p. 191, Vol. VI, 324.
[13] Ibid, Vol. II.

clergy but a number of so-called Coxians would not even accept these innovations of French fashion. Yet portraits of the Precisians have been handed down showing them proudly supporting the Beza ruff, as did the English nobility,[14] or the Zanchy collar which eventually became the bib of the Reformed Church. Both fashions which the common man, whose clothing we are now told the anti-Cox group wished to wear, had abandoned. Indeed, during the time of the Levellers, we find them still wearing long, exaggerated white collars which later became the uniform of many North American colonists. Indeed, in the youth of this writer in England, one could tell the Free Church clergy easily from their colleagues of the Established Church as they invariably wore the higher 'dog-collar'.

Percy relates how amazed Ridley was when he heard from Grindal of Knox's prejudices, responding with the words, 'I do marvel how he can or dare avouch them before the Englishmen that be with you.' Percy continues:

> Knox and his congregation were speaking different languages. He was talking European and they English. To him church unity meant a common confession and a common discipline; to them it meant a common worship. The Prayer Book to him was a local peculiarity of English law; to them it was the one concrete achievement of the English Reformation, the sole cement of a national church. He thought of it as a book imposed by Dudley; they as the book forbidden by Mary. He took it for granted that men whom England had driven out would at least avail themselves of a freedom which England had denied them; they were resolved to preserve, as their common bond in exile, the worship which had been proscribed at home.

Although Percy is obviously biased here against the English at Frankfurt and represents their position differently to the one they give themselves, he sees that here the problem is not so much a

---

[14] See Mark Gerard's famous painting of William Cecil, Lord Burghley.

matter of doctrine and experimental Christianity but of one form of culture against another. Thus, in striving to give a fair and balanced picture of the situation, Percy reveals his own one-sidedness. To complete the comparison, he ought to have explained how Knox was far more particular than Dudley concerning the legalising of his own favourite forms of discipline and how one of the reasons his faction gave for not accepting the Prayer Book, if we are to admit Neal as an authority, was that Mary had made it illegal. In spite of any influence Dudley might or might not have had on the legalising of the Prayer Book, he never prescribed the death penalty for nonconformity as such, which was Knox's custom.[15] Furthermore, Percy, in mentioning Dudley, forgets his own advice not to write off the works of good men because their lives ended on a negative note. Dudley's alleged weakness at the end of his life, does not take away two facts, the first being that Dudley was in the foremost rank of the early Reformers and the second being that the Dudleys played a most important role in the history of the Reformation in England and the American Colonies for over a century and half.

Modern Presbyterian critics of supposed Coxian vestments, must be reminded that many Anglicans did without them altogether, even during Laud's purge. However, at this time, their Presbyterian colleagues had been adorned with ceremonial clothing for generations. In short, it would have been difficult in 1554 to have found a group of Christians so anti-vestment in their approach as the 'Anglican' exiles at Frankfurt. Though a number of these Anglicans were prepared to face suspension and dismissal for not wearing robes after the Elizabethan Settlement, Knox merely took offence against English robes and prescribed Scottish (i.e. French and Italian) ones for his 'model' church. Whilst writing this passage, the author has before him a recent photograph of a well-known Scottish Presbyterian minister who represents an organisation which has published most radical 'anti-vestment' works. There he stands in his floor-length, flowing robes looking like Roman Catholic Chesterton's amiable 'Father Brown' himself. His robes, however, are black and

---

[15] *John Knox*, p. 198.

not the devilish white of the descendants of Aaron! Legality is thus preserved and hypocrisy hid. But, wait a minute – did not Chesterton's amiable Father Brown also wear black? Indeed, is not the long black caftan the traditional Mullah's robe? This is why the English Reformers teased too ardent lovers of Genevan fashions for dressing up in 'Turkish robes'.

Fox's biographer tells of a serious incident in the life of his son Samuel which nevertheless has an amusing side. Samuel spent some time on the Continent and was so taken up with the latest fashion there that on his return he presented himself to his father 'in a foreign and somewhat fantastical garb.' 'Who are you?' said Fox. 'Sir, I am your son Samuel,' was the reply. Fox retorted with 'O my son, what enemy of thine hath taught thee so much vanity?'[16]

Lloyd-Jones makes much of the point that Knox refused to admit the children of the excommunicated to baptism, though it would have been most difficult to find an English Reformer or any so-called 'Coxian' who would have disagreed with him. However, would Lloyd-Jones have baptised the children of those dismissed from Anglican fellowships who then sought fellowship with his church? There were many former Anglicans who had 'converted over' to the Westminster Chapel and had their children duly 'done' in Lloyd-Jones' days. Would Knox have accepted such who, in spite of being thrown out of one church, wished to join his?

Sitting in worship no improvement on kneeling
Nor was either kneeling, sitting or standing during certain ceremonies a point to fall out over amongst the so-called Coxians, who explained that false adoration of images could ensue from any bodily position. Yet Lloyd-Jones maintains that 'Quite on his own, and by his understanding of the Scriptures, he came to the conclusion that it is wrong to kneel in the reception of the Sacraments.'[17] This, for Lloyd-Jones, is yet another proof that Knox was a Puritan. Apparently, we are not to question the validity of Knox's hunch. However, Calvin himself, insisted that his communicants knelt on re-

---

[16] *Writings of John Foxe*, RTS, p. xxv.
[17] Ibid, p. 270.

ceiving the Lord's Supper, as was customary in all the Reformed churches. Concerning the Lord's Supper, it might well be argued that many of the Frankfurt Christians who did not support Knox, were even more Zwinglian than he was. Lloyd-Jones is surely inaccurate in depicting Knox as an ultra-Zwinglian in contrast to Anglican views of the Supper as a means of grace. Knox's argument that the Anglican celebration of the Lord's Supper could be interpreted superstitiously falls totally flat in view of his own Geneva Book rendering 'the Sacrament is a singular medicine for all poor sick creatures.' One could interpret this phrase most superstitiously if one were so inclined! Furthermore, Lloyd-Jones, as Knox, refers to the Lord's Supper and Baptism, as 'Sacraments' whereas the Anglican Nonconformists preferred to use the term 'Ordinances'. Otherwise, Knox's 1560 *Book of Discipline, II Of Sacraments*, is quite in unison with writings on the subject by Ridley, Grindal, Jewel, Fox etc., and even older writers such as Firth and Tyndale, regarding the spiritual and symbolic purpose of the ordinance. There is, however, one major feature in which Knox departs entirely from the bulk of his Anglican counterparts, especially Grindal, Jewel and Fox. In his *Book of Discipline* which he addressed to The Great Council of Scotland, advising them how to go about their daily religious and judicial business, Knox rails against the Nonconformist whom he calls 'idiots' who dare to celebrate communion without due authority from his newly set up church hierarchy. Concerning these Dissenters Knox tells his country's rulers, 'We dare not prescribe unto you what penalties shall be required of such. But this we fear not to affirm, that the one and the other deserve death.' Though Knox says '*We dare not prescribe unto you*', after 'proving' his point by a case-law reference to Darius on quite a different topic, Knox goes on to say, 'Therefore, the more earnestly *require we*[18] that strait laws may be made against the stubborn contemners of Christ Jesus, and against such as dare presume to administer His Sacraments, without orderly call to that office; lest, while there be none found to gainstand impiety, the wrath of God be kindled against

---

[18] My emphasis.

the whole.'[19] It is of interest to note that where the Dissenters whom Knox would put to death spoke of lovingly 'disciplining' church members in the environment of church fellowship, Knox, though he termed his work *The Book of Discipline*, merely proscribes 'punishments' for 'idiots' for breaking the civil law. A strange view of pastoral care.

It is ironic that such as Frankfurt exile Thomas Becon should be thought guilty of celebrating a popish Eucharist as he was one of the most outspoken critics of Rome on this subject and one who was more Zwinglian than most. He goes down in history as being a master of alliteration, telling the lovers of the Mass:

> Your peevish, popish, private pedlary pelting mass agreeth with the Lord's blessed supper and communion nothing at all.[20]

The pro-Puritan author of *The Lives of the British Reformers* tells his readers:

> Becon was one of the most laborious and useful writers and preachers among the British reformers. His publications exceed forty in number; some of considerable length. The earliest was printed in 1541, and the latest in 1566. They embrace a much wider range of subjects than the works of any other writer of that day. Several of them are upon the Romish controversy, and manifest a thorough knowledge of the subject, but the greater part of them do not directly relate thereto. Their contents are also exceedingly scriptural; frequently for pages together they exhibit a collection of passages from holy writ, illustrating in a very striking manner the subjects upon which the author is treating. All the reformers were 'mighty in the scriptures,' but Becon, especially, 'abounded' therein.[21]

---

[19] *The Book of Discipline*, XVI, For Punishment of those that Profane the Sacraments.
[20] See Carpenter's *The Church of England 597-1688*, p. 297.
[21] *Lives of the British Reformers*, RTS, p. 266.

These great works of Becon's were nearly all written from Frankfurt, just one of the many factors that show what a positive influence the exile at Frankfurt had on the English Reformation.

John Bale, too, can hardly be put in the popish camp concerning his views of the Supper. He easily rivalled Becon in hot alliteration, calling the priests, 'beastly blind babblers and bawds' and their church 'The madam of mischief and proud Synagogue of Satan.' For him, the popish mass:

> Serveth all witches in their witchery, all sorcerers, charmers, enchanters, dreamers, soothsayers, necromancers, conjurors, cross-diggers, devil raisers, miracle-doers, dog-leechers, and bawds; for without a mass they cannot well work their feats.

Bale is referring to the fact that nothing could be done in the world of deceit and devilry without the mass being appealed to, even if it were a Black Mass! Our modern conjurers remind us of this sordid fact when using part of the Latin Mass when waving their wands over their top-hats![22]

Actually, the forbidding of kneeling as also the forbidding of lay responses throughout the liturgy showed the acute clericalism of the Knoxian development which proscribed a full passivity on the part of the congregation. As S.C. Carpenter so rightly says, learning is doing for those who come under the gospel, 'For in all ages, while they constantly decline to take much notice of what is said, they are moved by what is done.'[23] Worship is hardly worship when it is only listened to and not practised. Neither is church discipline, one would think, anything to do with that name when it is left to the secular authorities alone to enforce it solely in the form of punishment.

Even though such as John Fox and Calvin himself thought Knox too radical in his views of 'the powers that be', his views were shared, more or less, by several Anglican exiles, including, Bishop

---

[22] *Works of Bishop Bale*, Parker Society, 1849, pp. 232-259.
[23] *The Church in England, 597-1688*, p. 277.

Ponet (or Poynet), Sampson and Gilby. Also the attempt to 'prove' that Knox was a Puritan, in contrast to the Frankfurt Anglicans, because he refused a bishopric from the hand of a Duke, is hardly a telling argument. Many Reformers swore to have as little as possible to do with Northumberland, who protected Knox and used him as a 'whetstone to sharpen the archbishop of Canterbury, whereof he hath need'.[24] Here it must be emphasised that Knox's generous church preferments in England were not church appointments but political patronages allowed him by secular dukes. Similarly, the Macedonian call from Scotland for Knox to leave his genuine church appointment at Geneva was instigated by the rebel lords and his ecclesiastical authority received from their hands. Furthermore, the question as to the nebulous distinction between Grindal's idea of a bishop and Knox's idea of a superintendent must be raised here.

Many a Coxian refused a bishopric
A good number of Knox's allegedly Non-Puritan fellow exiles also refused bishoprics. Indeed, Knox's main critic at Frankfort, David Whitehead not only refused a bishopric, and an Irish Archbishopric before leaving for Frankfurt, he declined to be elected Archbishop of Canterbury on returning to England! Sampson, who took the 'Anglican' side at Frankfurt, refused to become Bishop of Hereford, Miles Coverdale never returned to Exeter and Alexander Nowell politely rejected the offer of Coventry and Lichfield. Horn, well-known for breaking down altars with his own hands, had refused the Bishopric of Durham. Even Cox, after serving as Bishop of Ely for a number of years, eventually handed in his resignation. It would be a daring man who would challenge the Puritan credentials of Bale, Fox, Lever, Becon, Sampson and Humphrey, all of whom were offered high clerical posts, yet rejected them, though they opposed Knox in various degrees. Yet, though these men said no to offers of higher posts, it was because of their humility and call to preach rather than disagreement with Episcopacy.[25] All of these men looked

---

[24] See Collinson's *Archbishop Grindal*, p. 63.
[25] See Collinson's *The Elizabethan Puritan Movement*, Part III, The First Presbyterians, 2, The Circumstance of Its Assertion.

on the reign of Elizabeth and a stable monarchy as a gift of God to the Church. Later Knoxians and Cartwrightians have sought to show that Fox rejected Episcopacy but Whitgift has proved without a doubt from Fox's works that the English Puritan Reformer, who stood very close to Whitgift, differed greatly from Knox on these matters.[26] Concerning radicals who wished to raise up a Presbytery in place of the bishop's office, Collinson quotes Fox as saying, 'If I were a man to rage with them against bishops and archbishops, they would never have sharpened their arrows against me. They hate me because I prefer to follow moderation and public tranquillity.'[27] When the would-be Presbyterians started persecuting their brethren at Magdalen College, Fox exclaimed:

> My private wrongs I can bear; it is the church's danger that moves me. This kind of men, if they gather strength, will throw all into confusion. They are worse than the old monks, and would reduce all to Judaean servitude.[28]

When Fox found out that Samuel, his son, was being persecuted and his close friend Humphrey, now President of Magdalen, possibly in an effort to discredit Fox himself, the reforming Puritan, protesting at the puritanising of externals instead of sound Christian doctrinal and spiritual norms exclaimed:

> I marvel the more what turbulent genius has so inspired these factius puritans, that violating the laws of gratitude, scorning my letters and prayer to them, despising the intercession of the president himself, they practise this monstrous tyranny against me and my son, without warning or reason

---

[26] See a balanced discussion of this topic in V. Norskov Olsen's *John Foxe and the Elizabethan Church*, Chapter IV. The Church and Its Ministry. The entire Whitgift-Cartwright debate which is true Puritanism versus Precisianism, can be read in the Parker Society's 3-volumed edition of Whitgift's *Works*.

[27] *The Elizabethan Puritan Movement*, p. 121.

[28] Taken from Norskov Olsen's *John Foxe and the Elizabethan Church*, p. 158. Olsen depicts clearly Fox's dread of the church splitting which the self-styled 'Puritans' were causing.

given. I grant my son is not so pure and free of all blemish as are those thrice pure puritans; nevertheless in these blemishes of his I have not yet found any mote so great as the greater beams which one may perceive in their characters.[29]

John Fox was undoubtedly one of England's greatest Reformers and Puritans but it was those of Knox's and Cartwright's persuasion who persecuted such as him. Also Fox's views of religious liberty and freedom of conscience were a direct challenge to Knox's legalistic application of case law concerning 'heretics'. Knox's only true ally at Frankfurt was Whittingham but even he begged Knox not to cause schism and conformed to the Church of England in 1567. Later, Whittingham was to work hand in hand with the very people with whom Knox had refused to cooperate.[30]

The Knoxians break with the main-line Reformation
Modern Presbyterians who feel they have built their testimony on the example set by such as Knox and Cartwright and thus have a more anti-papist stand than the English Reformers will be surprised to find that the English awakened Christians, on the whole, suspected these early Presbyterians of having one foot still in popery. Hence their nick-name for the Knoxians was Precisians. They were called such by the English Reformers because of their legalistic love of nit-picking and overt fatuity with externals. They insisted that matters of ceremonies, order and discipline were necessary to salvation and must be considered as matters of faith and doctrine. This was seen by such as John Bale and John Whitgift as old Roman wine in new bottles. How could one claim to be Scriptural, Whitgift argued, when one believes that one's own peculiar view of govern-

---

[29] Ibid, p. 158.

[30] In this controversy, the Precisians evidently revolted against Humphrey's presidency, then dismissed Foxe's son because he supported his president and father's friend and used the whole affair to discredit Foxe and the church for which he stood. The irony here is that Foxe and Humphrey were amongst the most radical Non-Conformists in the Church of England, but obviously not radical enough for those who had made their radicalism their religion.

ment and ceremonies are necessary to salvation? This is a novelty 'strange and unheard of', was his comment.[31] So, too, the Precisians' virtually setting aside of Romans 13:1 made Whitgift state: 'Wherein differ these men, in this case, from the Papists? The Pope denieth the supremacy of princes: so do, in effect, these.'

Fox clearly agreed with Whitgift that it was the church splitting caused by the Precisians which was driving people back to Rome. Indeed, the Precisians' claim (so Cartwright) that clergymen should be exempt from civil law to regulate their behaviour was the teaching of Thomas á Becket.

Indeed, it was the political and revolutionary claims of the Precisians, who alone now claimed the right to be called Puritans, that brought evangelical Calvinism into lasting disrepute. A case in point is the life and witness of Samuel Ward, England's representative at Dort. Ward was a Puritan of the Puritans and headed Sidney-Sussex College, Cambridge which was considered *the* Puritan College. However, he refused to join the revolutionary, republican Precisian party, who dubbed themselves Puritans, because of their radical politics. He remained true to king and country, which was not difficult as James I fostered the Anglican Puritans at Cambridge. However, at the Revolution and the establishment of the so-called Protectorate, Wade was severely persecuted for being a papist i.e. one who refused to join the political revolution.

Taking anti-Anglican criticism with a pinch of salt

Readers may now realise that criticism of the 'Anglican' exiles at Frankfurt from Knoxian quarters must be taken with a very large pinch of salt indeed, and one could easily suspect that the critics are actually less reformed than those whom they criticise. Horton Davies, who accepts both sides in the Frankfurt debates as Puritan, nevertheless points out that the Knoxians departed from main-line Reformed thinking in numerous ways, adding 'They would probably have been surprised had they realised the extent of their diver-

---

[31] See Whitgift's *Works*, Vol. I, pp. 180-1. See also Dawley's *John Whitgift and the Reformation* pp. 139-141; 182.

gence from the customs of the Reformed churches.'[32] Indeed, it is demonstrably accurate to show that where the Anglican Reformers' 1552 order was quite in keeping with New Testament principles, that of the Knoxians was either Old Testament-bound or a mere creation of new traditions based on questionable views of church worship and discipline. As viewed above, Knox disagreed, at least during his years of exile, with the Reformed churches on vestments and the Lord's Supper and also with the public reading of Scripture portions. Knox also abolished Confirmation. This was because of his High Church view of baptism and his covenant thinking which toned down the need for teaching the re-birth and personal confession of faith, matters on which the Anglican Reformers insisted. This method of theologising away experimental religion was quite obnoxious to Calvin who did not think it un-Biblical to lay his hands on repentant sinners and bless them, calling those who objected to this alleged 'ceremony' Romanists and Schoolmen.[33] He argued in his *Tracts* that the rite of Confirmation[34] should be restored so that young people might be 'presented to God, after giving forth the confession of their faith.'[35] It is no wonder that the Baptists, after initially uniting with the Presbyterians at the Usurpation, quickly left them to practise their own teaching of baptism on confession of having experienced the New Birth. Sadly, most Presbyterian churches have not returned to the Reformed doctrine of Confirmation which leaves them open to the accusation that they always preach to their congregations as if they were all born-again Christians. The usual argument Presbyterians bring against Anglican Confirmation is that there is no guarantee that the confirmed are true believers. This argument loses all force when faced with Knox's *Book of Discipline XI, Concerning the Policy of the Church* where it dictates, 'We think that none are fit to be admitted to that mystery who cannot formally say the Lord's Prayer, recite the Articles of belief, and

---

[32] *The Worship of the English Puritans*, p. 38.

[33] See Calvin's 'Of Confirmation', Book IV, Chapter XIX, in Calvin's *Institutes*, (usually in Vol II of the two-volumed editions).

[34] Here, of course, the Romish rite of the crism with the *pax tecum* is not meant.

[35] See Horton Davies' *The Worship of the English Puritans*, p. 42.

declare the sum of the Law'. One wonders which chapter and verse of Holy Writ the Knoxians would quote to back up this piece of pure legal formalism. The Reformed Church which this author served for over a quarter of a century as a Religious Instructor, re-instituted Confirmation when it merged (for good or evil) with the Lutherans. Its Reformed nature was, however, preserved by its adopting the Heidelberger Catechism as its statement of faith.

The Knoxian argument that their 'Anglican' opponents used the sign of the cross, proved to be untrue, though even this was practised in other Reformed churches of that time, but more especially in Lutheran and mixed Lutheran and Reformed churches. None of the Coxians followed this practice. However, the Coxians did not challenge the celebration of Christmas, Easter and Whitsuntide to which the Knoxians objected. Here Cox's party were again closer to Calvin and Reformed traditions than Knox. The latter also departed from Calvin in abandoning the Absolution. Cranmer, in drawing up the Reformed Prayer Book, took over the Genevan form verbatim in the Order for the Visitation of the Sick, whereas Knox dropped it. So too, Cranmer added responses taken from the French Order which Knox also rejected. The Knoxians, unlike Calvin and the Church of England, not only objected to weekly communion, but objected to the celebration of communion with private sick people. Calvin placed the Lord's Supper at the centre of worship and, on visiting the sick, celebrated communion with them. Indeed, Calvin did not regard auricular confession in counselling as being anything but Biblical, though the Knoxians regarded it as superstitious. The Knoxians also departed from main-line Reformed practice by viewing marriage and burials as being outside of church fellowship and thus merely secular rites. Horton Davies quotes Scotsman Rutherford at the Westminster Assembly who argued that there was no more occasion for an act of worship at a man's leaving the world, than at his entering into it. One could hardly imagine more fitting opportunities than the birth of a child and the testimony of a beloved saint, now gone to glory to worship the Lord. One must also ask here why the Knoxians continued to marry couples in church when it was a mere secular act. If, as they argued, there was no Biblical authority for a 'church marriage', one must ask why they practised what was to them a meaningless spiritual ceremony. This paradoxical stance is nowhere better illustrated than the Synod of Fife's decision in 1611 to admit no one to the marriage bond who could not recite the Apostles' Creed. This harsh and surprising decree was rendered even more legal and tyrannical in the Culross Session of 1642 which threatened not only not to marry those unable to say the creed but heavily punish them for being so 'backward'.

Not the least of Knoxian divergences from the Reformed norm is his rejection of Scriptural sentences in the Sunday and baptismal services. Thoroughly Reformed liturgies such as that of the Second Prayer Book contained so many Bible readings that the entire Word of God was heard yearly. Calvin started his service with Scriptural sentences and the Waldegrave and Middleburgh versions of the Geneva model, used by Englishmen, start their service with the reading of a Bible chapter and a Scriptural exhortation. Finally, the Knoxians departed most radically from mainline Reformed doctrine and practice in their revolutionary politics and state-church relationships.

This is not the end of the story, however. Lloyd-Jones and other supporters of the Knoxian spirit, eagerly relate what 'reforms' Knox brought in but fail to relate what popish customs and laws Knox failed to abolish. Barefooted pilgrimages to the crucifix continued under Knox's rule and laws coupled with heavy penalties forbidding the eating of meat during Lent, set up by the Regent in February 1559 remained on the statute books until long after Knox's death. Furthermore, a rigid Romanism remained in parts of Scotland that England was not to see again, apart from brief Scottish influence in the North-West, until 1685-1688 when James II strove to re-introduce the papacy.

Sadly, when modern critics of the Church of England read English Reformers and Puritans such as Ridley, Cranmer, Grindal, Parker and Whitgift who claim that Knoxianism is contrary to God's Word and more allied to Rome than Geneva or Canterbury, as this writer has repeatedly experienced, they greet these utterances with scorn. They will not admit what the facts clearly teach, that not only the Frankfurt Nonconformists who opposed Knox at Frankfurt but the bulk of the English clergy after the Elizabethan Settlement, were in very many respects nearer to Poullain's French Reformed Church and that of Calvin's than the Knoxians and later Cartwrightians and they were further than the Precisians on many counts from Rome. Indeed, when the Westminster Assembly delegates, put under great pressure from their Scottish brethren, decided to outlaw the Church of England and present themselves as the Reformed Church, and bring in that chain to fetter Christian liberty, the Solemn League and Covenant, John Durel, the pastor of the French Church at Savoy, in his 1662 work *A View of the Government and Public Worship of God in the Reformed Churches beyond the Sea*, claimed that they were greatly deceiving themselves and that their ideas of what was Reformed were, 'mere *Chimeras* and *Ideas*; which, like the *Utopia* of *Sir Thomas More*, never existed but in their brain.' Indeed, the ideas of uniformity which they brought in were thoroughly Laudian in their comprehensiveness and no one, we would assume in his right mind, would pronounce the Reformed Church of England's last Archbishop 'Reformed'. Thus, in closing his chapter comparing worship of the Knoxian kind with the main-stream Reformation, Horton Davies concludes that the English and Scottish Puritans, arising from the Knoxians were closer to the Separatists than the main-stream Reformed churches. This is also the opinion of this writer after much careful and lengthy research. The Presbyterian revolution in England proved to be a shredder which divided the Reformed Church into a thousand denominational fragments which substituted organisational, legal, formal statutes, orders, declarations, constitutions and traditions for experimental fellowship and witness in Christ. Members of these denominational bodies now believed that adherence to their organisation and statutes marked them out as a true church. At the same time, they rejected fellowship with other Christians who were ruled by other outward forms as being apostate churches. Thus, instead of one Rome, England was now plagued with scores of them and the Reformation clock was put back over a century.

All the evidence points to the fact that Knox sought to set up a form of worship which was unique amongst the exiles. It is true that Knox did accept something approaching the Genevan order after 1556, but this was because of Calvin's authority and pressure against which even Knox dared not strive and also the moderate wishes of the Scottish lords. It was also not Knox's decision to set up the Order of Compromise (i.e. English Order of Geneva) but the democratic choice of the Genevan church made before Knox was called back to Geneva in 1556 to pastor the English church. The order was officially accepted on 10 February, 1556 through the advice and approval of Calvin himself. Knox, however, was still in Scotland in July, 1556 and probably left his home country that month for Geneva via Dieppe where his family, who had gone on before, were waiting for him. Thus the long-standing invitation to Geneva suddenly proved an urgent blessing and need for Knox[36] as, immediately after his departure, he was burnt in effigy and outlawed by his enemies for not answering a summons.

Furthermore, it was Thomas Lever, an Anglican Nonconformist, who ultimately took the initiative in drawing up this form in order to keep the peace and not Knox. The latter had rejected both the modified Prayer Book and Calvin's order, so Lever suggested a compromise. This was initially rejected by the assembled church but eventually Lever's idea of a compromise won the day. Incidentally, it was immediately after Lever had drawn up an 'Order as should be both godly without respect of the Book of Geneva or any other' i.e. neither Genevan nor Edwardian, that Knox and Whittingham sent Calvin the garbled, mock Prayer Book, Latin 'plat', saying that this was what the Lever faction were thrusting on the church, which had not the slightest basis in fact. Knox, even when he had a comparatively free hand in Scotland, did not produce anything as simple and effective as Calvin's orders of worship and discipline. Though the Order of Compromise continued to be used for a time in Scotland, the Book of Discipline Knox

---

[36] See Lang's Chapter VIII, Knox's Writings from Abroad: Beginning of the Scottish Revolution, 1556-1558 in his *John Knox and the Reformation*.

imposed was far more High Church and far more politically orientated than that form of worship as a peep into the strictures on the Lord's Supper alone will show. Indeed, the political theory which Knox developed from his case law understanding of the Old Testament ran totally counter to Luther's, the Reformed Church of England's and Calvin's more New Testament views. It most certainly ran quite contrary to the relatively peaceful methods of the bulk of English exiles now restored to their mother-country. This is illustrated by a letter of Matthew Parker's written to Sir Nicholas Bacon on 1 March, 1558 in which he says:

> At my last being at London I heard and saw books printed, which be spread abroad, whose authors be ministers of good estimation: the doctrine of the one is to prove, that a lady woman cannot be, by God's word, a governor in a Christian realm. And in another book going abroad, is matter set out to prove, that it is lawful for every private subject to kill his sovereign, *ferro, veneno, quocumque modo*, if he thinks him to be a tyrant in his conscience, yea, and worthy to have a reward for his attempt: *exhorrui cum ista legerem*. If such principles be spread into men's heads, as now they be framed and referred to the judgment of the subject, of the tenant, and of the servant, to discuss what is tyranny, and to discern whether his prince, his landlord, his master, is a tyrant, by his own fancy and collection supposed, what lord of the council shall ride quietly minded in the streets among desperate beasts? what master shall be sure in his bed-chamber?[37]

Writing to Sir William Cecil, now as Archbishop elect, Parker refers to Knox's 'turbulent reformation' by saying, 'God keep us from such visitation as Knox have attempted in Scotland.'[38]

---

[37] *Correspondence of Matthew Parker*, p. 61. This can only be a reference to Knox's and Goodman's books.
[38] Ibid, p. 105.

Summing up Knox's attempts to alter the course of the Reformation, Wilhelm Moeller in his gigantic *History of the Christian Church* says, 'From Geneva also, whither he returned (from Scotland) at first as preacher to the English congregation, he exercised a wider influence, proclaiming the theocratic doctrine of the Old Testament, that the authorities are bound, in accordance with the law of God, to do away with and severely punish idolatry.' Moeller also argues that Knox 'regards the gospel as the new law of God, the church as the external fulfilment and representation of the divine statutory will by a nation which devotes itself to the people of God and thereby enters upon the rights and obligations of Israel.' Moeller sees here the lasting influence of Schoolman John Major, Knox's tutor, revealing the Roman theology of the day. Moeller also argues that Knox's revolutionary politics of putting monarchs to death for holding contrary views to his standards of orthodoxy 'find their analogy in the doctrines developed by Romish theologians' which he also learnt from Major. Though Moeller rejects the idea that Major was the 'precursor' of the Scottish Reformation, he no doubt believes that Major made a substantial contribution.[39]

The fact that many modern writers refer to Knox's later order as *The Geneva Order*, causes confusion as readers are thus led to believe that Knox used Calvin's order. Actually, 'Anglicans' such as Fox and Humphrey adhered far closer to the theologico-political aspects of what has become known as Calvinism than did Knox. This is illustrated by the fact that whilst Knox, Goodman and Ponet were preaching regicide, Fox and Humphrey were teaching a broader form of democracy in which monarch, nobility and commoners could live together in harmony vouchsafed by gospel preaching and sound laws, the monarch being pledged to obey both as much as the commoner.

It is very difficult for modern Presbyterians who often confuse Knox's nationalism and politics with evangelical doctrine to realise that, in these matters, Knox was far from Reformed and reserved for clerics in power the same temporal rights that Rome claimed.

---

[39] Vol. III, *Reformation and Counter Reformation*, p. 339.

However, in banning bishops, he gave the magistrates church authority formerly held by the bishops of the church. Scotland was run on principles that destroyed the line between Christ and Caesar and strove to merge the two.

It is worthy of note that Dr Martyn Lloyd-Jones, in a chapter where he denounces the Englishman's love of compromise and eagerness to keep the peace, looks upon the extremes of Knox's politics as being 'a sign of true Puritanism'. Yet Knox's merging of Church and State was a compromise that few Englishmen had even thought of! Nor had the Scottish lords initially thought of such a combination and imagined that Knox was bringing in English ideas. They thus constantly teased him for becoming English in his ways and for the fact that he could not (or would not) any longer speak his mind in plain Scots. Yet, after denouncing the compromises of the English, Lloyd-Jones claims that Knox's brand of compromising Puritanism was ahead of Calvin's. With true undisguised revolutionary zeal, the famous Welsh physician says, 'I maintain that one cannot truly understand the revolution that took place here in England in the next century except in the Light of this teaching. Here was the first opening of the door that led to that later development.'[40]

We must be reminded that the Great Rebellion of 1640-1660 to which Lloyd-Jones so enthusiastically refers brought in Presbyterian tyranny over the consciences of Anglicans, Independents and Baptists and such a wholesale purge of the Reformed Church of England that it was nigh annihilated. The backlash against the Presbyterians enforced by Cromwell left the blood of such Presbyterian saints as Christopher Love on the tyrant's hands and his henchman Colonel Pride made sure that the Presbyterians joined the Anglicans as citizens of no political rights. During this rebellion, the ship of the church was smashed into the smithereens of militant denominations from which the Church in England has never recovered and the Presbyterians were lamed for centuries to come. Reformation was stopped and pseudo-state-church interference in man's liberty of faith and conscience reached a height hitherto unparalleled since

---

[40] *John Knox, the Founder of Puritanism* in *The Puritans*, p. 275.

Mary's bloody days.[41] Indeed, it was not until a century later in the Evangelical Awakening that true religion returned to England for a time but now the church which was most instrumental in effecting that revival has become but an insignificant small denomination among many others equally spiritless.

It is thus high time that this bubble of misunderstanding and artificial juxtaposition of sides were allowed to burst. Then it will be found that the theory concerning 'the troubles at Frankfurt' which has caused so much controversy over the years up to the present time is the result of later denominational prejudice, an anachronistic back-projection of later troubles. The drawing up of sides and parties most certainly does not do justice to the true events of 1554-55 in Frankfurt. Troubles there were, but they were for entirely different reasons than the acrimonious ones so often given. A deeper study of the circumstances will also show that most of those troubles were settled when the vast majority of the brethren on both imagined sides fellowshipped and served together in the same church at the Elizabethan Settlement. Indeed, the troubles which are imagined at Frankfurt occurred in reality almost a century later under totally different conditions and a totally different setting up of sides. Furthermore, this view, which brands some of Britain's greatest reformers as criminals, though nowadays sadly common, presents a totally false picture of both sides in the controversy, besides being guilty of chronological error and anachronisms. Knox's golden hour was to come when he stood at the head of his nation and rid Scotland of French and Roman threats but Knox's

---

[41] See John Walker's *An Attempt Towards Recovering an Account of the Numbers and Sufferings of the Clergy of the Church of England . .. in the Late Times of the Grand Rebellion*, London, 1714, for a detailed survey of Anglicans persecuted by the Cromwell regime. See *The Nonconformist's Memorial* by Edmund Calamy, Button & Son, 1802 for persecuted Presbyterians and Independents. See J. Jackson Goadby's *Bye-Paths of Baptist History* for a brief account of persecutions against Baptists during the Grand Rebellion and after; also W.T. Whitley's *History of British Baptists*, Revised Edition, Kingsgate Press, 1932. This author has not found a good survey of Baptists persecuted during this period which is of the depth and breadth of Walker's and Calamy's works. Such a study is most necessary in order to reach a balanced view of these times.

agitation at Frankfurt cannot be claimed as anything but a great set-back to the work of Reformation. The only true ally he had at Frankfurt was Whittingham but even this fiery spirit pleaded with Knox to be more tolerant and balanced and very soon left the Knoxian position. This left Whittingham for the rest of his life, under the wrath of the later Knoxians, who called him a lost leader and a backslider. [42] However the Anglican Puritans also looked upon him with suspicion and he remained something of a tolerated outsider.

---

[42] See Collinson's *The Elizabethan Puritan Movement*, pp. 121, 133, 154.

The order where

Morninge and Euening prayer shalbe vsed and sayde.

The morning, and eueninge prayer, shalbe vsed in suche place of the Churche, chapell, or Chauncell, & the minister shal so turne him, as the people maye best heare. And if there be any controuersie therin, the matter shalbe referred to the ordinarie, & he or his deputie shal appoynte the place, and the chancels shal remayn, as they haue done in times past.

And here is to be noted, that the minister at the tyme of the communion, & at al other times in his ministracion, shall vse nether Albe, Uestiment, nor Cope: but beyng Archebishop or Bishop, he shal haue and weare a rochet: & beyng a priest or Deacon, he shal haue and weare a surples only.

An order for morninge

prayer dayly throughout the yeare.

At the beginning both of morning prayer, and likewise of euening prayer, the minister shal reade with a loud voyce, some one of these sentences of the scriptures that folowe. And then he shal say that, which is written after the said sentences.

What time soeuer a sinner doeth repente hym of hys synne, from the bottome of hys heart: I wyl put all his wyckednes oute of my remembraunce sayth the Lorde. [Ezechiel xviii.]

I do know mine owne wyckednes, and my synne is alway agaynst me. [Psalm. lj]

Turne thy face awaye from oure sinnes (O Lorde) and blot out all oure offences. [Psalm. lj]

A sorowfull spyryte, is a Sacrifice to God: despyse not (O Lord) humble and contrite heartes. [Psalm. lj]

Rente your heartes, and not your garmentes, and turne to the lorde your God, because he is gentle and mercyful, he is pacient and of muche mercy, and suche a one that is sory for your afflicccions. [Ioel ij]

To thee O lord God belongeth mercy & forgeuenes, [Daniel ix]

C.i.   for

First page of the Order For Morning Prayer
in the Second Prayer Book of Edward VI., 1552.

Chapter Nine:
The Knoxians Appeal to Caesar

Whittingham asks the Senate to intervene

Now Whittingham, without seeking the backing of the church, which he obviously would not have gained, complained to John Glauburg, a Senator, about the Strasburg party whom he referred to as if they were a tiny faction of trouble makers in an otherwise united church of which he was the official spokesman. Again, he affirmed that the Coxians had come straight from England and were now throwing their weight about and had forbidden the church's minister to preach that day (Wednesday) and had appointed another in his place which 'would not be well taken'.[1] Again, we are left to puzzle over who this minister or preacher could be. The only pastor the church now had was Lever. As Lever got on well with all parties bar a very few individuals, it is impossible to imagine that the 'Coxians' had dismissed him, nor does the author of the tale give any background information to the subject apart from warning Glauburg that if he did not act, there would be further trouble in the church. It does seem as though Whittingham is speaking of Knox who had been asked by the church to stop interfering. It also seems odd that Cox was in a position to appoint and dismiss ministers if the church majority was against him. Acting, on Whittingham's testimony, Glauburg had the Wednesday meeting

---

[1] *Troubles at Frankfort*, p. 56.

stopped. Not wishing to toe the line with the church, Whittingham, obviously backed by Knox, had appealed to Caesar and Caesar acted.[2] However, Glauburg knew the true situation in the church and Whittingham's action backfired.

Glauburg now ruled that the church should draw up yet another form of worship. He then called for the French Minister, Valerand Poullain 'commanding him that two learned men should be appointed; and that he and they should consult and agree upon some good Order, And to make report unto him (Glauburg) accordingly.'[3] Poullain chose Lever and Cox as the two representatives who then asked Knox and Whittingham to join them. As this was quite against Glauburg's ruling, it was either done for the sake of peace following Knox's protests or simply because of the fair-mindedness of Lever and Cox. Poullain, for a reason not given by the author of *Troubles at Frankfort*, was now not allowed to stand on an equal footing with the committee of four and was given the task of keeping a record of the agreements. This was also not in keeping with Glauburg's ruling. This meant that the Coxians could not outvote the Knoxians and vice versa, making further progress a hard business. A measure of agreement appeared to have been reached when Cox put his finger on one of the central nerves of the Reformation, the public reading of God's Word. It had been the Reformers' practice to provide early morning lessons each day, one reading from the Old and one from the New Testaments. This had proved most successful in drawing in the unsaved and instructing them in the Word. Indeed, this was the method the Evangelicals of the Great Awakening such as Whitefield and Hervey turned to and which was again blessed by the Spirit. Not regarding the very many concessions the Anglican party had made, and the almost lack of concessions on the 'Knoxian' side, Knox and Whittingham now accused Cox and Lever of being uncooperative and called a halt to the discussions. Again the author of *Troubles at Frankfort* blamed Cox but the fact was obvious that though Knox would not budge an inch and Whittingham would only move a centimetre, Cox and Lever were always pre-

---

[2] *Troubles at Frankfort*, pp. 56 and 66.
[3] Ibid, p. 56.

pared to go the extra mile where fundamentals were not concerned, as they later gave abundant proof to Calvin. The public reading of God's Word was, however, one of those fundamentals. Knox believed this practice to be popish, arguing superficially that morning readings were practised at Matins, Matins had been used by the papists (though with a completely different form and aim in view), therefore the public reading of Scripture in morning worship was a papist ceremony. This dislike of old names, whatever their new meaning, was also probably why Knox detested the Litany, though it contained the soundest of Reformation teaching.[4] Knox also complained that Latin prescripts such as '*Domine labia, Deus in adjutorium, et Deus laudamus*' were used at Matins, which were words not found in Scripture. This is a double puzzle as though Latin was no longer used in morning worship after Edward's Second Prayer Book, Knox himself used Latin forms in worship throughout his remaining life. His argument that papist lips had spoken the above-mentioned Latin words, so they were to be condemned, would also condemn a good many phrases in Knox's own *Confessio Scoticana*. This was used in Scotland until superseded by the *Westminster Confession* in 1647, the latter only being accepted because it was 'in nothing contrary' to the *Confessio Scoticana*.[5] So too, both the *First Book of Discipline* and the *Book of Common Order* demand the use of the *Apostles' Creed* in public worship and at baptismal services as also do the Calvinistic catechisms such as Calvin's, Craig's and the Heidelberg. Perhaps an awareness of such incompatibilities in his argument moved Knox and the subsequent Church of Scotland to lessen their use of the ancient creeds.

During the Reformation, it had been ruled that Morning and Evening Prayers should be performed daily as a public service to enhance the spread of the gospel and so the Word of God could be

---

[4] Sadly, the strongest denunciations of popery such as those read by Jewel at Frankfurt, were removed in Elizabeth's reign.
[5] See Lindsay's *History of the Reformation*, Vol. II, p. 302. The Confession (in modern English), with The Book of Discipline, is appended to Knox's *History of the Reformation of Religion in Scotland*, Revised and Edited by Cuthbert Lennox, London, 1905.

heard in its entirety over the ecclesiastical year. As a number of the Frankfurt Christians, including Cox, had been instrumental in putting forward this Reformed and evangelical strategy, they did not wish to go back to pre-Reformation days.

It is noteworthy that Knox informs his readers that as soon as the topic of what he called Matins came up, 'then began the Tragedy, and our consultation ended. Who was most blame-worthy, GOD shall judge! and if I spake fervently, to GOD was I fervent!' In other words, Knox never sought a compromise or mutual agreement and he never queried his own protests but thought they were all from God. So, too, when Knox was asked to leave Frankfurt because of his attack on Charles V, the very man who had given Knox his freedom of worship, the Scotsman did not humbly admit that he had been somewhat too fervent but wrote himself, 'O, Lord GOD! open their hearts that they may see their wickedness; and forgive them, for thy manifold mercies! and I forgive them, O, Lord from the bottom of my heart. But that thy message, sent by my mouth, should not be slandered; I am compelled to declare the cause of my departing: and to utter their follies, to their amendment I trust; and the example of others who, in the same banishment, can have so cruel hearts to persecute their brethren.'[6]

Matins dated back to times of persecution when Christians met before dawn to avoid observation and worship undisturbed. Obviously the critical author of this account in *Troubles at Frankfort* and Knox himself are being knowingly sarcastic as the Edwardian Prayer Books had rejected the old Breviary services of Matins, Lauds and Primes and substituted them by one of the most important Reformed parts of the new Prayer Book, i.e. Morning Prayer, which included copious Scriptural exhortations, Scripture readings, profession of faith, prayers and thanksgiving. Each service goes through the entire presentation of the gospel to sinners, dealing with man's sins, the need for repentance, the kind of faith and worship acceptable to God and the love, hope, pardon and mercy to be found in Christ. Certainly, to deny these elements is to deny all that the Reformation stood for. To object to such a presentation of the

---

[6] *Knox's Account of his banishment*, from *Troubles at Frankfort*, pp. 66-67.

gospel, renders the objector a matter of suspicion regarding his Reformed credentials. The First Edwardian Prayer Book Morning
Prayer had started with the Lord's Prayer but the Reformers did
not wish to give the impression that they were addressing the congregation as if they were all born again Christians, so they substituted this in 1552 with a depiction of sin and the need for repentance.[7] Though the author of the *Troubles at Frankfort* account sneers
at the use of Morning Prayers, no part of the Prayer Book had more
influence on it from the French Forms and Continental Reformers
such as the Pole John Laski, the Italian Peter Martyr and the German Martin Bucer. Indeed, the Absolution in which it is stated that
'He pardoneth and absolveth all them that truly repent and unfeignedly believe His Holy Gospel,' is very similar to the one used by
Laski when he pastored the Belgic (Walloon) Church in London
during Edward VI's reign. In doing away with these Reformed elements in morning worship, Knox separated not only from Lutheran[8]
but also Continental Reformed and Reformed Church of England
practice.

Knox's and Whittingham's second appeal to the magistrates to rule their church

Now, some time between 20 March when Whittingham called on
the Senate and 22 March when Glauburg visited the English church
to tell them of his new ruling in the light of the church's inability to
reach a compromise, Knox and Whittingham decided to draw up
an appeal to the secular arm again, claiming rather illogically that
they spoke on behalf of the 'congregation', yet also maintaining
that the large body of newcomers were acting in defiance of the
imperial city and abusing the Senate's authority.[9] Unlike the letters

---

[7] See Daniel's *The Prayer Book*, Morning Prayer, p. 78 ff.
[8] One might fairly say that the First Prayer Book contained a substantial amount of
Lutheran influence, whereas the Second Prayer Book was more according to the
traditional 'English' doctrines of grace as taught by Bradwardine, Wycliffe and
the earlier English Reformers often termed 'Calvinism'.
[9] The letter, called *The Supplication to the Senate*, is undated but the author of
Troubles at Frankfort places it between 20 March, when Whittingham visited
Glauburg and 22 March when Glauburg gave the congregation the Senate's ruling.

before and after Knox's short but stormy stay in Frankfurt, no signatures were appended. Obviously very few signatories could have been found. Lever, the acting pastor, was certainly not privy to the deceit. After a very long preamble, the appeal states:

> Now, of late days, certain of our countrymen came to us, who have endeavoured, by all means, to obtrude that huge volume of Ceremonies upon us; to break the Covenant; and to overthrow the liberty of the Church granted by your benevolence. And, no doubt, this they enterprize and mind to do under the title and name of your defence; whereby they may abuse the authority of your name to satisfy their lust (desire).
>
> We are here compelled to omit things which would make for our Cause, no less rightly than profitably: but we remit to our brethren for concord's sake.
>
> You have here, most honourable Senators! a Brief Sum of Case and Contention; whereby you may easily understand what to judge of the whole matter.
>
> What manner of Book this is, for the which they so cruelly contend, ye may consider by the Epistle that CALVIN lately wrote unto us: in the which he hath signified his mind, as well plainly of the Book, as also of the uprightness of our Cause.
>
> We could have pointed out unto you the foolish and fond things of the Book: but, passing over an infinite number of things, this one we bring for many; the which shall be necessary well to be marked.
>
> Within these three years, arose a great conflict between Bishops of the Realm and the Bishop of GLOUCESTER, Master HOOPER, a man worthy of perpetual memory, whom we hear to be burned of late, on February 9 1555. This man being made Bishop by King EDWARD, there was obtruded by other Bishops the same Order, according to the Book, a Rocket and a Bishop's robe. This man, being well learned and a long time nourished and brought up in

Germany, as soon as he refused these proud things that I marvel at, was cast into prison: and, at length, by their importunity overcome and relenting, he was compelled, to his shame, to give place to their impudency; with the common grief and sorrow of all godly minds. (took advice from the Continental Reformers)

'But wherefore speak you of these things' will you say, 'that appertaineth nothing to us?' Yea, verily, we think it toucheth you very much. For if these men, armed by your authority, shall do what they list, this evil shall be in time established by you; and never to be redressed: neither shall there for ever be any end of this Controversy in England. But if it would please your honourable Authority to decree this moderation (arbitration) between us. That this whole matter may be referred to the judgement of the five above named (Calvin, Musculus, Martyr, Bullinger and Viret): not we alone that are here present; but our whole posterity, yea, our whole English nation and all good men, to the perpetual memory of your names, shall be bound unto you this great benefit.

We might have used more words in this Narration; for we feared not that we should lack reasons: but rather that time should fail you, letted (hindered) with more serious Business. Therefore we, by these things, leave the rest to the consideration of your Wisdoms.[10]

Here Knox's and Whittingham's grossly exaggerated position, which amounted to sheer lies is clearly seen. The so-called Coxians were presented not only as enemies of the church but enemies of and traitors to the state powers. They were furthermore accused of bringing in 'a huge volume of ceremonies'[11] which were now being imposed on the church. None were named by the two troublemakers and none had been introduced. Indeed, it can be clearly demonstrated that the Anglicans kept to former agreements far more

---

[10] *Troubles at Frankfort*, pp. 57-58.
[11] Ibid, p. 57.

closely than the Knoxians' small minority. Equally groundless was the accusation that the new majority had broken the church's covenant as the Frankfurt exiles had had several covenants and the last one was especially short-termed to meet the new situation of the newcomers from Strasburg. Indeed, it was only when the newcomers showed their willingness to adhere to the *Liturgy of Compromise* that Knox began to complain. Furthermore, the Frankfurt church had specifically promised the Strasburg brethren that if they were willing to settle down for a longer period, they were prepared to discuss revisions with them. That the Strasburger group had come a fortnight or so before they were expected, and the short term agreement was to run out, is neither here nor there,[12] besides, they clearly kept to both the letter and the spirit of the *Liturgy of Compromise*. Thus, all the evidence points to the fact that it was the Knoxians who wished to end the provisional order and not the Anglicans. So, too, the accusation that the new majority were abusing the rulings of the Senate was a grave matter in those days where the death penalty was used for even small acts of disobedience to the authorities.

Again, as in their complaint to Calvin, the Knoxians repeatedly argued that there were worse things to report but their modesty forbade them. Such idle talk was a most un-Christian stratagem to employ. If the Knoxians could not amass real proof against those whom they so bitterly opposed, they ought, for Christian decorum's sake and for the sake of church unity, to have desisted from such gossip-mongering which endangered the standing of their church and even the lives of their brethren. Nor was the Knoxians' reference to the letter from Calvin a fair move as its strictures in no way applied to the group of men whom Knox wished to denigrate.

Knox loved to use such words as 'cruel' and 'tragic' to describe the testimony of those whom he could not win over to his point of view. Yet how are we to regard the fact that Knox and Whittingham again resorted to the old tale of Hooper's resistance to the vestments as probably not one of those opposed by the two Precisians

---

[12] The Strasburg party, however, had originally planned to move to Frankfurt in February, 1555.

would have disagreed to a great extent with Hooper? Furthermore, Hooper and his followers in the Church of England would have nothing to do with any trimmings, 'feathers' Hooper called them, that could possibly be associated with popish misuse. Thus, in his early Reformation days, he would not have cloths on communion tables as this represented to him the old *corporas* cloth of the popish priests which covered the sacrament on the altar.[13] Other Reformers overcame this ceremonial difficulty by placing a carpet on the table as at Parker's consecration. Ninian Winzet, in his *Four Score and Three Questions*, teased Knox on this issue as the Scotsman placed a white cloth on the communion table before officiating, which to many signified the *corporas* or canopy cloth of the papists.[14] This was one of the very many ceremonial uses, Winzet pointed out to Knox, where the Scottish Reformer professed to rest on Scripture alone but whose actions were not defensible by Scripture alone. Lever, whom Knox saw as one of his major opponents, Sampson and Whitehead went way beyond Hooper's protests, and Knox's practice in the matter of vestments. Unlike Hooper, they would not even wear the surplice and four-cornered hat, nor the Genevan Robes and 'Calvinistic' clerical cap. Here, once more, Knox, in his misplaced zeal, stood truth on its head. Indeed, the brethren at Frankfurt were continually discussing Fox's work on the martyrs and Reformers. In his short biography of Hooper, placed in Book VI of his *Acts and Monuments*, Fox takes up the problems Hooper faced and relates how the popish vestments against which Hooper protested were a thing of the past.[15] Concerning Calvin, Musculus, Martyr, Bullinger and Viret, both sides were in close correspondence with these men, who were obviously greatly embarrassed by this over-emphasis on 'things indifferent'. The out-

---

[13] Hooper did much radical pioneer work as a Reformer though he became more moderate towards the end of his life. His detailed thoughts on the Supper are recorded in his *Answer to the Bishop of Winchester's Book*. Hooper's *Sermons upon Jonas* also deal very much with the subject of the Supper.

[14] See Watt's *John Knox in Controversy*, Lecture Two: Ninian Winzet.

[15] Sadly, the full biography is omitted from modern versions of Fox's work as also the various CD versions available. Readers will find a copy in Legh's *Fathers of the English Church*, Vol. V, pp. 3-43. The reference to former clerical wear is on page 9. See also Olsen's *John Foxe*, p. 166.

come, however, was that the men appealed to, whatever their own inhibitions, recommended the English exiles not to allow such externals to stop them continuing the work of the Reformation together.

Glauburg takes charge of the situation

On 22 March, 1555, Glauburg presented the magistrates findings before the congregation. They should adopt the same doctrines and ceremonies as the French church. Lever, Cox and Whittingham agreed at once. According to the author of *Troubles at Frankfort*, on listening to Glauburg, Cox replied 'I have read the French Order; and do think it to be good and godly in all points.' He then advised all to comply with the magistrates' ruling, the result being 'the whole Congregation gave consent.' We notice that whatever the imaginary difficulties were that Knox and Whittingham whispered in the Senate's ear, the church was behind Cox and, according to the author of *Troubles at Frankfort*, followed his leadership.

In his reports of his dealings with the Senate, Knox, followed somewhat slavishly by Whittingham, whom he used as his spokesman, always acted as if he represented the majority of the church against 'cruel' opposition from an extreme High Church minority i.e. the true low church majority in the congregation. Furthermore, he continually stressed before the magistrates that the original order of July, 1554, which he had broken continually himself, still applied. As the magistrates were kept up to date by both sides, they knew this to be a myth as Knox was not party to the original proceedings of the church and Whittingham, with the entire church body, had long departed from them. Furthermore, the Senate had repeatedly emphasised that the church could worship as she felt fit but they must remain at peace with the French church and with the Senate.

As in previous attempts to win the Senate to their side against the church majority, Knox's new ruse back-fired. The Senate eventually appointed a lawyer (Glauburg's nephew) as arbitrator and he came down fully on the side of the new majority, yet this was not until the Senate had asked Knox to leave the city.

Thomas McCrie accuses Cox of two-facedness

Much of the doubt thrown on Cox's actions at Frankfurt by contemporary critics of the English Reformation can be traced to an unwillingness of later Presbyterian writers to accept Cox's peacemaking actions at their face value. The author of *Troubles in Frankfort* complains that the majority were either 'most cruel, barbarous, and bloody' or 'bloody, cruel and outrageous',[16] with not a shred of evidence given to back up such a severe judgement which thus appears ludicrous in its total exaggeration. However, no writer appears to have influenced his readers so negatively as Thomas McCrie (1772-1835), who has done perhaps more work than any to depict Knox as the great British Reformer who did more than any other to rescue Britain from Rome. In his enthusiasm to rescue Knox from adverse criticism which had admittedly gone to other extremes, McCrie sought to paint a black and white picture of Knox versus Cox which was detrimental to both men. Knox is depicted as having a super-human greatness, whereas Cox, in all his actions, is presented as double-faced, dishonest and mean. Thus, throughout his *The Life of John Knox*, McCrie intersperses his analysis with highly personal, subjective, negative remarks concerning Knox's opponents which he never seeks to justify by providing documentary evidence. When Knox quarrels with the Cox party, it is because Knox is piously 'indignant', but when the Cox party protests at the the Knox party's action, it is because Cox is 'insolent' and knows no better. When, however, for the sake of peace, Cox accepted the rule of the magistrates to use the French order of worship, McCrie tells us, 'To this peremptory injunction the Coxian faction pretended to a cheerful submission, while they clandestinely concerted measures for obtaining its revocation, and enforcing their favourite liturgy upon a reclaiming congregation.'

The Coxians immediately agreed to Glauburg's ruling

The interesting point here is that, though the author of *Troubles at Frankfort* tells us that all the 'Anglicans' agreed to accept

---

[16] Op. cit. pp. 59-60.

Glauburg's dictate, he says nothing concerning Knox's reaction, though he tells us that the French Order was carried out in the congregation at the very next meeting 'to the comfort and rejoicing of the most part.' The question is, was Knox, who had refused to adopt the French Order on being invited to pastor the church one of the exceptions to the 'most part'? We turn to Knox's own account of the troubles at Frankfurt in vain for an answer as Knox, though he emphasises all the events where he felt that he had won a point, totally ignores the matter of Glauburg's intervention and Cox's agreement with the majority to adopt the French Order. McCrie mentions the fact that Knox refused to use the French Order on his arrival at Frankfurt, but, like the author of *Troubles at Frankfort* and Knox himself, he does not comment at all as to how Knox accepted Glauburg's ruling. If Knox had accepted this with open arms, it would have backed up McCrie's argument and also shown that Knox could change his mind without rancour. If Knox had continued to reject the French Order, then it would have been better for McCrie to keep quiet on the matter. McCrie did keep quiet.

After quoting McCrie as his authority, G. Barnett Smith in his *John Knox and the Scottish Reformation* tells us: 'Dr. Cox, a high-churchman who had been preceptor to Edward VI, had been the chief disturbing spirit, in consequence of the determined effort of himself and his partisans to introduce fully the English service.'[17] Lang is a little more guarded when he says, 'Cox had accepted the Order used by the French Protestant congregation, probably because it committed him and his party to nothing in England.'[18] He thus concludes that 'Knox acted the most open and manly part.' This is sheer negative speculation and does not take into account that most of the English exiles were preparing to settle down in Germany and looked upon the churches in exile as their permanent spiritual homes. The evidence shows that the Anglicans were industriously learning German so that they could settle down in that country and, as Mary was still relatively young, there was no indi-

---

[17] John Barnett Smith, London, undated, p. 35.
[18] *John Knox and the Reformation*, p. 58.

cation that their exile would not be a long-term matter. Thus their actions were because of their present situation and not because of compromise built on what they envisaged might happen in England in an indistinct future.

Many exiles were reluctant to return to England

Many, such as Sandys and Ponet, sought and obtained Frankfurt citizenship. Others bought houses, and even factories and settled down as teachers, printers, leather-workers, weavers and dyers. Indeed, the English became so successful as traders and craftsmen that the Frankfurt historians Hermann Meinert and Friedrich Bothe write that they were far more industrious (weit überlegen)[19] than their Frankfurt neighbours and the guilds protested at the fierce competition which had sprung up. Coverdale took over a German parish in Bergzabern. Many of the English exiles were so full of praise to God for the opportunities open to them on the Continent that they lived every day for what it brought them in tasks for the Lord and their minds were riveted on those tasks. Sandys told his Strasburg friends in a rousing, evangelical sermon:

> Could we wish for more at the hands of God than, being banished and constrained to forsake all the profits and comforts which we enjoyed at home in our native country, here amongst aliens and strangers to find a city so safe to dwell in, maintenance so competent for our needful and reasonable sustentation, such grace in the eyes of the godly magistrates under whom we live, such favour and respect to our hard estate, such free liberty to come together, to call upon God in our common prayers, to hear his word sincerely and truly preached in our own natural tongue, to the great and unsearchable comfort of our souls; finally, all things so strangely and almost miraculously ministered and brought unto our hands, as doubtless we could never have

---

[19] See Bothe's *Geschichte Frankfurts*, p. 343 and Meinert's *Auszüge aus den Frankfurter Ratsprotokolle*, pp. XVII ff.

found here, if the Lord himself had not gone before, as it were, to make ready and to provide for us? O what tokens of mercy and special favour hath our kind and gracious Father shewed us in this our exile and distress for his gospel, in these our sorrowful and afflicted times! We have lost the saving truth at home, and found it abroad: our countrymen are become our enemies, and strangers are made our friends: being persecuted by our native rulers, foreign magistrates have shewed us favour. In banishment we have a place to dwell in: in anguish we abound with comfort; and, as the apostle speaketh, 'having nothing, we are as possessing all things. Therefore, dear brethren, having received these so great and rare graces at the merciful hands of our good God, I may justly, as one of your poor helpers in these holy labours, use the words of St Paul, which in the beginning I recited; exhorting and beseeching you, 'that ye receive not this grace of God in vain.' Be not an unthankful people: neglect not the great benefit now offered unto you: approach with all reverence, and present yourselves as humble petitioners before the Lord, and careful servants before our God. For I say unto you, As Jacob said in his journey towards Mesopotamia: *Vere Dominus est loco isto*: 'truly God is here', even present amongst us. We do clearly and plainly perceive that, our fathers and mothers, our friends and familiars, having forsaken us, he hath received us as his dearest.[20]

Fox relates in his *Acts and Monuments* how Sandys was sitting at dinner with Peter Martyr when the news of Mary the Bloody's death arrived. Martyr could not conceal his joy at the news but Sandys was sad. He feared that being called back to England, he would be called back to a life of misery. He was most happy to be

---

[20] Sermon on 2 Cor. VI, *We therefore, as helpers, beseech you that ye receive not the grace of God in vain*, from *Sermons by Archbishop Sandys*, Parker Society, 1842, p. 296.

in exile! Grindal, who had been a close friend of Sandys' since their childhood, accompanied him back to England, cheering him up on the way. Grindal's love for Germany and German theology caused him often to be teased for his 'Germanical Nature'.

Sandys' saintliness

Stalwart Edwyn Sandys, clearly placed amongst the Puritans by Daniel Neal, suffered much for Christ's sake and was persecuted by Romanists and Precisians alike. Whilst imprisoned in the Tower of London under Mary, he led his jailer, John Bowler, to Christ. Bowler had been called 'a very perverse Papist'. Sandys was thus transferred to Marshalsea and the jailer there also bowed under the gospel. Indeed, he could have walked out of prison unguarded on several occasions but for his witness' sake, he stayed until freed by the Knight Marshal. Bishop Gardiner was furious and tried to stop Sandys leaving the country and put a price on his head. However, those who were in a position to betray Sandys helped him escape to Germany.

Sandys, like Cox, believed that if one first preached Heaven, earth would take care of itself. Therefore he did not become a legalist regarding externals merely for the sake of the Precisians who placed these before faith. He felt that their extremely militant campaign against the Church of England could only force the establishment to answer back in the same tone to protect their own interests which the Precisians denied them. Thus Sandys wrote in his will:

> I am now, and ever have been persuaded, that some of their rites and ceremonies are not expedient for the Church now; but that in the Church reformed, and in all this time of the Gospel, they may better be disused by little and little, than more and more urged.[21]

---

[21] Taken from Heaton's *The Puritan Bible*, p. 212.

The Frankfurt exiles re-reform England

Once back in England, any comparison of the list of names under
the exiles' letters from Frankfurt and those of the greatest defenders
of Protestantism during the Elizabethan period, reveals that the Frankfurt exiles were the most active in overturning the Marian papacy.
Collinson points out how Cox, Scory, Whitehead, Horn, Aylmer,
Sandys and Jewel 'opened the way' for the defeat of the papists on
returning from exile.[22] Indeed, a good number of the Coxians, including Cox himself, had trouble in England for sticking to their
Frankfurt ideals. Cox is well known for his personal criticism of
Elizabeth and his refusal to become her chaplain unless she removed the crucifix and candles from her private chapel.[23] Cox's
frustration with Elizabeth's love for externals for diplomacy's sake
forced him to hand in his resignation, which his death prevented.
Cox, with fellow Frankfurt exiles Grindal and Whitehead, immediately pressed for reforms in the first year of Elizabeth's reign.[24]
Incidentally, Strype's list of those responsible for the Elizabethan
Prayer Book which in externals was less 'Reformed' than Edward's,
is decorated by a number of 'Knoxian' names alongside moderate
Coxians.[25] This shows that Knox's influence over them, if it ever
had been strong, soon dwindled when faced with the practical reality of reforming England. Furthermore, the Frankfurt Anglicans
had been in close touch with the imprisoned Reformers, especially
Ridley, and discussed these matters with them. Ridley told his
former chaplain Grindal that Knox could not defend his views from
the Word of God and that his criticisms of the Anglican's position
were misrepresentations. A further letter of Ridley's to Grindal is
extant in which the imprisoned Reformer says:

---

[22] *Archbishop Grindal*, p. 89.

[23] See Strype's *History of the Reformation*, Appendix Numb. XXII, pp. 50-52 for
Cox's letter refusing the offer of a chaplaincy on the above-mentioned grounds.

[24] See Strype's *History of the Reformation*, Appendix Numb. IV, pp. 4-6 for their
proposals, also signed by Parker, Bill, May and Pilkington. Collinson calls
Pilkington 'the most puritanical of all the Elizabethan bishops.' *Archbishop
Grindal*, p. 50.

[25] *History of the Reformation*, pp. 289 ff.. Cole and Poullain were at Geneva,
Beesely at Frankfurt. Collinson describes Cole as a 'prominent Frankfurter'.

Alas that our brother Knox could not bear with our book of common prayer! matters against which although, I grant, a man, as he is, of wit and learning may find to make apparent (i.e. plausible) reasons; but I suppose he cannot be able soundly to disprove by God's word.

The reason he maketh against the Litany and the fault per 'sanguinem et sudorem', he findeth in the same. I do marvel how he can or dare avouch them before the Englishmen that be with you.

As for private baptism, it is not prescribed in the book; but where solemn baptism, for lack of time and danger of death, cannot be had, what would he in that case should be done? Peradventure he will say, it is better then to let them die without baptism. Sir, for this his 'better' what word hath he of the scripture? and if he hath none, why will he not rather follow that that the sentences of the old ancient writers do more allow, from whom to dissent without a warrant of God's word I cannot think it any godly wisdom? And as for the purification of women, I ween the Word *purification* is changed, and it is called thanksgiving, (but the book is taken from us, and now I do not perfectly remember the thing; but this I am sure of, the matter there said all tendeth to give God thanks, and to none other end). Surely Mr Knox, in my mind, is a man of much good learning and of an earnest zeal: the Lord grant him to use them only to his glory!

Where ye say, ye were by your magistrates required gently to omit such things in your book as might offend their people, not as things unlawful, but to their people offensive, and so ye have done, as to the having of surplice and kneeling; truly in that, I cannot judge, but, that both ye and the magistrates have done right well; for I suppose in things indifferent, and not commanded or forbidden by God's word, and wherein the customs of divers countries be diverse the man of God, that hath knowledge, will (not?) stick to forbear the custom of his own country, being there where the people therewith will be offended; and, surely, if I might have done so much with our magistrates, I would have required Mr Alasco[26] to have done no less when he was with us.[27]

This passage is omitted by Coverdale and Fox in their collections and Patrick Collinson in his most studious work on Grindal suggests that it was because of Ridley's criticism of Knox which the two English Reformers felt might harm the Reformation if published.[28] Sadly, however, the Reformation *was* harmed and as modern Dissenting opinion has been trained to see the Anglicans as the sole cause of such harm, it is now correct of Collinson and others to balance off the picture. Collinson also shows that the procedure of Grindal and his party was 'almost normative among the English exiles' and he quotes the brethren at Wesel who affirmed that it would only be because of 'singularity or disease of mind' to utterly reject the Edwardian Prayer Book. Finally on this issue, Lang's claim that Knox's part concerning the acceptation or rejection of the French forms was more manly than the majority's is impossible to evaluate as Lang gives no information whatsoever as to how Knox took the news.

Knox proves too controversial a figure for the Frankfurt magistrates

Returning to the more immediate situation at Frankfurt, after the majority of the church, led by Cox, Lever and Whittingham had both accepted the Senate's ruling and put it in practice, a further matter disturbed the congregation. This was the news of Knox's political writings against Emperor Charles V (Mary's cousin and

---

[26] The Polish Reformer à Lasco who was placed by Edward VI as Superintendent of the foreign Reformed churches in England.

[27] *Works of Ridley*, pp. 533-535. See also Letter XXX from Coverdale's collection in the same volume, p. 386 ff.. Strype gives one of Grindal's letters to Ridley and part of Ridley's reply in his *The Life and Acts of Archbishop Grindal*, pp. 11 ff.

[28] *Archbishop Grindal (1519-1583): The Struggle for a Reformed Church*, Jonathan Cape, 1979, pp. 75-76.

Father-in-Law), which now placed the Frankfurt church under strong suspicion as the city was under direct imperial rule.

According to Whitehead,[29] when the Frankfurt exiles had become familiar with Knox's politics, they discussed the matter with his 'intimate friends', and advised against him remaining in the church. It appears that these friends, in turn, gave Knox the advice to leave but he refused. Then, two members of the church, Edward Isaac and Henry Parry, following Whittingham's example,[30] turned to the Senate for arbitration and revealed to the Senate the contents of Knox's book *A faithful Admonition made by John Knox unto the Professors of God's Truth in England*. The Senate then approached Whittingham and asked him concerning Knox's character, and requested *sub poena pacis*, that he should produce a 'true and perfect' rendering of Knox's book in Latin by one o'clock that same day. The magistrates then ruled that Knox should not preach until a decision concerning his character and work had been reached. After due deliberation, they called for Williams and Whittingham and asked them to tell Knox that he must leave the city at once, otherwise, should the news that Knox was still in Frankfurt reach the Emperor's Council at Augsburg, he would be called before the same. Commenting on this event, Edward Arber states:

> As Knox himself tells us, pp. 67, 68, his banishment from Frankfort was not the work of the new Anglican Church as a whole: but entirely the act of two members of it: Edward Isaac, of Kent; and Henry Parry, who had been Chancellor of the Cathedral of Salisbury.[31]

This statement is highly misleading as when the pages cited are turned to, we find Knox arguing that Isaac and Parry were backed by Richard Cox, John Bale, William Turner, John Jewel 'and others'. This would mean that not only men who had been chiefly responsible for his calling were now against him, but leading Non-

---

[29] *Original Letters*, Letter to Calvin, September 20, 1555.
[30] So Edward Arber, *Troubles at Frankfort*, p. xvi.
[31] *Troubles at Frankfort*, p. xvi.

conformist, anti-vestment William Turner, a Puritan of the Puritans was, too. Turner,[32] who became the Dean of Wells, was so against the wearing of clerical uniforms that it is said he trained his dog to snatch off the four-cornered hat of visiting clergy, so that they could be presented to his church in decent array. This also would refute Knox's later defence that those who called him to the ministry were always for him. This fact alone also puts later criticism to flight which maintained that Knox represented the 'Puritans' and 'Non-conformists' and his opponents were High Church Conformist Anglicans. Incidentally, Cox and the Turners were the best of friends and when Turner died, Cox married his widow and thus angered Elizabeth so much that she had Cox called before the Star Chamber and threatened with severe punishment.

The author of *Troubles at Frankfort* says of the supposedly 'new Anglican Church' action against Knox, that they 'assayed, by a most cruel, barbarous, and bloody, practice, to dispatch him out of the way.' Though the Senate gave every sign that they were glad to be rid of such a dubious political character in their midst, putting on the best face possible in the circumstances, the author of *Troubles at Frankfort* tells us that 'it seemed that the Magistrates abhorred this bloody, cruel, and outrageous, attempt' and had advised Knox to flee, not so much from the Emperor as from the 'Anglicans'![33] The writer has obviously quite forgotten that it was Knox and Whittingham who first started accusing their brethren before the magistrates of treachery.

These rather contradictory reports of Knox's dismissal have given rise to a large variety of interpretations amongst Knox's biographers as to why he was asked to leave Frankfurt, according to whatever axe to grind, bias or even hagiographical purpose the authors had. Barnett Smith tells us that 'Knox was compelled to leave his charge after a few months', adding 'the magistrates completely absolved him', leaving the question open as to why Knox was compelled to leave if the magistrates absolved him. Howie

---

[32] See Turner's fine reforming work *The Old Learning and the New* (1548), *Fathers of the English Church*, Vol. IV, pp. 599-672.
[33] Ibid, pp. 60-61.

informs his readers that the Senate secretly advised Knox to depart, arguing that they could not save him if Mary and Charles consorted to harm him. Lang says that Knox was 'dismissed'. Laing, as Hanko after him, says that Knox quite simply resigned. McCrie here, is closer to the 16th century reports when he says that the magistrates 'desired Whittingham to advise his friend privately to retire of his own account.' Lloyd-Jones affirms that Knox was 'driven out from Frankfurt'. All these accounts, except Hanko's, varied as they are, assume that somehow the Senate only wanted Knox to go for his own health's sake; that they had not the slightest wish to criticise him and that they themselves were antagonistic to the so-called Coxians. That Knox was an extremely uncomfortable figure for the Senate appears to have escaped their attention. Nor do they seem to respect the fact that it was a question of the vast majority of the congregation leaving Knox or Knox leaving them. For all concerned, the latter choice was more practical and peaceful. Perhaps however, when all is said and done, Whittingham's account is nearest to the truth, he related in a letter to Calvin, that Knox 'was ordered to quit the place' by the Senate, whatever the reason.[34]

Dr George Sprott of North Berwick and Dr Peter Lorimer of the English Presbyterian College, London conclude that the only real reason for Knox's expulsion was that he was a 'violent man'. Under the heading The cause of Knox's expulsion, Sprott writes:

> Many of his (Knox's) opponents were almost as hostile to ceremonies as he was, and suffered much for it after their return to England. Strype says, 'They were anxious that so violent a man should be removed from any control over the Church, and hence their complaint to the magistrates,' and Dr. Lorimer was much of the same opinion. 'It was not worth while,' he writes, 'for Cox and so large a party of supporters to come to Frankfurt to make so small an amount of changes, for upon their own showing to Calvin they had no wish to press for the restoration of any of the ceremonies which were offensive to some . . . It was mainly

---

[34] *Original Letters*, Vol. 2, p. 765.

to rid the church of the pastorate of Knox and the eldership
of Whittingham . . . The feeling of the churchmen like Cox
and his party was that the Church of England was ill-repre-
sented in the Church of Frankfurt – the principle church of
the exiles – by men like Knox and Whittingham, men of
the minority, not of the majority.'[35]

As these comments were made by men who cannot be said to
have an over-Anglican bias and by men who have done pioneer
research into the matter, their words speak volumes. However, it is
a too speculative hypothesis to believe that Cox and his party settled down in Frankfurt with their wives and families with the sole
intention of ousting Knox. Moreover, Knox had not changed his
views radically at that time and was not even in Frankfurt when
initial contact between Frankfurt and Strasburg was made. Nor is it
technically correct to say that Knox had a pastorate in Frankfurt as
he neither claimed the title for himself, nor did he take on pastoral
duties on his arrival in Frankfurt.

Reading the extant Lord Mayor's books and the Corporation
minutes of the City of Frankfurt, sheds much light on this matter.
The Senate urged the English to integrate themselves into the Frankfurt citizenship, become burgers, pay tax and have a say in the
affairs of the city. They made it quite clear to the French, English
and Dutch that if they did not do so, they could expect no support
from the city authorities and were people who would not pay their
way and stood outside the peace of the town (Stadtfrieden). This
latter term was the basis of Frankfurt law and order.
Stadtfriedensbruch (breaking the peace of the city) was one of the
severest crimes in the city and punishable with 'life and goods'. It
must be added that every burger had to pay Burgergeld, a kind of
tax, in order to finance the hospitality given to refugees. Those
refugees who merely claimed hospitality and citizens rights but
refused to become citizens and help pay their way were considered
parasites and very often asked to leave, unless they had sponsors.

---

[35] Sprott, pp. 222-223.

Almost every eligible Englishman in the years 1554 and 1555 became a Frankfurt citizen and paid their taxes. Knox refused point blank and thus set himself outside of the Frankfurt political and social society. Such stubbornness was usually taken as an insult to the city and to the Emperor. However, the Glauburg family were noted humanists and had reserved the right to apply the old laws leniently in certain cases. Thus the fact that Knox was asked to leave rather than fined, thrown into prison and hanged, for which the city had every legal right, shows how magnanimous the Senate was. Knox's own writings show that he feared this would happen. Yet this mild and merciful expulsion is so often called persecution by Knox's supporters. Knox himself never showed such leniency to the 'idiots', as he called them, who claimed the same kind of treatment at his door.

After giving a farewell sermon on the evening of 25 March at which 'fifty persons, or thereabout', i.e. half of the congregation, were present, Knox left Frankfurt for Geneva on the following day. That day, the Senate told Whittingham that they wanted no more trouble and that the magistrates had granted the church full freedom to use the Second English Prayer Book, should they wish. Whittingham was to report back to the church, to inform them of the Senate's decision. Suspecting that Whittingham might cause further trouble, and not even inform the church concerning their new freedom, on 26 March the Senate sent a lawyer, Adolphus Glauburg, John Glauburg's nephew, to the congregation and told the rest of the church of the Senate's ruling. Whittingham said that he would obey the Senate's ruling for him to keep quiet but he reserved the right to join another church and take others with him. The congregation, of course, stated that they did not wish to see the church again divided. At this, Whittingham asked the Senate's permission to dispute the matter with them. The Senate refused. Now Gilby visited John Glauburg and undiplomatically sought to play the uncle against his nephew. Glauburg was not pleased. He told Gilby that the vast majority of the church were in unity and he did not want odd-men-out disturbing the peace. Obviously suspecting that Whittingham was behind this move, Glauburg called for him and 'straight charge was given him, that he should meddle no more in that matter.'[36] Overlooking the fact that the lawyer was acting on behalf of the Senate, McCrie perpetuates Gilby's unacceptable theory by saying that though Glauburg was on the side of the Knoxians, Cox and his nephew intrigued together.[37] Even the rather biased author of *Troubles at Frankfort* shows that this theory cannot possibly be true.

This evidence shows how totally inaccurate is the traditional pro-Knoxian account of the Scotsman's speedy exit from the Frankfurt church. Percy strives to put himself in Knox's shoes and think his thoughts as he travelled on his round-about way through Switzerland and France back to Scotland:

> It is not difficult to imagine Knox's feelings as he journeyed up the Rhine, and his own words show them clearly enough. Outside Switzerland Protestantism had now only one foothold in Europe: the Lutheran States and cities of Germany. These had been won back in the very hour that England had been lost ... And now Frankfurt had just shown how insecure was this foothold in Germany, how powerful Nero still was in the lands of the Empire.
>
> That, however, was the least of it. Who had appealed to this persecuting Caesar? Who by his own brethren of the English Church, driven into exile by Caesar's son? This English Church itself could find no place for him. It was partly his own fault. On the whole, he had played the part of a peacemaker, but in his original discussions with Grindal and Lever he had wounded susceptibilities by a curious pernicketiness about minor points.[38]

The fact was that it was Knox, followed by Whittingham and a few others, who had appealed to their 'Nero' on a number of occasions, thus angering their church and, at last, causing two individu-

---

[36] *Troubles at Frankfort.* p. 71.
[37] *Life of John Knox*, p. 53.
[38] *John Knox*, p. 197.

als to turn the method that Knox had instigated against him. Knox could not possibly complain of being persecuted at the hands of Charles V, a most different person from the Nero with whom Percy compares him, as he had misused both the hospitality of the church and the city. If Knox was persecuted, it was thus by his own hand. Nor could Knox say that the church had no place for him as they had agreed to keep Knox on as preacher in spite of his disregard of their own views concerning worship. On the whole, Knox was still highly respected by the Frankfurt church though his 'pernicketiness' had proved too much for their patience. Nevertheless, the records show that the Frankfurt church kept offering the Knoxian faction the hand of peace.

Philip Melancthon

Chapter Ten:
The Aftermath of Knox's Retreat

The 'great schism' myth exploded

It is now that later interpreters begin to exaggerate the outcome of the supposed schism that ensued on Knox's dismissal. Neal tells us repeatedly, without giving the slightest evidence, that the original Frankfurt church moved to Geneva en bloc.[1] On the other hand, Fuller states that only eighteen men, whom he names,[2] left the church. None of these people left the church in the wake of Knox who only stayed at Geneva to break his journey to France and Scotland. When a party did depart from Frankfurt over six months after Knox left, it was to various cities. Indeed, so few were the exiles who moved to Geneva in comparison to those who moved elsewhere that some authorities do not even mention the relatively small number of Genevan bound Englishmen at all. James Gairdner, for instance, writes that the controversy at Frankfurt 'led to secessions from the congregation to Basle and Aarau.'[3] As Bale eventually led the Basle group and Lever the Aarau brethren, it would appear that it was basically the Prayer Book men who left rather than an imagined 'Knoxian' party. This was part of the usual coming and going that had prevailed at Frankfurt since the church's first days. Some

---

[1] *History of Puritanism*, Vol. I, pp. 80-81.
[2] *Church History of Britain*, Book VIII, p. 732 (Separate Section p. 32).
[3] *A History of the English Church in the Sixteenth Century from Henry VIII to Mary*, p. 392.

of these went to Zürich to sit under Bullinger, some returned to Strasburg to sit under Peter Martyr and after a few months followed him to Switzerland to escape Lutheran opposition in Germany. Indeed, the Lutherans were now putting pressure on the Frankfurt Senate against the English and French churches. Others English exiles left Frankfurt for Emden and still others, such as 'Foxe, with a few more' on Fuller's list, settled in Basle. Sampson and Bale, who do not appear on Fuller's list, also moved to Basle.

The times were most turbulent and the Lutherans began to clamp down on the Anglicans concerning their view of the Lord's Supper which approached that of the Swiss Reformers rather than Luther. A good number of the Frankfurt church, for instance, at one time, moved to Wesel when they heard that Miles Coverdale with Richard and Catherine Bertie were planning to settle down there. Again because of Lutheran opposition, some of the Wesel church left for Poland, some for Bergzabern and some for Aarau. Neal is incorrect in his account of Whittingham's flight to Geneva as he stayed at Frankfurt for some time, not wishing to create a schism. When he did move, it was initially to Basle. He later moved to Geneva when the exiled churches began to draw together again, faced with common enemies such as Rome, the Lutherans and the Augsburg decrees and a common hope, i.e. the possibility of a quick end to Mary's reign.

Even Thomas Lever, whom Knox looked upon as his major opponent, eventually moved to Aarau from whence he strove diligently and with great success to mediate between the so-called Coxians and Knoxians. Grindal, Fox, Sampson and Goodman found it now impossible to print their works in Germany but found acceptance in Switzerland. Even there, however, the long arms of the German princes exerted pressure on Swiss printers to either delay the printing of English works or reject them. Much was thus printed clandestinely. Knox too, according to Calvin's testimony, published his later radical works in Geneva clandestinely, that is, without checking with Calvin or Beza who were by no means in agreement with their contents. Calvin took this affront well, but Beza was quite annoyed.

Thus it can in no wise be said that all those who left Frankfurt did so in order to support Knox. Indeed, it is very obvious that it was only a very small minority who eventually left for Geneva. Deducting those who travelled elsewhere from Fuller's list, we find that no more than fifteen, at the very most, of the Frankfurt congregation of approximately 100 members can have moved to Geneva late in 1555. It is also hardly probable that they departed for Geneva in the hope of one day coming under Knox's ministry as he was over the seas and far away and there was no immediate signs that he would return. A more sure reason was that Calvin had written to the Frankfurt church and promised them a safe haven and more independence as a church in Geneva. The fact is that there was no English church at Geneva until 1 November, 1555. Furthermore, we know from the writings of such as Humphrey and Fox and the Parker Society records that, during the periods of exile, Melancthon, Bullinger, Martyr, Pellican, Lavater, Gesner, Gualter, the Prince of Wittenburg, the Danish Royal Family[4] and many other church and political leaders encouraged the English exiles to seek asylum in their territories. Cities such as Zürich organised special funding for their British guests.

The history of the English refugees at Wesel alone suffices to put to flight the idea that it was the bulk of the Nonconformists and the more Puritan who left Frankfurt for Geneva. The congregation of English refugees in the city had no constituted church of their own. The Wesel church held to a mild form of Lutheranism and allowed the English to worship in the Augustinian chapel in their own language, using their own forms. However, much pressure was put on them to accept the Augsburg Confession. They were not allowed to celebrate communion or baptise themselves, these ceremonies being performed by German Lutherans in German. This meant that the English had to accept a form of consubstantiation, performed by a priest wearing vestments called *Chorröcke*. When Knox and Whittingham wrote to Calvin concerning imagined ceremonies going on in the English church, the English refugees in

---

[4] This was only initially as Lutheran opposition to the Reformed faith grew in Denmark.

Wesel were corresponding with Calvin, Melancthon and Laski concerning real ceremonies which were being forced upon them by the city's churches. Unlike the picture of Calvin given in *Troubles at Frankfort*, Calvin told the English at Wesel as early as 13 March, 1554,[5] when the first refugees were arriving from England, not to be bothered with such minor matters and accept the Lutheran demands as they were one with the Wesel church in essentials. Melancthon wrote in 1556 to the city authorities, pleading with them to be more tolerant towards the Englishmen's wishes. However, Jan Laski urged the refugees not to compromise at any cost. As the refugees, on the whole, followed Laski, the Wesel authorities asked them to leave, which they did in two or three batches from 1555-57. Now the members spread across the Rhineland with the bulk going, not to Geneva, but to Frankfurt. In other words, rather than a mass exodus of Puritan men leaving Frankfurt, they were but a trickle in comparison to the large number of the staunch Puritans, including the Berties and Laski who moved to Frankfurt from Wesel.[6]

Yet, when one reads through the contemporary Frankfurt City records, it can only be considered a miracle that any English remained in Frankfurt at all. The French became very possessive of the White Ladies Chapel which was still in the ownership of the nunnery and only loaned to the exiles. When the English were refused their own building, the French Walloons became more difficult and, instead of taking turns with the English on Sundays, they extended their services, locked the doors and kept the English waiting on the streets until they were allowed in. This is probably why Knox started holding meetings in his private house and not merely to set up a rival church to that of Lever. Furthermore, the White Ladies Chapel was very dark and cold and both congregations longed for better accommodation. The English were given Allerheiligenkirche (All Saints) on 29 October, 1555. That was good news but very bad news was to follow.

---

[5] See Rudolf Schwarz, *Johannes Calvins Lebenswerk in seinen Briefen*.
[6] See *Die Reformation in der Stadt Wesel*, pp. 37ff; 144-145. The Berties later followed Laski to Poland.

The English were becoming more and more successful in business and complaints from the Frankfurt craftsmen were growing. It appears that the French and Dutch were faring just as well and Poullain had become a profitable weaver alongside his pastoral duties. There were now 2,000 foreign tradesmen and craftsmen in Frankfurt. Inflation hit the town and the foreigners had to shoulder the blame. In 1555, the senate decided to double the taxes which had remained constant for many years. The wealthy in Frankfurt now protested that it was the English who had brought the city to its bankrupt state and so they argued that they must be extra taxed and not the rich landowners and patricians. Anti-foreign feelings became so strong that ideas of banning the foreigners competed with ideas of fleecing them. Now the Lutheran ministers joined the protesters and argued for the expulsion of the Anabaptists as they called the Anglicans and their fellow Reformed churches. At first the humanist Senate supported the Reformed churches but gradually were argued down by the Lutherans and the patricians. Laws were passed curbing the influx of refugees which hit the English church in Wesel hard as they were being expelled by the Lutherans and had hoped to find asylum in Frankfurt. Many of the French and Dutch now even left Frankfurt. Though many English also left, many others took their place, spotting loop-holes in the administration. All these matters had nothing whatsoever to do with Knox's expulsion and merely shows how those who do not know the true historical facts are sadly often very quick to establish imaginary ones.

It is often forgotten in the heat of the Coxian-Knoxian debate that the first large body of exiles to arrive in Geneva were the Italians who looked to Peter Martyr as their leader. They were given the church of Marie la Nove in which to worship. When the English exiles, pastored by Goodman and Gilby applied for a building, they were given Marie la Nove to share with the Italians under similar conditions that the Frankfurt English had with the French. It is ironic to think that Knox who blasted his trumpet against three very earthly Marys because of their regentships and queenships, should, in the following year, become the pastor of a church whose building was dedicated to a Mary whom popish tradition proclaimed as the Queen of Heaven!

New controversies in Frankfurt

It is clear that those Frankfurt exiles who moved to Switzerland did not form a homogeneous whole. Whereas problems to do with finance and distribution of charity plagued the Frankfurt church in succeeding months, there was no further trouble similar to that caused by Knox. The same controversy, however, now raged amongst the English exiles in Switzerland but there was no clear dividing line between them, if there ever had been at Frankfurt. They could be united, for instance, on the non-use of vestments but be divided on the question of Godparents. Bale and Cole were quite shocked to find that they had jumped out of the frying pan into the fire. Added to this came the growing dissatisfaction with Knox's extreme revolutionary politics and demands for violence. This was too much for peaceful Fox who eventually broke with the Knox party on this issue and reproached their leader.[7] McCrie tells us that Knox 'did not excuse his 'rude vehemencie' and inconsidered affirmations, which may appear rather to proceed from choler than of zeal and reason; but signified, that he was still persuaded of the principle propositions which he had maintained.'[8]

The constant movement of exiles between Switzerland, Frankfurt and other areas

The congregation at Frankfurt continued to number between sixty-five and just over a hundred as there was a constant coming and going due to ever-changing ecclesiastical, social, financial, occupational and political factors. As many modern critics tend to limit their studies to what happened to the few who left for Geneva, the important fact that most of the so-called Anglicans also left Frankfurt within the following months and years is overlooked. Yet num-

---

[7] See V. Norskov Olson's *John Foxe and the Elizabethan Church*, especially p, 186 and 188 with footnotes.
[8] *Life of John Knox*, 1892 reprint, p. 73. The original letter is in Laing, Vol. 5., p. 1 ff.

bers who left were always replaced by newcomers. Indeed, when in December, 1558, William Kethe (Keith), a former Frankfurt man and author of the metrical version of the Old Hundred, was sent by the Genevan brethren to Aarau and Frankfurt with the express purpose of being reconciled to the 'Coxians' remaining there, the Frankfurt congregation replied, on 3 January, 1559, to say that there were only *four* of the original members still present but all these and those who had left had long forgotten the differences and regarded the Genevan members as their brethren.[9] Kethe was also sent to Basle, Strasburg and Worms with the hope of reconciliation with the brethren who had moved there. Kethe, according to Laing, was probably a Scotsman and assisted in translating the Geneva Bible. Again, according to Laing, and Collinson, his sphere of service became England.[10]

This leads to the second factor which again is almost always overlooked by critics of the Frankfurt situation. Though there was a large exodus of Frankfurt members in 1555-6 who eventually settled down in Basle, Geneva, Aarau and Zürich, there was an equally large flux of exiles from Switzerland to Germany and other countries. So that in spite of Frankfurt losing members, in the autumn of 1555, Grindal says that the church was still the largest of all the Continental exile congregations.[11] Arber, a pro-Knoxian, speaking of the Frankfurt church between 1556-7, i.e. a year after many of the members had departed for reasons given above, estimates the number of male members at sixty-two. A year later, when adding up the number of separate signatories under the New Discipline debate, we find over a hundred male members in the church. If we add women and children, as many exiles had their families with them, the number would at least be trebled.

Writing to Ridley on 6 May, 1555, Grindal told him that peace was now reigning at Frankfurt due to 'the Prudency of Maister Coxe and other which met here for that purpose.'[12] Knox who had been so

---

[9] *Troubles at Frankfort*, pp. 223-226.

[10] *Works of John Knox*, Vol. VI, pp. 572-5, including Kethe's metrical translation of Psalm 94. Collinson's *The Elizabethan Protestant Movement*, p. 150-151.

[11] *The Remains of Archbishop Grindal*, p. 239.

[12] Ibid, p. 239.

particular in his criticism of almost everyone and everything, though always backing down when looked upon for *his* solution, had gone. However skilled in Reformation practices Knox was to become, his short stay at Frankfurt was not his finest hour and it is no wonder that he merely skimmed over the events in his *History of the Reformation of Religion*. Grindal, obviously breathing a sigh of relief confessed to Ridley in the above mentioned letter that now Frankfurt could get on with the business of evangelising and edifying, dealing with experimental religion instead of externals and 'So that now we trust God hath provided for such as will flye forth of Babylon, a resting Place, where they may truly serve hym and hear the Voice of their true Pastor.'

The Troubles at Frankfurt were greater amongst the Belgians than the English

Though English-speaking commentators tend to claim that those nearest to Poullain were also nearest to Calvin in the controversies at Frankfurt, and that Poullain's pastorate was one of peace and that of the English one of great controversy, it must be emphasised that from the point of view of the Precisians amongst the French, Belgian and Dutch, Poullain was seen as anti-Calvinistic and constant reports reached Calvin's ear that Poullain was not toeing the Genevan line. Much of this criticism was totally exaggerated but criticisms of Poullain passed on to Calvin often resembled closely those criticisms of the English passed on to Calvin by Knox and Whittingham. Though in the case of the English, it was the critics who lost out, in Poullain's case, it was he who lost out to the critics. It is an ironic act of history that one of the reasons why Poullain eventually fell foul of the Senate, whom Calvin supported, was the same which caused Calvin's own dismissal from Geneva in 1538. Poullain barred his critics from communion.

Calvin had not intervened directly in the case of false allegations against Lever and Cox in which the Knox party drew the shortest straw. So this time, Calvin decided to resolve matters himself. He journeyed to Frankfurt in the late summer of 1556 via Strasburg. On this occasion, however, the refugee church he had pastored in 1538-41 refused to allow him to use their pulpit. As soon as he reached Frankfurt, Calvin consulted with the Glauburgs. He also asked Horn, now pastor of the 'Anglicans', and Jan Laski, now Superintendent of the Dutch church, to help him sort the matter out. The pastors and the Senate now set up a 'Schiedsgericht' (court of arbitration) under Calvin's chairmanship. Nicolas Walet as elder of the French Church and four other city dignitaries were appointed as arbitrators. The events show perfect concord between Calvin and the 'Anglicans', a fact not even mentioned in passing in *Troubles at Frankfort* and other pro-Knox 'histories' of this period. There was also perfect concord between Laski and Poullain, the latter pleading with Calvin not to come to a decision independent of Laski.

Horn and Laski strove to defend Poullain from accusations which could not be proved, but it turned out that Poullain could also bring forward no evidence to convince the court that he had any strong reason for his disciplinary measures. Although the whole matter was a storm in a tea-cup, Calvin appeared to listen more earnestly to those rumours which claimed that Poullain was anti-Genevan. The Swiss Reformer thus weighed down the scales against Poullain who was asked to hand in his resignation.

Though Calvin appeared to be making a balanced decision in court, a letter he wrote to Musculus was a scathing condemnation of Poullain, stating that no punishment would have been too severe for him,[13] without the least evidence being cited. It was quite clear, however, in the whole disciplinary case that Calvin was more worried about protecting himself from criticism than seeing that Poullain received a fair deal.[14] As he told Musculus, in order that peace should reign, Poullain had to go. However, Dalton emphasises that the majority of the church were for Poullain.[15] The other pastors in Frankfurt were shocked at what had happened, complaining that the whole matter of Calvin's intervention had been kept secret from them. They refused to debate the matter with Calvin after the trial, though the Senate urged them to do so. Now that Bucer was dead, Calvin was the undisputed leader of the Continental Reformed and

---

[13] "Obwohl Valerand jeder Art von Strafe wert gewesen wäre".
[14] The letter is reproduced in Baur, p. 256.
[15] Dalton, pp. 474-475.

the (mostly) Lutheran preachers confessed that they did not feel themselves competent enough to debate with him. This could, however,
merely mean that they could not dispute in Latin as there had been
several cases of embarrassment on their side in their disputes with
Poullain. Furthermore, in the controversies which led up to the disciplinary court, it is obvious that Poullain leaned to his old tutor
Bucer with whom he had stayed in the 1540s and certain critics, as
in the case of the English, wished to play Geneva against Strasburg
as if they represented two different theologies. That this was an ill-
meant scheme is obvious as Calvin built his own Genevan order on
that of Bucer's at Strasburg. Poullain had been a co-worker with
Bucer for several years as also had Calvin so both could be called
Bucer's disciples. Bauer points out that Calvin held principally to
the church order that he found at Strasburg in compiling his Geneva
works and was strongly influenced by Bucer in other respects.[16]

Poullain had always enjoyed the best of fellowship with Bucer
and Calvin, until his time at Frankfurt. However, Poullain's pastorate was now at an end. One of Poullain's Dutch critics described it
as, 'of, for the main part, an almost constant narrative of disunity
and strife.'[17] Obviously this critic had not known Poullain in France
and England where his reputation had been second to none for learning and piety and for his enormous organisation talents. Poullain
was heart-broken and planned to return to England. Now out of
grace with the Senate, they refused him a passport. Poullain was
thus forced to stay in Frankfurt where he sought to work with
Lutherans in coming to a joint understanding of the Lord's Supper.
Poullain had difficulties publishing his views and is thought to have
died, according to a letter written by Cnipius to Calvin on 2 April,
1558, at forty years of age.[18] After these affairs, the French church
entered into violent controversy as to whom should be accepted as
a church member or not.

---

[16] Bauer, p. 144.

[17] 'Grootendeels een bijna onafgebroken verhaal van oneenigheid en twist.' See
Bauer, p. 228.

[18] Cnipius wrote '*Valerandus piae memoriae*.' See Meinert for further references
to this correspondence and the Ratsprotokolle entries concerning Calvin's visit
to Frankfurt.

This over-view of Poullain's pastorate is necessary here to show how the critics of the English church under such as Lever and White-head, grossly exaggerate the controversies there and totally play down the lack of unity amongst the Belgians in fellowship and doctrine. Poullain is invariably described by them as peaceful, constant Calvinistic orthodoxy itself whereas Cox and Co. are described as chaotic controverts. Yet the so-called Coxians and Poullain enjoyed the best of fellowship. Actually if we are to use such a title as 'Troublemakers at Frankfurt', this would fit the Walloon church the most. However, this church was multi-national, having a congregation of French, Belgian, Dutch, Spanish and English so that it had a much more difficult task in keeping unity than the British had.

The election of new pastors, preachers, elders and deacons at Frankfurt

On 26 March, all the ordained men of the English church comprising former deacons, deans, vicars, bishops, doctors and professors who had joined before and during Knox's short period of stay at Frankfurt, came together to discuss the future of the church. Goodman was apparently the only one who wished to work out yet another church order and discipline but the others said they would adopt the freedom the Senate had given them but would avoid giving the church too much of an English face. This was one of the reasons why they dropped 'Anglican' titles and elected a pastor, two ministers or preachers, four elders and four deacons. Here, again, reports of how these offices were manned vary. One side emphasises that the appointments were discussed *in plenum* and others that they were elected behind locked doors by all the ordained men. As most of the men in the congregation, however, were ordained, there need be no diversity in the two accounts. Whittingham wrote to a friend in England, complaining that they had 'neglect(ed) all Orders in the Election of their Ministers and other Officers.'[19] This probably meant that at the election, the candidates received no bonus because of their former positions in the

---

[19] *Troubles at Frankfort*, p. 74

church hierarchy. The custom at Frankfurt, imposed on the church by the Senate, was that before new church officers were voted in by the church, all former pastors, preachers, elders and deacons should lay down their offices and the vote should thus be solely amongst what they called 'private men'. It is also worthy of note that Cox did not seek office and the pastor whom they elected, Whitehead, was one of the most Nonconforming men in the church. Though Knox had warned the Senate of all the popish titles and 'huge volume of ceremonies' the 'Coxians', if given power, would reintroduce, Whitehead was just the man to prove that Knox's 'prophecy' was wrong. In comparison to Whitehead, Knox could safely be called a High Churchman. Under their new church government, the Frankfurt believers pledged to do away with the surplice, not to use crosses and not to perform dubious ceremonies such as private baptisms, in short, they did away with all that Knox said they would reintroduce in abundance. One very important step of moderation and reconciliation that the new church government adopted appears to be overlooked by all pro-Knoxian commentators and would take all the wind out of their sails. Kneeling at the reception of the bread and wine during the Lord's Supper was abolished. This shows, how hollow, unjust, and downright scandalous were Knox's warnings to the Senate, Calvin and the exiled churches. Knox had not budged one inch in his anti-Coxian position but the Coxians had bent over backwards to live in peace with their brethren. All that indeed separated the Coxians and the Knoxians now was the public reading of God's Word as a single act of worship and instruction and the spoken responses of the congregation. Both these were features on the part of the Coxians which were fully in keeping with mainline Reformed worship.

A most subjective historian

It is here that Thomas McCrie proves himself to be altogether too biased to deserve the name of an objective historian. With deep sarcasm, he says of the church that was led by one of England's major Nonconformists who was sequestered from his living because of his refusal to toe the ceremonial line: 'They could now lift up their faces in the presence of the Church of Rome herself and cherish the hope that she would not altogether disown them!' This is pseudo-Christian polemics at its basest! Furthermore McCrie tells his readers sarcastically that Whitehead had been elected 'bishop, or superintendent over the pastors,' whereas the contemporary records clearly state that the Frankfurt church specifically rejected both the notions of a bishop and superintendent and elected one pastor only to shepherd the one church. This was in stark contrast to the conduct of Knox who, though he had given up his pastor status, still reserved the right to Lord it over the other pastors and preachers such as Lever and Whitehead. The fact that the brethren now elected only one pastor was probably to save the church from the embarrassment caused by formerly inviting three shepherds to lead the flock. Once bitten, twice shy! However, Hudibras greets us again as we are reminded that, on arriving in Scotland, Knox had superintendents placed in the churches.

It is interesting to note that McCrie, Fuller and others who base their interpretation of the events on the texts in *Troubles at Frankfort* only, make quite a display of the (albeit highly questionable) theory that it was the ordained men who elected the church officers. This is a most unfair criticism indeed as it was not only Knox's own practice to elect ministers without any reference to the will of the church whatsoever, but this was also the practised view of the few Knoxians who strove to promote Presbyterianism in Elizabethan England.[20] In their various Books of Discipline, it was invariably stated that the election of ministers should be carried out 'without the knowledge and consent of the church.'[21] It must be also borne in mind that the congregation at Frankfurt was composed almost entirely of ordained men, including many former bishops and Professors of Divinity. Probably conscious of the false criticism that their ministers were elected according to what became the Presbyterian pattern, the 'Anglicans' of Frankfurt emphasised in their letter to

---

[20] See Knox's 1560 *Book of Discipline*, IV. Concerning Ministers and their Lawful Election.

[21] See Chapter I The Book of Discipline in Part 6 of Collinson's *The Elizabethan Puritan Movement*.

Calvin below, that their church officers had been chosen by common vote.

That the Knoxians and their later supporters are quite unjust in their 'democratic' criticism of the 'Anglicans' method of 'voting', is proved by the fact that the French Walloon church only voted on candidates recommended by the Presbyters as did Calvin both at Strasburg and Geneva.

The Frankfurt Church inform Calvin of their situation
With Knox gone and new church officers elected and more or less total freedom of worship given them by the Senate, the Frankfurt church decided to write to Calvin on 5 April, informing him of their progress. At the time of writing, no one but Knox had left the church and it was six months before some would leave for Geneva at Calvin's invitation. The fact that no schism had occurred must have strengthened the Frankfurt brethren's determination to gently rebuke Calvin for his 'easy-believism' in accepting the most biased and one-sided criticism from Knox and Whittingham. It was not the first time that Calvin had erred in this way. Acting on vicious gossip, he had rebuked Melancthon, urging him to be more firm in his attitude to the Interimist and Adiaphorist controversies, though he had not compromised as Calvin was led to believe. This error of judgement on Calvin's part, prompted by mal-intentioned 'advisors' was not a mere rumour spread by Calvin's enemies but pointed out by his own successor Beza.[22] Thus, to rectify such misinformation, the Frankfurt party wrote:

> GREETING. After that our very dear brother Thomas Sampson had communicated to us sometime since the letter that you wrote to him touching our common controversy with certain brethren, we considered it a mark of our duty and regard to you to inform you, as early as possible, of all that has been done, and with what design. But though it may perhaps seem to you somewhat late to write to you, when

---

[22] See Beza's explanation given in *Zurich Letters*, Second Series, p. 126.

the matter is altogether brought to a termination; yet we im-
plore you by Jesus Christ, not to suppose that the delay has
arisen from any desire unduly to undervalue your authority.
For it both is, and ought to be, most highly esteemed and
regarded, not only by ourselves, but by the world at large.
But since your reverence was many days' journey distant
from us, and because there was great hope that all that controversy could be settled with less inconvenience between
the brethren themselves, we were unwilling to disturb your
most important meditations by our trifling and domestic con-
cerns. But though we are very loth to suspect our brethren of
any thing that savours of insincerity, we are nevertheless
somewhat afraid that the whole affair and case has not been
set before you with sufficient explicitness. For neither are
we so entirely wedded to our country, as not to be able to
endure any customs differing from our own; nor is the authority of those, fathers and martyrs of Christ so much regarded by us, as that we have any scruple in thinking or acting in opposition to it. And we have not only very frequently
borne witness to this by our assertions, but have at length
proved it by our actions. For when the magistrates lately
gave us permission to adopt the rites of our native country,
we freely relinquished all those ceremonies which were regarded by our brethren as offensive and inconvenient. For
we gave up private baptisms, confirmation of children, saints'
days, kneeling at the holy communion, the linen surplices of
the ministers, crosses, and other things of the like character.
And we gave them up, not as being impure and papistical,
which certain of our brethren often charged them with being; but whereas they were in their own nature indifferent,
and either ordained or allowed by godly fathers for the edification of our people, we notwithstanding chose rather to lay
them aside than to offend the minds or alienate the affec-
tions of the brethren. We retain however the remainder of
the form of prayer and of the administration of the sacraments, which is prescribed in our book, and this with the
consent of almost the whole church, the judgment of which

in matters of this sort we did not think should be disregarded. With the consent likewise of the same church there was forthwith appointed one pastor, two preachers, four elders, two deacons; the greatest care being taken that every one should be at perfect liberty to vote as he pleased; except only that by the command of the magistrate, before the election took place, were set forth those articles lately published by the authority of King Edward, which contained a summary of our doctrine, and which we were all of us required to subscribe. For what kind of an election, they said, must be expected, unless the voters shall previously have agreed as to doctrine? Certain parties, who had before manifested some objection, subscribed to these articles of their own accord. Some few declined doing so, of whose peaceableness nevertheless we entertain good hope.

We have thought fit to write thus fully to your kindness, that you might ascertain the whole course of our proceedings from ourselves. Our liturgy is translated into French, and the articles above mentioned have very lately been printed at Zurich. Did we not suppose that they would easily be met with among you, we should take care that copies should be forwarded you. But we pray your kindness not to imagine that we have aimed at any thing else throughout this whole business, and this we testify before the Lord, than the purification of our church, and the avoiding of most grievous stumbling-blocks which otherwise seemed to be hanging over us. May the Lord Jesus very long preserve your piety to us and his church! Farewell, Frankfort, April 5 (1555).

Your piety's most devoted English exiles,

RICHARD COX	EDMUND GRINDAL
DAVID WHITEHEAD	JOHN BALE
RICHARD ALVEY	ROB. HORN
THOMAS BECON	THO. LEVER
EDWIN SANDYS	THO. SAMPSON

Here is a letter full of grievances but void of rancour. There is no name-calling but all the accusations from the Knoxians are refuted one by one and shown to have no basis whatsoever in fact.

The letter starts by naming Sampson who also signed the letter. This was a strategic move as Sampson was highly respected by Calvin and known to be a man of God whose faith was sound and unadulterated by outward trimmings. Sampson's Nonconformity was, however, extreme and often he was even nonconforming to himself. Thus he could make great friends and even enchant Queen Elizabeth to take his side, yet be found most offensive by others. In a letter to Beza, Bullinger added a paragraph to warn him of Sampson, writing:

> This, however, I freely confess to you, that I have always looked with suspicion upon the statements made by master Sampson. He is not amiss in other respects, but of an exceedingly restless disposition. While he resided amongst us at Zurich, and after he returned to England, he never ceased to be troublesome to master Peter Martyr of blessed memory. He often used to complain to me, that Sampson never wrote a letter without filling it with grievances: the man is never satisfied; he has always some doubt or other to busy himself with. As often as he began, when he was here, to lay his plans before me, I used to get rid of him in a friendly way, as well knowing him to be a man of captious and unquiet disposition. England has many characters of this sort, who cannot be at rest, who can never be satisfied, and who have always something or other to complain about. I have certainly a natural dislike to men of this stamp.[23]

Those modern authors who put Sampson in the High Church and Hyper-Anglican sector perhaps have never read his works against the wearing of ecclesiastical habits. Nor do they apparently know how he strove with Laurence Humphrey to work out a Non-

---

[23] *Zurich Letters*, Second Series, p. 152.

conformity in the Church of England that so angered the conforming feelings of Knox and his state church ideas that he asked the
Church of England to discipline such Nonconformity. Sampson
would not wear the four-cornered clerical cap, nor would he have
music and organs in church. He argued that once a minister was
ordained, he had free liberty to preach with or without the church's
order of worship as he thought fit. Such ideas were certainly not
Knoxian! Happily, there is an extant letter from Sampson, one of
those the Frankfurt members referred to above, which shows what
a balanced position Sampson took in the Frankfurt debate, despite
his reputation, and how he described everything to Calvin exactly
as it was with no over-biased comment or criticism of his brethren.
Sampson also brought Calvin up to date on affairs in England:

> Thomas Sampson to John Calvin, Feb. 23, 1555
> I do not cease from doing here as I did at Lausanne,
> that is, I am expecting a reply from your kindness. And
> indeed I am more anxiously expecting it, in proportion as
> I perceive the flame is lighted up with increased vehe-
> mence amongst us English. For a strong controversy has
> arisen, while some desire the Book of Reformation of the
> Church of England to be set aside altogether, others only
> deem some things in it objectionable, such as kneeling at
> the Lords Supper, the linen surplice, and other matters of
> this kind; but the rest of it, namely, the Prayers, Scripture
> lessons, and the form of the administration of Baptism
> and the Lords Supper, they wish to be retained. Some
> contend for retaining the form, both because the Arch-
> bishop of Canterbury defends the doctrine as sound, and
> also, because the opposite Party can assign no just rea-
> son why the form should be changed. They exclaim on
> the other hand, that the sole object of these persons is the
> establishment of ceremonies. You see, most excellent
> Calvin, how Satan is permitted, both at home and abroad,
> to rage against the English. May God have compassion
> upon us! and I entreat you, by Christ our common Sav-
> iour, to give your best consideration to these disturbances

of ours, and shew me how we may best remedy this present evil. I well know how much weight the authority of your letters will have with both parties in the settlement of this dispute.

I have few things, and those far from pleasant, to tell you about the affairs of England. On the dissolution of parliament the bishop of Winchester summoned before him all those who were in prison in London for the word of the Lord, in number eighty, and he urged them by promises, rewards and threatenings, to sign their recantation. All persevered most steadfastly, these two only excepted, Barlow, formerly bishop of Bath and Wells, and Cardmaker, archdeacon, I believe, of the same church: for these submitted to him. Five of them, after a few days, were again brought to trial, condemned as heretics, and, as we say, delivered up to the secular authority to be burned. Whether the execution has taken place, I know not; but all the English are of opinion that they will most assuredly suffer. Their names are Hooper, Rogers, Taylor, Bradford, Saunders; all of them formerly celebrated as ministers of the word. The three bishops are still alive, and it is thought that a conference will be held between them and Pole. Philip has not got possession of the crown. The bishops are authorised to seize at pleasure upon all suspected of heresy. You see, excellent sir, the state of England; I commend it to your prayers and those of your church. Farewell, and write to me in return. In haste. Strasburg, Feb. 23. 1555,

Yours,

Thomas Sampson'[24]

The picture of an ideal Continental Reformation and a half-baked English Reformation is quite false

Anti-Anglican authors such as Neal tend to use an idealised picture of the Continental Reformers, especially the French, as a yardstick

---

[24] *Original Letters*, Vol. I, pp. 170-172.

to measure the orthodoxy of their own countrymen. Such an imagined yardstick, however, can only be of service if one realises that
the Continental churches were going through exactly the same problems as the English churches and it is not a question of comparing a
supposed Reformation 'ideal' with the turbulence of the English Reformation. Indeed, this method of comparison invariably backfires
on those who see either a united and rigid anti-episcopalianism, anti-
vestiarian, or even anti-clerical stand amongst the Continental Reformed churches. First of all, these churches were not as thoroughly
united as the Reformed Church in England had been under Edward
VI and was to be after the Elizabethan Settlement. Nor can one say
that where they were reformed, they were, as a whole, more reformed than the English churches. Furthermore, countries such as
Denmark, Norway and especially Sweden had experienced thorough-
going Reformed churches, with the Scriptures in their own tongues
before even Germany, yet they kept the Episcopacy as a Scriptural
order, though they rejected Apostolic Succession. The great Reformation which started in Finland parallel with Luther's work in Germany and produced such fine men as Peder Särkilaks, Martin Skytte
and Mikael Agricola was Episcopal through and through. In Western and Southern Europe, Charles V, and his ideas of an imperial
church involving an ecumenical mixture of Roman Catholic and
Reformed teaching, prevented a large area of the European Continent from adopting the more thorough nation-wide Reformation
experienced in England. Furthermore the Interimistic and
Adiaphoristic controversies in 'The Holy Roman Empire' concerning 'things indifferent' such as vestments and certain traditional ceremonies was fought out with much more violence and even bloodshed on the Continent than the case was in England during Edward's
and Elizabeth's reigns.

Indeed, it could be rightly argued that the controversy of the
Continental British exiles regarding ceremonies and vestments was
a reflection of the controversies going on in a number of European
countries which the exiles then took with them to England after their
exiles under Henry and Mary. The Adiaphora[25] controversy, for in-

---

[25] *a*- not + *diaphoros* different.

stance, so eagerly taken up by the Knoxians, was a thorough-going Lutheran nit-picking war, originally fought out by Melancthon and Flacius and exported to Britain by the Precisians. The ensuing vestment and order controversies were therefore to a great extent fought out by those who had tasted new fashions on the Continent and wished to introduce especially French forms into British ecclesiastical dress. It was a clash of culture, politics and tradition rather than faith and doctrine. Scottish antagonism to a church which had 'an English face' is quite understandable as the Battle of Pinkie which left the Scots heavily defeated[26] was still fresh in memory and there was still no lasting peace between the countries and the threat of war accompanied most of Knox's ministry in Scotland. It was also no wonder that Scotland took to French forms so readily as, at the time of the Reformation, they were under the rule of Mary of Guise and of Mary Stuart, i.e. they were a French dependency. The English preferred to stick to their own understanding of the ministry, monarchy and English dress. Lawrence Humphrey, one of the most radical of Nonconformists saw this problem and wrote that John Jewel, after the Knox debacle, was:

> ... employing all the spare time from his more necessary studies, in seeking to appease, by word of mouth and epistle, the contentions among his brethren, arising from difference of opinion concerning ceremonies and church discipline, which they brought not with them from England, but like scattered seed, they received from the nature of the place and soil where they were dispersed.[27]

Jewel's fellow-labourer in exile continues:

> These small jarring strings, which have so much troubled the sweet harmony of our church, he then sought, by all means, to put in tune, exhorting them, as brethren, to lay

---

[26] 10 September, 1547. The English, according to John Hooper's report to Bullinger, had 17,000 and the Scots 30,000 troops. *Original Letters*, Vol. I, pp. 43-44.
[27] See Life of Bishop Jewell, *Fathers of the English Church*, Vol. VII, p. xxi.

aside all strife and emulation, especially about such small
matters; lest thereby they should greatly offend the minds of
all good men; which thing, he said, they ought to have a
principle care of.

It is a strange irony of history and a sure sign of the weakness of
the flesh that Knox and his few English followers have been praised
by succeeding generations of Precisians for bringing back needy
reforms from the Continent, whereas, in reality, they spread Continental, denominational bickering, based on external fashions
throughout Britain. Lloyd-Jones criticises the Frankfurt majority
for being prepared to compromise on these small matters as if it
were a great evil to contend against.[28] Indeed, so taken up with the
idea of no compromise regarding inessentials is this modern writer
that he sees Puritanism as standing or falling on the colour of a
gown! Methinks that a little English love of compromise would
have saved the British church from being rent down the middle
because of a Turkish robe, a Genevan hat, or an English surplice or
the ancient toga, tunics and capes from which such clothing developed as a matter of fashion and taste.[29]

The Knoxian policy was always that misuse rendered usage
useless, i.e. anything ever used in a wrong way by others could
never be used correctly again. Thus if a Romanist clergyman wore
a certain hat, all Protestant pastors must adopt a new form of head-
gear or go bare-headed. If a Romanist was thought to kneel at communion, even if this was a great rarity, the Protestant must sit or
stand. The English Reformers, on the whole, were above such non-
sense. A phrase they often used was *abusus non tollit usum*, i.e.
misuse does not prevent right use. They were, however, prepared
to give way to weaker brethren on certain externals for the sake of
peace and because they were truly things of indifference. However, when a schism breaks away from its mother church in order
to set up a different system based on imagined 'pure' ceremonies

---

[28] *The Puritans*, p. 277.
[29] See especially Lloyd-Jones' essay Puritanism and Its Origins in his *The Puritans*.

and traditions, what guarantee is there that it will not reap adepts rather than Christians? When that schism seeks to enforce conformity on pain of death and by means of the secular arm, what guarantee is there that this will not lead to absolute tyranny? Latimer, the great preacher of the English Reformation, abhorred any idea of enforced faith and the use of the secular sword (as opposed to the Word of God). Most of the English Reformers believed as he did, especially that fine body of men gathered at Frankfurt and so often denigrated by Presbyterian denominations. Yet Knox judged them to be idolaters and idolaters must be punished by death! It is a sad comment to the origin and development of Presbyterian and Independent dissent that such fine doctrine of grace men as Cox, Lever and Fox were persecuted by the emerging Presbyterians in the 16th century and the very men who had co-founded Calvinism in the form of the Five Points at the Synod of Dort (1619), were likewise hunted down and 'punished' by the Precisian Presbyterian Junta.[30]

On the other, more positive side, it is often forgotten in the heat of debate what an enormous amount of agreement in doctrine and even liturgy there is between the Genevan and Anglican forms of doctrine and worship. Calvin was as much influenced by early Continental and English Reformers such as Gottschalk and Wycliffe as were the Anglicans and he was also much in debt to his contemporaries, Farel, Zanchy, Martyr, Bullinger and especially Bucer. These men were used of God to renew both Continental and English Reformed thinking and for the compiling of the English Prayer Book. Nor do critics of the English Reformation take into due account the enormous influence Calvin and the French Reformers themselves, including Frankfurt's Valerand Poullain, had on the English liturgy.

It is often argued that the Church of England relied too much on the Early Fathers and too little on Scriptural doctrine, but if one compares Calvin's works point for point on these matters one must

---

[30] The English historical form of the word 'Junta', indicating an oppressive administrative body, is 'Junto' but as the former neutral word 'Junta' is now used widely negatively, I may be excused for using it.

reach the conclusion that such as Parker (the great Anglican historian and Archbishop), Jewel, Whitgift, Grindal and Abbot, were more reserved in their appeals to the Fathers beyond the apostolic period and first three centuries. Calvin was perhaps more interested in the continuing development of the theologies of the Fathers because of his great interest in ecclesiastical law and the Fathers' conceptions of the state.[31] It is interesting to note, however, that when the relatively small party of Knoxians left for Geneva in the autumn of 1555, their arguments to prove that they were not forming a schism were based on the pronouncements of the so-called Fathers and of Calvin and Bullinger. Sadly, the church majority appeared to be no better in such a debate. Much of the discussion centred around whether Calvin had actually defined schism as 'a cutting off from the body' or not and what the Church Fathers had to say about it.

Though Calvin was quoted by the Knoxians as justifying their breech with the Frankfurt brethren, his teaching clearly considers Knox and his few followers to be in the wrong. Writing in Book IV, Chap. I, Section 13 of his *Institutes* on Schism, Calvin condemns the Precisians, claiming:

> For where the Lord requires mercy, they omit it, and give themselves up to immoderate severity. Thinking there is no church where there is not complete purity and integrity of conduct, they, through hatred of wickedness, withdraw from a genuine church, while they think they are shunning the company of the ungodly. They allege that the Church of God is holy. But that they may at the same time understand that it contains a mixture of good and bad, let them hear from the lips of our Saviour that parable in which he compares the Church to a net in which all kinds of fishes are taken, but not separated until they are brought ashore. Let them hear it compared to a field which, planted with

---

[31] See Chapter 1:2 'Bildung des Geistes' in de la Tour's book *Calvin – Der Mensch – Die Kirche – Die Zeit.* Also Chapter 1:2 'The Sources of the Institutes', in Wendel's *Calvin.*

good seed, is by the fraud of an enemy mingled with tares, and is not freed of them until the harvest is brought into the barn. Let them hear, in fine, that it is a thrashing-floor in which the collected wheat lies concealed under the chaff, until, cleansed by the fanners and the sieve, it is at length laid up in the granary. If the Lord declares that the Church will labour under the defect of being burdened with a multitude of wicked until the day of judgment, it is in vain to look for a church altogether free from blemish (Matth. xiii.).

The only concrete reason Knox and the Knoxians had from separating themselves from the Frankfurt fellowship was that they disapproved of responses from the congregation, the public reading of Scripture and morning worship according to a modified Prayer Book order. A close study of Chapter I, Book IV entitled *Of the True Church. Duty of Cultivating Unity With Her, As the Mother of All the Godly* in Calvin's *Institutes* will reveal clearly that, according to the Swiss Reformer, such behaviour was Schismatic. Likewise the reason given by Fox that he could not stand the behaviour of the young people in the Frankfurt church which was one of several reasons why he left, must be questioned. The young people cannot have been in the majority and thus a disciplinary weakness in the congregation, not usually discussed by historical analysts, seems to have been apparent.

The Continental Reformers were more balanced than the Knoxians

Another point, often forgotten by critics of the Reformed Church of England is that the Continental Reformers such as Calvin, Luther, Martyr, Bucer, Bullinger, Gualter and Zanchy were mostly men of balance in minor matters and had a measure of tolerance unknown to the Knoxians and the more radical of the budding Puritans. For them, whether one wore a round cap or a square cap, was purely a matter of personal taste and fashion, whereas to the radicals that such as Neal often supported, it was a matter of saving importance. Thus we find William Turner giving Bullinger a dressing down, comparing him to Melancthon,[32] and Samaritans who limped on both feet, and suggesting that his honour and integrity were at stake and even his doctrine. Why? Because Bullinger had advised the English Reformers to get on with the process of preaching the gospel instead of squabbling over caps and gowns. For Turner such a squabble was necessary to purify the church.[33] For Bullinger, such a purification would have been merely whitening sepulchres.

In comparing the French orders which later Scottish Reformers made so much of, claiming they adhered to them, it must be remembered that they were compiled during a time of persecution and exile. It is often forgotten that even Farel and Calvin were persecuted Frenchmen in exile. At the time of the Frankfurt troubles, Henry II (1547-59) was at the height of his persecuting power. Thus the forms drawn up amongst the French who remained in their home country under persecution concentrated on the church as a secret and underground fellowship which had no relationship to the State as such. This was roughly the situation, though with far less intensity, under Mary of Guise and Mary Stuart in Scotland during Knox's reforming work there. On the other hand, the Anglican forms developed during the reigns of Edward and Elizabeth when the Reformers were able to exert a great influence on a state who was very much open to their plans and where persecution, compared to the situation on the Continent and for a great part of this period in Scotland, was at a low minimum. Hence, the English Reformers neither pleaded for a Church which had nothing to do with their country's way of life, nor for a Church which ruled that country. They sought rather for a co-existence of Church and State within the limits imposed by Christ when He ruled that Caesar had a God-given realm of influence, not only the Church. They thus taught that the State, whatever the faith of its members, was ordained by God and to be obeyed or face the consequences of diso-

---

[32] Turner had obviously been influenced here by Calvin's misinformation concerning the German Reformer.

[33] Letter LI, William Turner to Henry Bullinger, 23 July, 1566, *Zurich Letters*, Second Series, Parker Society, pp. 124-126. See *Fathers of the English Church*, Vol. IV. for samples of Turner's fine work *The Old Learning and the New Compared Together*.

bedience. As the French forms developed within a church dilemma, hidden from the State, a situation such as the English mutual acceptance of Church and State was not envisaged. When the British Presbyterians took over the French forms and sought to plant them on British soil, they also strove, more than the French and far more than the Anglican Reformers, to overthrow the State to make it subject to the Church. This was most certainly the policy of Knox, a policy which came to a head in the teaching of Samuel Rutherford in his revolutionary work *Lex Rex*. Here we do not have the teaching of Christ concerning the distinction between Caesar and God, nor the Pauline teaching that the powers that be are ordained of God but the teaching that the powers that be are subservient to the Church and church forms and that they are ordained of God only in so far as they obey God along the paths set by the Church, in this case a Presbyterian order. Thus, if the magistrate is thought to be un-Christian by his subjects, those subjects have every right to punish him by death. Rutherford even teaches that a Christian does not break against the rule 'love thy neighbour as thyself' when the magistrate gets in the way and thus has to be killed, thus standing Romans 13:1-8 on its head.[34] Knox's and Rutherford's politics are argued as being thoroughly Biblical. This is to a very negative extent true. The Bible refers to them, yet not with acclamation but condemnation. As critics of Knox and Rutherford were quick to point out, theirs was the idea that the commands of God are equal to the will of the people illustrated by the Jews wishing for a king. The result was that they received an earthly Saul only to be compelled by God to drop him for the real God-given prophet, priest and King, David the forerunner and type of Christ Himself.

However, the English and Scottish Presbyterians were far from consistent in their choice of the French customs. The brethren in France, Switzerland and the Low Countries practised private wor-

---

[34] It was through reading *Lex Rex* many years ago as a student of Civics that finally helped put me off Scottish Presbyterian politics (realising that Continental and American Presbyterians did not necessary follow them) and it was Campbell's honest but frightening book *The Triumphs of Presbyterianism* that saved me from accepting such attempts to mingle the affairs of Caesar with God's and use the sword Islam-like to gain inner Christian peace.

ship, private communion and private baptisms. So did the Reformed
Church of England to a very limited extent. Especially the French
had to work this way as any public testimony of this kind was strictly
forbidden on pain of death. In order to separate completely from the
Reformation Church of England, the Presbyterians banned these
French practices as popish and therefore devilish, little realising
that they were the very marks of a church fully separated from the
papal system.

Furthermore, the cry of the early Presbyterians had always been
for a parity of ministers, a view they shared with the early Anglican Reformers, yet the French forms which the post-exile Presbyterians took over reflected a highly organised underground hierarchy which included, apart from the normal three fold division of
church offices taught by the Reformers, the *consistoire*, the *colloque*,
the *synode provinciale* and the *synode nationale*. This is perhaps
why, in imitating the French, yet politicising their orders, the Scottish Presbyterians soon found themselves abandoning the simple
structures of the Anglican Reformers and adopting a seven-tier ministry that reminded critics very much of the Roman structure of a
seven-graded hierarchy.

Thus the Knoxians lost that element of the French Church which
was its greatest blessing and which kept the Church in France alive
during generations of persecution. This was what they called their
ceaux de religion in contrast to a politic-cum-religion. In losing
their position of a church within a state for a state which is a church,
the Scottish Presbyterians departed Rome-wards from the separated character of those whom they initially sought to follow. In all
these matters, the relationship between the Church ministry, Convocation, Queen and Parliament accepted by the Reformed Church
of England proved a most practical and workable Middle-Way.

Calvin quite misinformed concerning the Coxians

Coming back to the Frankfurt letter, the Frankfurt brethren go on
to tell Calvin patiently that he has been misinformed as to their
allegedly acting against the Senates ruling and introducing 'offensive and inconvenient ceremonies.' They stress that though the
magistrates gave them liberty to draw up the order of their choice,

they abstained from all such ceremonies i.e. all those that Knox always said they would introduce and apparently had told Calvin that they had introduced. All that was retained was by majority vote. The use of the phrase 'almost the whole church' is very important here as it is claimed by so many enemies of the English Reformation that the vast majority were against the new order. The supposed 'Knoxians' had not yet left, yet they comprised an insignificant minority of the church's members. So, too, the Frankfurt brethren showed that they had ministers appointed by the majority vote of the church in a very similar way to the French and Emden orders, so greatly respected by later Presbyterians. There is no sign whatsoever of Anglican High Churchmanship here! Actually the idea of letting each man vote as he pleased was practised by the Frankfurt church in keeping with later free churches and stood in direct opposition to the form of electing church offices used by the early English and Scottish Presbyterians whom many would define (quite wrongly) as the first 'Puritans'. It was also a procedure insisted upon by the Frankfurt authorities. When the few Koxian dissidents complained to the Senate, they were told that they were protesting against a democratic vote.

The last paragraph really puts Calvin in his place. If he wanted to know how the Frankfurt worship was conducted, he need not have read Knox's 'plat' as that showed nothing of the kind. He could have read the real thing in his own language printed in Switzerland if he had taken the trouble. Again, the writers of the letter emphasised that though there had been some objection, as is usual in Christian debate, few had voted against the order.

Recapitulating the charges levelled against the 'Anglicans' in the light of their letter to Calvin

We have already seen that McCrie, building on Knox's prognosis of the terrible papist things that would happen if he were not there to stop them, informs his reader that once Knox had left, Rome was left free to take over at Frankfurt. A more recent writer, A. M. Renwick, sums up the entirely erroneous myth that has developed from such negative flights of biased imagination. Ignoring the problems at Frankfurt before Knox and Cox arrived, he writes:

The peace (at Frankfurt) was rudely disturbed by the arrival of Dr. Cox (formerly Chancellor of Oxford university), and a fresh band of English refugees. Although received with every mark of Christian generosity, they immediately became exceedingly aggressive, insisted on a full-fledged Anglican service, and paid no attention to the contract made with the French Church, or the agreement reached in the congregation itself.[35]

It must be presumed that the 'disturbance' of which Renwick accuses Cox is merely the fact that Jewel, who was not of the Cox-Strasburg party was asked to preach by the pastor and did so with great acclamation on his first Sunday in Frankfurt and when the litany was read, 'the people answered'[36]. Jewel also confessed that he had signed a popish pledge in acknowledgement of Mary but now deeply regretted it. This, says eye-witnesses was taken positively and with great sympathy and understanding by all. The Strasburg men were, indeed, received warmly by the members of the church but most coldly by Knox. The Coxians never, ever, were aggressive in demanding a fully-fledged Anglican service, not to mention a Roman mass! On the contrary, they accepted every single demand of Knox, including not kneeling at the communion. What were then the differences? The differences were solely to be found in Knox's view of himself and his own importance and can be reduced to two Reformation principles which Knox believed he could neglect. Though the Coxians were one mind with Knox concerning abolishing crosses, salt at baptism, candles, private baptisms, crucifixes, kneeling and several other ceremonies listed in these pages, when faced with their plea concerning the public reading of the Scriptures and the public response of the congregation, Knox firmly told his brethren that they were to do his will entirely or be accused of popery and devilry. To back up his threats, he claimed that he was appointed of the Lord to make no concessions whatsoever. Thus, if such as Lloyd-Jones believe that Frankfurt

---

[35] *The Story of the Scottish Reformation*, p. 61.
[36] Knox's expression.

was the birthplace of Puritanism and Puritanism takes the Knoxian line, then they believe that Puritanism is based on Knox's stubborn refusal to accept these two features of Reformed worship. Knox was, it must be emphasised strongly, prepared to break up and then leave a church on these two sandy and shaky grounds alone. Once Knox had left Frankfurt, however, the Coxians carried on as usual and if Knox had returned, he would have found a church which suited him fine but for two tiny items against which one would think no man of Christian virtue or common sense would protest.

Calvin replies to the Frankfurt letter

Calvin's reply must have partly cheered and yet mostly disappointed the Frankfurt brethren. There is no shade of apology but merely the statement that Calvin is glad that things are not as he was led to believe. Then he goes on to take this back and write as if he did not believe a word of what the Frankfurt Christians had told him. He also confessed that he had been working underhand, persuading dissatisfied members to join him at Geneva, on the basis that what they had told him of the Frankfurt situation was true. It thus becomes obvious that the exodus of the eighteen members in September was not so much in protest of the Senate dismissing Knox but because of Calvin's interference in the local church's affairs, acting on quite false presumptions. Indeed, the author of *Troubles at Frankfort* presents the matter as if Calvin's interference in the church's matters had prompted the letter of complaint signed by a handful of members and presented to the church on 17 August of that year.[37] Calvin's strange and quite inexcusable letter reads:

> To the Worshipful my loving Brethren in the Lord, Master RICHARD COX and the rest of the Englishmen which now remain at Frankfort.
>
> PERADVENTURE, I ANSWER your Letter, Worshipful Friends, and Brethren, more slowly than either ye hoped, or looked for: but forsomuch as ye know the ways, for a time, so to be beset with thieves that no messenger almost

---

[37] *Troubles at Frankfort*, p. 81.

could pass from hence to you, the excuse of my long delay towards you shall be the easier.

I expressed my mind frankly to our beloved Brother, THOMAS SAMPSON, of that whereof I was informed by the Letters of certain men as touching the Contention unluckily stirred up among you. For certain of my friends found themselves grieved that you would so precisely urge the Ceremonies of England; whereby it might appear that ye are more given and addict(ed) to your own country than reason would.

I confess that I heard certain reasons alleged on your behalf, which would not suffer you to depart from the received Order: but they might be soon and easily confuted. Now, as I counselled mine own friends which dissented from you, somewhat to yield, if they might conveniently; so it offended me, that there was nothing granted or relented on your Parts. Because there was no man named unto me; I durst not enterprise to meddle with the matter, lest my credit should incur the suspect (suspicion) of rashness. Now that ye are more mild and tractable in this Controversy, and that ye have, as ye say, stilled the matter with quietness; I am very glad.

Verily, no man, well instructed, or of a Sound judgement, will deny, as I think, that Lights, and Crossings, or such like trifles, sprang, or issued, out of Superstition. Whereupon I am persuaded that they which retain these Ceremonies in a free choice, or when they may otherwise do, they are over-greedy and desirous to drink of the dregs: neither do I see to what purpose it is, to burden the Church with trifling and unprofitable Ceremonies, or as I may term them with their proper name, hurtful and ostensible Ceremonies; when as there is liberty to have a simple and pure Order. But I keep in, and refrain myself: lest I should seem to begin to move a new Contention of that matter which, as you report, is well ended.

All good men will allow the Pastors' and other Ministers' Elections with common voices: so that none (can) complain that the other part of the Church was oppressed fraudently, and with crafty practices. For it standeth your Wisdoms in hand to consider, That how much commodity the goodness of the Senate doth deserve; so much envy shall you be guilty of, or charged withal, if you have abused their lenity or gentleness. which were so well affected towards your nation. Yet I would not have this so taken, that I go about to be prejudicial to any man: but I had rather shew plainly what may be said; than to nourish an ill opinion by silence, or in holding my peace. But certainly this one thing I cannot keep secret that Master Knox was, in my judgement, neither godly nor brotherly dealt withal. If he were accused by the subtle suggestion of certain; it had been better for them to have tarried still in their own land, than unjustly to have brought into far countries the firebrand of cruelty to set on fire those that would not be kindled. Notwithstanding, because it grieveth me (even) to speak slightly of these evils, the remembrance whereof I would wish to be buried in perpetual forgetfulness; therefore I only counsel you, not without a cause, to be wounded (minded?) that ye apply yourselves to make them amends for the fault committed.

When I heard that the one Party was minded to depart from thence; I earnestly admonished them, as it became me, that if they could not well remain there, that the distance of place should not dissipate, or rent in sunder, their brotherly agreement; for I feared much, lest that some privy grudge of the former Contention remained. And certainly nothing could more comfort my heart than to be delivered from this fear. For if any (should) haply come to us; it would grieve me that there should be, as it were, but a suspicion of any secret debate between you.

Therefore, as touching that ye have written of your agreement; I desire that it may be firm and stable: that if it chance the one part to go to another place; yet that you, being so sundered by distance of places, may keep sure the holy band of amity: for the fault already committed is too much, although through discord it creep no further. Wherefore it shall well beseem your Wisdoms, that ye may be friends. to purge diligently whatsoever remaineth of this breach.

Fare ye well, Brethren! The Lord succour you with his aid; and govern you with his Spirit! pour his blessings upon you, and mitigate the sorrow of your exile!

From Geneva, this last of May, anno 1555.

Yours,
JOHN CALVIN.[38]

Calvin's letter examined

Calvin's accusation that the Frankfurt church was using 'Lights and Crossings', can only have been a product of Knox's phobia that once outside of his jurisdiction, the Coxians would bring in the abundance of ceremonies that he constantly prophesied. He seems never to have grasped the point that this was the last thing that the Coxians wished to do and they lagged behind Knox in nothing concerning ceremonies. Indeed, Knox had a far more difficult time in Scotland banning lights and crosses from his own churches than the English Reformers had in Elizabethan England. At one point, it would appear that such items were only to be found in the Queen's chapel for allegedly 'diplomatic purposes' when receiving Spanish guests. Cox protested strongly against this and risked the Queen's anger on several occasions because of such protests. The compiler of this section of *Troubles at Frankfort* makes a very lame attempt to explain Calvin's protest away by suggesting that the Swiss Reformer merely meant that if lights and crossings have been done away with in the work of Reformation, how much more should other ceremonies be done away with. Obviously Calvin said nothing of the kind and the Frankfurt church understood him in the only way possible and protested strongly in their reply to this faulty accusation. This apparent ignorance on Calvin's side is difficult to understand as the evidence suggests that Calvin knew perfectly well what was in the Second Prayer Book. Indeed Wilhelm

---

[38] *Troubles at Frankfort*, pp. 78-80.

Moeller argues in Vol. III of his mammoth work *The History of the Christian Church* that the Second Book of Common Prayer was drawn up 'with the co-operation of Calvin and Bucer'. Furthermore, Cranmer also called upon the help of Coverdale, Hooper, Ridley, Rogers, Martyr, Fagius and Laski in this work showing that it was drawn up by a representative cross-section of the Puritan Reformers.[39]

Knox and Whittingham had always argued that the Senate was fully on their side, against the majority party and Calvin still wrote as if this were a fact, utterly ignoring what the Frankfurter party had to say. It is plain from the details given by the compiler of the 1554-55 account of the troubles at Frankfurt that, though he strove to give the impression that the Senate was on the Knoxian side, all the facts he records show that the Senate came down on the side of the Coxians. Calvin's insistence that the Coxians should allow dissenters to leave Frankfurt for Geneva without bearing them any grudge was partly because of the debate which sprang up on both sides concerning the definition of the word 'schism'. Some felt that should a party break off and found another church based on another faith and order, this must rightly be called a schism. Naturally the Knoxians did not wish to go down in history as the schism that broke away from the Reformation party. Sadly, both sides appealed more to the early church fathers than the Bible and when the eighteen left for various other towns, the matter as to whether they had created a schism or not was left to later history to decide. The other reason is, of course, that after the Augsburg decree the Anglican and Calvinist parties in Germany were classified as illicit religions and Knox's meddling in international politics, demanding death to emperors, kings and queens had not helped matters.

Meanwhile, at Geneva, whether because of language difficulties or the heat of fierce argument, or because of Knox's most prejudiced report during his brief stay at Geneva before departing for Scotland, Calvin was led to believe that the Frankfurt church were now against all reforms and were defying the German authorities, wishing to remain 'English' at all costs.

---

[39] Op. sit. Vol. III, 1517-1648, p. 209.

Whitehead rebukes Calvin for his gullibility

Nonconformist Whitehead, the new pastor of the Frankfurt church, had been fuming in the background against the fiery Scotsman who ought to have taken over his pastorate. He had been shocked to the core to find that Knox's religion during his brief stay at Frankfurt had consisted of nit-picking of the most exaggerated kind. When the Frankfurt dissidents had indeed left, he now felt that fine words and diplomacy had failed and he must tell Calvin straight that he was misinformed, that he had helped to split the church and had acted foolishly in his most biased taking of sides. There is much tit-for-tat in the letter but, knowing Whitehead's character and the fact that he in no way fitted into the picture the Knoxians painted of those they opposed at Frankfurt, it would be folly not to take Whitehead's defence seriously. It must be used to gain a balanced picture of the troubles. Assisted by the new preacher Thomas Becon, another Nonconformist if ever there was one, other church officers and Cox, Whitehead wrote on 20 September, 1555:

> As we were awaiting the arrival of certain of our breth-
> ren, to whom your letter seemed especially to apply, we
> were prevented from answering it, most learned Calvin, so
> early as either the case itself required, or as you probably
> expected. But now, since all hope of their coming to us is
> taken away, it has seemed good to us who are here, to make
> at length some reply; partly indeed, lest by our silence we
> should seem unmindful of our duty to you, and partly, lest
> we should seem to betray our excellent cause. And, first.
> we desire you to be fully persuaded of this, that we regard
> you with entire veneration and love, both by reason of your
> singular godliness, and also of your especial pre-eminence
> in the most valuable attainments. But we consider it as a
> matter of exceeding regret, that our late letter was not alto-
> gether satisfactory to you in removing all your scruples.
> This, however, we must ascribe to those parties to whom
> you appeared to be a fit object for them to endeavour to
> deceive, and one whose authority they might shamelessly

abuse for the purpose of disturbing our church. For it seems very evident to us, that they would never have ventured to raise such a disturbance, had you not refrained in that letter of yours from pouring as it were cold water on the flame. Your letter was to them like the club of Hercules, by which they easily believed that they could beat down all their opponents. And, indeed, your name ought deservedly to have influence both with us, and with all godly persons. But if you had been well acquainted with their devices, if you had been sufficiently aware of their boldness and wicked designs, we have no doubt but that you would never have suffered them to come near you, much less to impose upon you as it were in so barefaced a manner. Indeed we consider it impossible to entertain any doubt of your candour and impartiality, as soon as our case shall have been clearly made known to you, and their artifices exposed. But through your letter is not a little annoying to us, inasmuch as it seems to brand us and bring us in guilty of such great offences, yet we hope that you have another ear in reserve for our reply.

Receive, therefore these few remarks in answer to your letter.

These friends of yours complain that 'we are too precise in enforcing the English ceremonies and unreasonably partial to our own country.'

These, indeed, we pertinaciously retain, as knowing them to be very godly: this, however, has never been done by us in a precise manner; for we have abandoned some of them for the sake of your friends, which might at that time have been piously adopted. But we make this concession to the love of our country, to which, forsooth, we are too much inclined. These, your friends, however, are altogether a disgrace to their country; for whatever has been bestowed from above upon our country in this respect, with exceeding arrogance, not to say impudence, they are treading under foot. You must know that we do not entertain any regard for our country which is not agreeable to God's holy word. Neither in the mean while are we so ungrateful to our country, nor have we so cast off every feeling of humanity, as rashly to despise the benefits which God has bestowed upon it. Nor have we such a mean opinion of the judgments of our countrymen, who resisted ungodliness even unto blood, as that by reason of the clamours of individuals, possessing no weight whatever, we should brand them with the foulest marks of papistical impiety. You 'heard the reasons which would not allow us to depart from the received form.' You heard them, indeed, but not from us, and probably not all of them. And, indeed, we have very little doubt but that you would easily refute them: but we are confident that the best reasons of our conduct will stand good before the judgment-seat of God. You say that 'it offended you that there was no concession or relaxation made to them an our parts.' And you might justly have been offended, had no concession been made. But as this is a barefaced and impudent falsehood of theirs, you can judge for yourself in what light they must have regarded you. You object to us 'lights and crosses.' As for lights, we never had any; and with respect to crosses, if we ever made use of them, these friends of yours have not imposed upon you. But consider again in what estimation they must have held you, when they presumed to assault you with so many manifest falsehoods. They also falsely lay it to our charge before you, that we wished to 'burden the church with trifling and unprofitable ceremonies.' Our ceremonies are very few, and all of them of no little use towards the advancement of godliness. But it is no wonder that our ceremonies appear redundant, and even burdensome, to those persons who exclaim against the public reading of the word of God as an irksome and unprofitable form. But from those words of yours it is quite evident, that you are entirely ignorant of almost all the circumstances of our case. For we have nothing, we are well assured, which either in your judgment, or in that of any godly man, will appear to be either unprofitable or injurious. But you are right in restraining yourself; or you would otherwise, as the mountebanks do, fight to no purpose against things which have no existence. We are quite ready to give you an account of the ceremonies we make use of here, whenever you please; and, whatever our cavillers may have muttered against them, we have more reason, we think, to apprehend the dissatisfaction of many persons by reason of their fewness rather than of their number.

To return now to the other points of your letter. 'All good men,' you say, 'will allow the pastors and other ministers to be elected by the common voice, so that others do not complain that a part of the church has been oppressed fraudulently and with crafty practices.' This assertion is certainly a stinging one, and would have wounded us severely, had not its point been blunted when it fell upon us. Nay, we allow it to be a thunderbolt; but it has not reached the object at which it was aimed. It is neither a novelty to us, nor a matter of surprise, that men, conscious of being in the wrong, will at length proceed to assert what is untrue. But it certainly turned out contrary to all our expectation, that you should so lend your ears to them, as to incline in some measure to that party. For what kind of an election ours was, we call to witness God, our conscience, our whole church, and the very magistrates themselves, of whose authority and advice we always availed ourselves. But we will explain to you at another time, if we are compelled to do so, the means by which others have attempted to undermine the church, and consequently to overthrow it; what indirect artifices they have made use of, and by what turbulent proceedings they have laboured after their own exaltation; and also, what a heavy charge that is which you seem to insinuate, that we have abused the lenity of the magistracy. We wish, however, that those persons who are filling your ears with these calumnious and slander-ous accusations, had never abused our lenity, the kindness of the magistrates, and your authority, which has given them no small encouragement to stir up this controversy. God forbid that we should abuse any persons whatever, much less those excellent magistrates who have deserved so well of us. But if you could bring your mind to believe that we were so lost to shame, how could you possibly think that the magistrates, discreet and worthy men as they are, would either be so stupid in regard to our cause, as not to find out our trickeries, or that they would suffer them, when detected, to go unpunished, and even regard us with greater kindness than before? In detecting the arti-fices of your friends, which, nevertheless, they knew how to devise and manage with much more ingenuity than we do, they were of such quick scent, that they immediately smelt them out, and their opinion of them is no secret.

But leaving these things, let us return to the business of Knox, wherein you greatly desire godliness and brotherly love an the part of those who were implicated in it. We will, therefore, briefly and truly explain to you the history of the whole affair. There were, at that time, certain parties in our church, who, instructed by long practice and experi-ence, were able easily to foresee and conceive beforehand in their minds the evils that were either already impending over our church, or might happen to it in future. These per-sons understood that Knox had published a certain book, which they perceived would supply their enemies with just ground for overturning the whole church. For there were interspersed, in this publication atrocious and horrible cal-umnies against the queen of England, whom Knox called at one time the wicked Mary, at another time a monster. And he exasperated king Philip also by language not much less violent. When these men had read this infamous libel, attached as they are to true religion and to our church, they considered it neither profitable nor safe to ourselves that Knox should be received with favour by our church. One of them, therefore, called upon the intimate friends of Knox, and pointed out to him that it would be most advisable for Knox to leave the church, and depart to some other place; and this he earnestly recommended him to do. Not succeeding in this, our friends, having more closely considered the danger which without doubt was hanging over them, thought it right to proceed in a different way. The matter was at last brought before the magistrates, with no other view than that Knox might be ordered to quit the place. When the magistrate was made acquainted with the case, and had also discovered that the emperor was defamed in that pamphlet; considering that a man of this kind might easily occasion danger, not only to our church, but also to his state, he ordered him to leave the city.

Thus you have the whole affair as it really took place; nor would we for the sake of our friends evade the subject, by holding back any thing, or obscure it by our relation of it. Something was conceded to Knox. For our party had observed some other things in him, which we have now purposely forborne to mention, but which induced them to desire his departure. But these clearly were the reasons which drove our friends to this step, and it was altogether in this way that they got rid of that affair. But what an occasion for disseminating falsehoods these authors of confusion thence laid hold of, what dreadful language they uttered, what disturbance they excited, must be matter of wonder to every one who is unacquainted with their character: especially when they even prevailed upon you to write concerning men who were in every respect innocent, that 'it had been better for them to have remained in their own country, than to have brought over to a distant land the firebrand of unjust severity.' If those who occasioned Knox's departure from hence had been in any way known to you, you would assuredly have dealt more gently with them. For scarce any man living is more remote from cruelty than, by the grace of God, those persons both are and have been. Certainly, when an account of what they had done was demanded of them by our pastor, they gave such a straightforward statement, that, scrupulous as he is in every thing else, he had nothing whatever to find fault with. For you cannot but be aware, how unbecoming it would have been in us impotently to rage in half-muttered abuse against magistrates; not, perhaps, because they do not deserve it, but because of the office imposed upon them by God. This we can assure you, that that outrageous pamphlet of Knox's added much oil to the flame of persecution in England. For before the publication of that book, not one of our brethren had suffered death but as soon as it came forth, we doubt not but that you are well aware of the number of excellent men who have perished in the flames; to say nothing of how many other godly men besides have been exposed to the risk of all their property, and even life itself, upon the sole ground of either having had this book in their possession, or having read it; who were perhaps rescued from the sword at greater cost and danger of life than the others offered their necks to it. But enough of these things.

You piously exhort us that, if we perceive that the minds of some parties are wounded not without cause, we should endeavour to make amends for the injury. But when you have left no stone unturned to heal those persons who have inflicted their wounds upon themselves, and have nevertheless lost all your pains, what can you possibly do for them? You say that you have 'diligently admonished those who are minded to leave us, that their departure should not rend asunder the agreement of the brethren.' We wish that your wisdom had foreseen this, and that the authority of your letter had not given encouragement to the former quarrel, before you had heard the other side of the question. We wish that your sagacity had anticipated what was the tendency of their designs, namely, to open faction, to say nothing more. For they themselves now presume to write that they are ready to maintain the lawfulness of their secession from our church. We certainly hoped, indeed, when we wrote to you, that our reconciliation would have been lasting; and your friend Whittingham, with all the rest of his party, except three or four, had given in his adhesion to our church. But oh? like true Proteuses, they now make subterfuges, and shamefully desert us, under I know not what pretence. We know not whence this change of sentiment has arisen; but we leave you to judge what opinion must be entertained of those persons who tell you that they leave the church solely an account of ceremonies which even they themselves dare no longer affirm to be ungodly, or can prove to be at variance with the word of God, or in any way unprofitable. We pray God to bestow upon them a better mind; and we earnestly entreat you no longer to mix yourself up in so hateful a business, lest some disparagement should arise to your reputation, which we desire should at all times be most honourable and holy. May the Lord Jesus preserve you as an especial ornament to his church!

Frankfort, Sept. 20, 1555.

Your admirers,
DAVID WHITEHEAD, Pastor   RICHARD ALVEY
RICHARD COX   HENRY PARRY
THOMAS BECON, Minister of the Word of God
BARTH. TRAHERON   THOMAS COTTISFORD

Whitehead's mention of Knox's indirect but nevertheless causative part in the Maryan persecutions reveals one of the great tragedies of the Reformation period. Whitehead is reserved and restrained in his remarks on it, thinking primarily in terms of the damage it did to the cause of God and truth in England. This false step on Knox's part has long proved an embarrassment to the Reformed cause in general and that of Scottish Presbyterianism.

Wotherspoon warns against the danger of giving the matter too much emphasis but says:

> Laing thinks that to ascribe the change of policy (i.e. of Mary etc.) entirely to the publication of the 'Faithful Admonition', would be to ascribe too much importance to it, but 'there can be no hesitation in believing' that its terms May have contributed in no small degree to evoke the spirit of persecution; and this is probably a fair statement of the case.[40]

However, the more immediate concern of the Frankfurt magistrates was that in his *An Admonition to Christians*, Knox had called Charles V, 'no less an enemy to Christ than was Nero.' Yet it was Charles who had given the English Protestant exiles asylum in his cities, the leading one being Frankfurt. Christopher Goodman, who joined Knox at Frankfurt but sought for peace between the parties, also wrote extreme revolutionary literature which provoked Mary's anger. In his introduction to *Troubles at Frankfort*, Edward Arber comments: 'How Knox could write such violent books, in such dangerous times, is another mystery in his life.'[41] Fox, who was torn between Knox and Cox, can only have meant Knox and Goodman and possibly also Ponet (Poynet), when he wrote:

> About the 5th of October (1554), and within a fortnight following, were divers, as well householders as servants and apprentices, apprehended and taken and committed to sundry prisons for the having and selling of certain books which were sent into England by the preachers that fled into Germany and other countries; which books nipped a great number so near, that within one fortnight there were little less than threescore imprisoned for this matter.[42]

---

[40] Wotherspoon, p. 30. For Laing's full comment see *Works* III, p. 256.
[41] *Troubles at Frankfort*, p. xvi.
[42] *Acts and Monuments*, vi. p. 561.

Knox's notorious book could not have come at a worse time. Charles V had made enormous concessions to the Protestants but the Frankfurt Senate obviously thought that the British exiles were now making their own case impossible in the eyes of Charles' Augsburg conference. Whether Knox directly influenced the negative decision against non-Lutheran Protestants or not, does not appear to be recorded but it cannot have helped the matter and Charles was in close touch with his near relation Mary who was greatly offended at Knox's radical politics.

Nor can we chide Whitehead for telling Calvin not to interfere so negatively in matters that had little to do with him and also not to pronounce such dogmatic judgement on his brethren in Christ based on mere hearsay. The English Reformers deserved better treatment from their Swiss counterpart. The Frankfurt Christians must have been puzzled to find that Calvin tended to support the more revolutionary and politically minded faction amongst the British and take the side of those who made much of externals. Was this because his system came closer to Knox's view of a State-Church under a Presbyterian-type ministry? However, in assisting Knox, and a few English opponents of the English monarchical system and the English Reformation under Edward and later under Elizabeth, Calvin obviously put his hand into a wasp's nest and lost much of his influence with leading English Christian politicians such as Cecil and Knollys.[43] Thus it was the more moderate politically, but equally sound theologically, Martyr, Zanchius and Bullinger, who became the major Continental partners of the English Reformation, though Calvin was always greatly respected. With all his great theological strength, Calvin was no political leader and the way he aided and abetted the more politically minded of the British Reformers was quite disastrous. Furthermore, Calvin was not always prepared to stand up for what he had said and done and, in order to keep his peace, left those whom he had encouraged to rebel to face the consequences themselves. Struggling to detach

---

[43] Several members of the influential Knollys family were members of the Frankfurt church during their exile.

himself from Elizabeth's and Cecil's accusation[44] that he had influenced Knox and Goodman in urging the Germans and British to revolt against Emperor and Queen, Calvin wrote:

THE messenger to whom I gave in charge my commentaries upon Isaiah to be presented to the most serene queen, brought me word that my homage was not kindly received by her majesty, because she had been offended with me by reason of some writings published in this place.[45] He also repeated to me, most illustrious sir, the substance of a conversation held by you, in which you seem to me more severe than was consistent with your courtesy, especially when you had been already assured by my letter, how much I promised myself from your regard towards me. But though sufficient reasons prevent me from vindicating myself by a serious discussion, yet lest I should seem by my silence to confess, in some measure the consciousness of having done wrong, I have thought it right to state, in few words how the matter stands. Two years ago John Knox asked of me in a private conversation, what I thought about the government of women, I candidly replied, that as it was a deviation from the original and proper order of nature, it was to be ranked, no less than slavery, among the punishments consequent upon the fall of man; but that there are occasionally women so endowed, that the singular good qualities which shone forth in them, made it evident that they were raised up by divine authority; either that God designed by such examples to condemn the inactivity of men, or for the better setting forth his own glory. I brought forward

---

[44] Hilaire Belloc, a most bigoted critic of the English Reformation, calls Cecil 'the author of Protestant England' and 'the true artisan of that prodigious change'. See his *Characters of the Reformation*, p. 193 ff. i.e. chapter on William Cecil.

[45] Knox and Goodman published revolutionary works in Geneva before moving to Frankfurt in 1554 but in 1556-7 Knox published the work which upset Elizabeth the most i.e. *The first blast against the monstrous regiment and empire of women*. In 1558, Goodman published his *How superior powers ought to be obeyed of their subjects, and wherein they may lawfully be disobeyed and resisted.*

Huldah and Deborah; and added, that God did not vainly promise by the mouth of Isaiah, that queens should be the nursing mothers of the church; by which prerogative it is very evident that they are distinguished from females in private life. I came at length to this conclusion, that since both by custom and public consent and long practice it has been established, that realms and principalities may descend to females by hereditary right, it did not appear to me necessary to move the question, not only because the thing would be invidious, but because in my opinion it would not be lawful to unsettle governments which are ordained by the peculiar providence of God. I had no suspicion of the book, and for a whole year was ignorant of its publication. When I was informed of it by certain parties, I sufficiently shewed my displeasure that such paradoxes should be published; but as the remedy was too late, I thought that the evil which could not now be corrected, should rather be buried in oblivion than made a matter of agitation. Inquire also of your father-in-law[46], what my reply was when he informed me of the circumstance through Beza. And Mary was still living, so that I could not be suspected of flattery. What the books contain, I cannot tell; but Knox himself will allow that my conversation with him was no other than what I have now stated. But although I was moved by the complaints of some godly men, yet, as I had not been informed in time, I did not dare to make any decided opposition, lest greater confusion should ensue. If my easiness has occasioned any offence, I think there would have been just reason to fear, lest if the subject had been brought under consideration, by reason of the thoughtless arrogance of one individual, the wretched crowd of exiles would have been driven away not only from this city, but even from almost the whole world; especially since the mischief could not now be remedied, otherwise than by applying a mitigation. I am indeed exceedingly and undeservedly grieved, in

---

[46] Sir Antony Cook. His daughter Mildred was married to Cecil.

proportion to my surprise, that the ravings of others, as if in a studied pretext, should be charged upon me, to prevent my book from being accepted. If the offered present were not acceptable to the queen, she might have rejected it by a single word, and it would have been more candid to have done so. This certainly would have been more agreeable to myself, than to be burdened with false accusations, in addition to the ignominy of a repulse. However, I shall always reverence both the most serene queen, and shall not cease, most illustrious sir, to love and respect yourself also, for your most excellent disposition and your other virtues, although I have found you less friendly to me than I had hoped, and though you say nothing about mutual good-will for the time to come. From this however, I am unwilling to draw any unfavourable conclusion. Farewell, most accomplished and esteemed sir. May the Lord evermore be present with you, guide, protect, and enrich you with his gifts. Geneva. As I am in doubt whether my former letter has reached you, I have thought right to send you a copy.[47]

[JOHN CALVIN.]'

Goodman gave quite another account of Calvin's interest in his and Knox's publications when writing to Peter Martyr five months earlier than the above letter from Calvin's pen, assuring the Italian that he had 'requested the judgement of master Calvin' before publishing his revolutionary book.[48]

Having principally given quotes from Presbyterians and Anglicans in this paper, it will be refreshing to have a noted Baptist historian give his views concerning Calvin's meddling in revolutionary politics. Quoting from a wide range of works, Stephen Brachlow comments:

---

[47] *Zurich Letters*, John Calvin to Sir William Cecil, pp. 34-36.
[48] Christopher Goodman to Peter Martyr, 20 August, 1558, *Original Letters*, Second Series, p. 771.

Despite what has recently been called Calvin's 'almost inflexible opposition to political resistance'[49] Calvin thus became, as Michael Walzer has argued, an 'inexhaustible source of sedition and rebellion' for succeeding generations of Calvinists.[50] While radical Puritans shared much of the Genevan reformer's conservative bias and the intensity of his passion for order at any price, it is likely that his acknowledgement of the validity of resistance in certain circumstances also provided a kind of ideological grammar for the political rhetoric of the more rigorous disciplinarians in Elizabethan England, as it did throughout the wider international Calvinist community.[51]

---

[49] Hopfl, *Christian Polity of John Calvin*, pp. 171-2.
[50] *The Revolution of the Saints: A Study in the Origins of Radical Politics*, New York, 1976, p. 23.
[51] *The Communion of the Saints: Radical Puritan and Separatist Ecclesiology 1570-1625*, OUP, 1988, p. 237.

Augsbourg

Chapter Eleven:
Coming to a Balanced Conclusion

The Conformity versus Nonconformity Myth
More recent writers, such as James Heron in his *A Short History of Puritanism*, are clearly mistaken in making this controversy out to be a battle between Arminians and Calvinists, Episcopalians and Presbyterians, Nonconformists and Conformists, Puritans and Anglicans. No such clear divisions were present. Both the majority in the controversy, dubbed 'Anglicans' by such as Heron and Edward Arber, and the minority, dubbed 'Puritans' were Calvinists to a man. Even the taunt of 'Episcopalian' falls flat in the case of the Frankfurt majority as they elected pastors and preachers, not bishops. They had even elected Knox! When Knox left, the church with an 'Anglican' majority, elected Nonconformist Whitehead as his successor. For these men, whether one was called 'bishop' or 'presbyter', was a matter of indifference and purely a utility question. So, too, the quite unjustified generalisation that the split was a matter of Nonconformists versus Conformists has no evidence whatsoever to stand on and is a misuse of contemporary terms. In the 16th century, the Nonconformists were a most influential part of the Church of England and embraced every function within the church from deacon to archbishop. The idea that a Nonconformist was a Non-Anglican came with the Great Rebellion. The fact is that both sides contained the entire range of churchmen from moderate Conformists to fairly radical Nonconformists. Whitehead, whom Arber

believes was the 'Anglican' ringleader and a Prayer Book man, was an Ultra-Nonconformist and certainly too Nonconformist for the like of Knox. Indeed, the most outspoken Frankfurt opposition against Knox was from the more radical Nonconformists. Wrong also is the polarisation of the terms 'Puritan' and 'Anglican'. The modern denominational tendency to make their own highly differing systems synonymous with 'Puritanism' fails completely in the light of contemporary usage. There is sadly a concerted attempt by new religious groups to define Puritanism solely in Lloyd-Jones' terms of Separatists, Presbyterians and radicals. This is to empty the term of most of its historical and all its spiritual meaning and takes the reader's attention from the great work of grace in the 16th and 17th centuries. No wonder that Hollywood invariably portrays the Puritans as being enemies of mankind! Such definitions would include the wildest, militant Arminian and anarchistic revolutionaries gathered under that umbrella term Fifth Monarchy men. It would also place such misguided souls as John Goodwin on pedestals which should rightly be reserved for true Puritans and Reformers such as Whitaker, Perkins, Hall, Usher, Featley, Crisp and Owen. As Baxter, a Puritan himself, recorded, the term was used of anyone who showed an earnest concern for religion. Who would deny that exiles Bale, Cox, Grindal, Jewel, Sandys, Becon, Lever, Sampson, Coverdale and Whitehead were Puritans? Who could possibly postulate that they were less Puritan than Knox without utterly changing the meaning of the word? Such facts, which one would imagine were indisputable, are summed up by Douglas Campbell in his well-documented two-volume work *The Puritan in Holland, England, and America*, led him to state:

> Among the people of England at large the name came finally to be applied to all those who were religious and moral, and who, either by word or life, protested against the irreligion and immorality of the time.

The author, one of the few that has sought to study Puritanism as an international movement of the Spirit, goes on to say:

Strictly speaking, as will be shown in its proper place, the name was confined to those Calvinistic members of the English Church who sought its reformation from within.[1]

Edward Arber in his 1907 Introduction to *Troubles at Frankfort*, admittedly calls the Knox party the 'Calvinists' and the Cox-Grindal-Bale party the 'Anglicans', coming down on Knox's side. Yet he is far more balanced than most commentators, arguing that the 'Anglicans', in the controversy were mostly 'noted puritans'. He also points out Knox's inconsistencies and adds, 'How Knox could write such violent books, in such dangerous times, is another mystery in his life.' He also comments 'Then, amazing as it seems to us, in men who made God's Word their sole rule in everything, these Frankfort Calvinists regarded the Public Reading of the Scriptures in Divine Service "as an irksome and unprofitable form"' and claims that the Frankfurt opposition to Knox were well able to defend themselves against Calvin's misinformed criticisms. Furthermore, it must be asked, Why make Frankfurt and Knox the source of an imagined Anglicanism versus Puritanism? Basle went through the same inner debates producing also a minority of over-zealous 'brethren of the purity' as Bale called them. These purists, as the overwhelming majority of those from all the churches in exile, realised that they had more scope to carry out their particular views within the Church of England than without.

Knox was not the hero of the day
Far from being the hero of the day, in 1554-5 Knox, who had only turned from Rome some eight years before, was not yet up to the Reforming standard of many fellow church members. These were defenders of Reformed principles in the mother tongue, irrespective of national or even international politics. Knox was still a lover of Latin forms of worship not only in 1554 but even when he returned to Scotland in 1559 to find the Reformation well under way. He even put a garbled version of the English Prayer Book into Latin! He insisted, too, on having the Scots order of worship trans-

---

[1] *The Puritan in Holland, England, and America*, p. xxvii.

lated into Latin,[2] the *Confessio Scoticana* only being replaced by
the Westminster Confession in the middle of the following century.
Knox obviously preferred Latin to any other language. He had equally
obviously difficulties with the English tongue and lacked the English Exiles' ability to preach and teach in several Continental languages. Most of the complaints such as Whitehead, Grindal and
Ridley had against Knox were that he pronounced judgement on
English texts which he had obviously misunderstood. His reforms
were more in the realms of church order, discipline and politics rather
than doctrine. In these matters, however, to argue that Knox was
more 'Reformed', more 'Puritan' or more 'Nonconformist' is to rob
the words of their spiritual and doctrinal content. It is a travesty of
history and the truth for modern authors to enhance their own denominational preferences by setting up non-existent sides. Indeed,
the Frankfurters were Nonconformist almost to a man and their
church order was simple and Biblical in comparison to the seven-
tier[3] system Knox had as his ideal, i.e. 1. Over-regional and regional
presbyteries, 2. superintendents, 3. ministers, 4. teachers, 5. elders,
6. deacons, 7. readers. Knox's method of 'electing' the Higher Clergy
was through direct appointment by the Lords and Privy Council
with the churches merely given the right to protest. Furthermore,
Knox was hardly Nonconformist or even Puritan in his love for
ceremonies and enforced unity and the direct interference of the political arm in inner-church and inter-church matters. Also, in the
matter of the liturgy, there is no trace of an anti-liturgical movement
on the Knoxian side whatsoever and the Frankfurt clash was to do
with which liturgical order was to be used and not over the use or
disuse of a liturgy. The point of issue was not Dissent against Conformity but to which prayer book one must conform. Here the Coxians
showed themselves to be, on the whole, more flexible, i.e. more tol-

---

[2] The Latin version roughly as it now stands probably dates from 1572. It is attributed to Patrick Adamson who later became Archbishop of St. Andrews and was
excommunicated by the provincial synod and his revenues confiscated so that he
ended his days living on charity.
[3] The papists had a seven-tier system whereas the Anglican Reformers held to a
three or four-tiered system.

erant, than the Knoxians. It also cannot be denied that much of Knox's often superstitious fear of using the Edwardian Prayer Book was that it bore an 'English face'. Thus as Horton Davies suggests, 'it was the principle of subscription, rather than the formulary to be subscribed'[4] that prevented Knox from remaining a minister of the Church of England. In point of fact, Knox insisted far more than such as Archbishops Parker, Grindal, Whitgift and Abbot on absolute subscription to his orders. When Knox supported the Elizabethan Reformation, it was to compliment them when he thought they had been strict against Dissenters and encourage them to become even stricter where he thought they were too lax.

This latter interest in the English situation highlights the main thrust of Knox's so-called reforms. Ninian Winzet, though a papist, complains of Knox's fussiness concerning ceremonies and externals which could not be allied to Scripture at all. Indeed, Winzet told Knox that he trampled his own Scriptural principles and doctrines in the mud. Hugh Watt, in his otherwise most sympathetic work on *John Knox in Controversy*, states that in the initial years of Knox's coming to power, his opponents were seldom chosen from the papist forces but were almost all 'on his own side of the fence'. Most of Knox's controversies were about his own preference of certain forms and ceremonies before others and thus he placed himself outside of the main spiritual thrust of the Reformation. The trouble those on Knox's side of the fence had with him was that he wished State and Church to conform to his principles alone. Knox was able to gain acceptance for his ideas of absolute state-controlled uniformity in religion in Scotland, but he was quite unable to enforce them at Frankfurt, let alone England. Any church unity, however, that is enforced by ecclesiastical tyranny, state legislation, or royal decree is bound to fail as it lacks the real unifying factor of oneness in Christ. This is where all the modern criticism levelled at the so-called Coxians is shown to be a mere back-projection of unspiritual, denominational bickering. Contemporary evidence shows that the overwhelming body of English exiles, whether of Emden, Duisburg, Frankfurt, Wesel, Strasburg, Aarau, Basle,

---

[4] *The Worship of the English Puritans*, p. 115.

Zürich or Geneva, dropped their external differences and resolved by the power of the unity Christ had given them in the gospel to proceed and progress in the work of Reformation in England. Whom God had so wonderfully drawn together, let no man put asunder.

It must be also emphasised here that Continental Reformers such as Bullinger and Calvin never agreed to Knox's views concerning his 'Christian State'.[5] Sampson, on the majority side, was as firm a denouncer of church hierarchies and papist customs as was Whittingham on the minority side. He was, however, like Grindal, very much influenced by Bucer's more moderate works. Moreover, even Whittingham censured Knox and begged him not to cause schism. Before Knox arrived, the Frankfurt church was local, free and democratic and had less formal structure than many a contemporary or later Presbyterian or Anglican order of service. Indeed, arch-Nonconformist David Whitehead sided with and led the majority because he found them more Reformed and had a better Christian spirit than the Knoxians. Whitehead protested to Calvin that the Knox faction had 'bold and wicked designs', almost scolding him for allowing himself to be influenced by their 'bare-faced manner'.[6] Whitehead also complains to Calvin of Knox's politics as 'infamous libel' couched in 'violent language'. We must further note that Knox at Frankfurt, refused to work with Bale, Fox, Jewel, Whitehead, Grindal and a host of other staunch Puritans who are now named by Knox's admirers depreciatingly 'Anglicans' because they sought a compromise with Knox rather than to follow him blindly. These men were of the purist Reformed calibre and thus can truly be called 'Puritans', though 'Reformers' is a more descriptive word. We must also remember that they were men of the deepest learning, a good many of them being trained in Divinity, others had degrees and post-graduate qualifications in literature, languages and law, and thus the argument that Knox outdid his Frankfurt opponents in academic ability cannot be justified. Admittedly, Knox's education is veiled in obscurity, biographers such as Schaff/Lee arguing that

[5] See *Knox versus Calvin*, in *John Knox and the Reformation*, Andrew Lang, p. 47, Longmans, Green & Co., 1905.
[6] David Whitehead and Others to John Calvin, 20 September, 1555.

he never even took a degree. It is known that he began to learn Greek in middle life and Hebrew even later. He could thus hardly compete with leading university men such as Cox and Bale and great expositors and theologians such as Grindal and Jewel. Whittingham, however, had unquestionably high academic qualifications. Yet one could not call him a pioneer of the English Reformation as he was absent from England from the reign of Henry onwards and had led a cosmopolitan life of study at the Continental universities and French-speaking Reformed circles. He, as the Coxians, felt more at home with the order of service he was used to, and thus pressed for a modified French form as eager as Cox pressed for a modified English form.[7] Several of the Frankfurt exiles such as Bale were in Christ and preaching the gospel decades before Knox.[8] Furthermore, Anti-Anglican Heron calls Knox's English church at Geneva which he led for a brief period after leaving Frankfurt, 'The First Puritan Congregation'.

It was not, however, Calvin's Geneva that immediately succeeded Frankfurt but Bucer's Strasburg. This was to a great extent because of Peter Martyr's teaching there. Due to Lutheran opposition, Martyr moved to Zürich and Geneva and many English exiles followed him. So, too, many moved to Switzerland to be under Bullinger's ministry. Perhaps the biggest attraction in Switzerland was the free press. The Lutherans had clamped down on British publications because of their alleged affinity to Zwingli, especially regarding the Lord's Supper. Christopher Froschauer at Zürich and Osorinus at Basle welcomed British works. The press at Geneva was rather more politically-minded and issued many a British revolutionary pamphlet, including Knox's calls to revolution and terrorism but this was offset by the great work of the Genevan Bible, which had drawn a number of British exiles to the Swiss city to work on it, Whittingham and Coverdale being two of the best known translators. It was

---

[7] See *The Life and Death of Master William Whittingham, Dean of Durham, who departed this life, Anno Domino 1579, June 10: Written by a Student of the Temple, about 1603*, included in the 1907 edition of *Troubles at Frankfort*.

[8] Schaff/Lee say that Knox first publicly professed the Reformed faith at forty. Dates for Knox's birth vary from 1505-1515, thus exact dating is impossible.

Grindal, however, who had the Genevan Bible introduced into England for use in the Anglican Church where it went through many editions bound up with the Book of Common Prayer. This alone shows that the work of the Genevan exiles was not in the direction of Knox who would never have linked the Word of God with the English Prayer Book in such a way. It is of note here that almost all the exiles who were ministers or wished to enter the ministry, whether they were in Geneva, Zürich or Basle, left for England in 1558-9 to take up Anglican orders. Thus obviously Heron's 'Puritans' were, or became, Anglican almost to a man and they were far more interested in preaching and teaching than giving up that calling because of the particular 'uniform' of the day. At this time, the most debated point amongst the anti-clerical garb lobby was the wearing of a four-cornered hat, which gradually fell out of use almost on its own accord. Indeed, the more a minority protested against hats etc. the more the Queen and the majority fought for the freedom of retaining them. If the so-called left wing had accepted that they were indifferent matters and certainly not central themes of the ministry, the ecclesiastical fashions then worn would most probably have disappeared in a short time. Cox's advice to get London doctrinally and experimentally reformed first, and then the rest of the country would follow and then tackle secondary issues was accepted by the vast bulk of the so-called Puritans.

That this was the most practical solution is shown by the fact that most of the exiles, whether from Frankfurt, Emden, Strasburg, Geneva, Zürich or Basle, became leading clergy and, throughout their teaching and preaching ministry were most lenient in matters of dress-conformity and even those who made a great issue against caps and surplices such as Sampson, Whittingham, Lever and Humphrey were given influential posts and allowed to preach in strategically very important points such as at St Paul's Cross. When they did get into bother for their views, there was always a Grindal, Jewel or Fox to help them out. Yet such bitter critics of the English Reformation as Thomas McCrie can write that because of the English Reformers unwillingness to follow Knox 'I am not surprised at the defeat of every subsequent attempt to advance the Reformation in England.'[9] Here we have the old problem that Whitefield had with the Erskines. The Anglican was willing to fellowship with all who loved the Lord so that he could win some for Christ. The Marrow Men, mighty preachers themselves as no one can doubt, nevertheless put their denominational differences before such denomination-less seeking out the lost and even refused to acknowledge the success in Christ other soul-winners had. Thus McCrie, writes off the entire Reforming work of what was perhaps the Golden Age (so Toplady) of the English church, because it was not conducted under Knoxian formalism.

Sadly, many preachers in the succeeding Episcopalian-Presbyterian controversies preached down externals more than they preached up the gospel and their external religion came to be regarded as 'Reformed' by a number of ordinary folk. This can be compared with the reputed 'reformed' antics of Dean William Turner who trained his dog to jump up and pull the caps off the heads of conforming ministers. However, to describe such action as 'Puritan' and that of the faithful Anglicans 'popish' as later Dissenters have done, is to forget what true reformation of religion is all about. We moderns also tend to forget that much of the arguments of the Dissenters, especially the later Presbyterian-minded critics within the Church of England, against vestments were merely against a particular form. They condemned the Anglican gowns as Aaronic and therefore Jewish, but they adorned themselves in the garb of Turkish merchants in their efforts to introduce a new fashion in churchwear. Here we have the story of the mote and the beam in all its force! Several Baptist ministers known to this writer, have fiercely condemned the Church of England's pre-Revolution ministry outright because her ministers preached in gowns,[10] yet the members of their choirs, who include paid professionals, perform their 'Revivals', 'Concerts', 'Musicals' and Church service 'Intervals' in colourful popish robes singing graduals as if they were an assembly of pontifical priests. We need not look to modern times for such 'Puri-

---

[9] *Life of John Knox*, p. 54.
[10] They did not know that very many of them indeed did not.

tan' parades of splendour. When Cambridge was at its Puritan height
with such luminaries as Samuel Ward and John Preston at its head,
James I visited the university to find the scholars lining the streets
dressed in dandified versions of the Puritan round hat, with short
gowns of diverse bright colours and hanging sleeves, revealing multi-
coloured stockings beneath. There is nothing like a break with tradition to boost the fashion market![11]

True Puritanism's cradle, nursery and school was in the Church of England

It must also be remembered that throughout the all too short life of
the pre-Rebellion Reformed Church of England, the majority of
Continental Reformers were certainly closer to their Anglican brethren than to the Precisian rebels in their ranks.[12] Thus if the word
'Puritanism' has any positive meaning at all, and is to be viewed as
an expression of purity of life and gospel teaching, then Patrick
Collinson is thoroughly justified in saying, 'Puritanism was to take
root within the established church and within its beneficed ministry,
not to any significant extent outside of it.'[13]

Whilst remembering this truth, it is also worth noting that the
Anglican Nonconformists would have had a far harder fate if they
had made their protests in the stiffer kind of uniformity which Scottish Presbyterianism demanded and which was thrust on the English
for a short time at the Usurpation.[14] Very quickly, Anglicanism was
outlawed and Dissent from the new Presbyterian establishment became more popular than it ever was under the former national church.
The dwindling number of Presbyterians were compelled to eat humble pie and beg the 'Supreme Governor' of a new Church of England to come and rule them. What was broken has sadly never been
put together again.

---

[11] See *Worthy Dr. Fuller*, p. 27.
[12] See, for instance, John Abel's letter to Bullinger, 6 June, 1566, *Zürich Letters*,
Second Series, p. 117 ff..
[13] *The Elizabethan Puritan Movement*, p. 59.
[14] See, for instance, Kenneth Dix's assessment of the Presbyterian Puritans in
Faith or Force.

However, what modern Reformed men appear incapable of doing, our 16th century Fathers in Israel succeeded in doing. We must go back to them for examples of unity and how brothers can walk together because they are agreed on 'the one thing needed'. The end of the story concerning the troubles at Frankfurt is an end which gives us all cause for optimism in seeking unity amongst the brethren. After the Frankfurt church had sent several letters to Geneva for the purpose of reconciliation, on 15 December, 1558, the Genevans wrote to all the other churches which they felt that they had wronged or grieved in any way. It is a beautiful study in reconciliation:

Geneva's Eirenicon to the exiled churches, 1558

AFTER THAT WE heard, dearly Beloved! of the joyful tidings of GOD's favour and grace restored unto us, by the preferment of the most virtuous and gracious Queen ELIZABETH; we lifted up our hearts and voices to our heavenly Father: who hath, not only by his due Providence nourished us in our banishment, preserved us and as it were carried us in his wings; but also heard our prayers, granted our requests, pitied our country, and restored his Word. So that the greatness of this marvellous benefit overcometh our judgements and thoughts, how to be able worthily to receive it, and to give thanks for the Same.

And when we had, with great comfort, weighed the matter, to the intent that we might, at the least, shew ourselves mindful of this most wonderful and undeserved grace; we thought, among other things, how we might best serve to GOD's glory in this work and vocation of furthering the Gospel of our Saviour JESUS CHRIST.

And because [*in Order that*] all impediments and cavillations of adversaries might be removed; it seemed good to have your godly counsel and brotherly conference herein, which we desire to learn by this bearer, our loving brother KETHE: that we might all join hearts and hands together in this great work; wherein, no doubt, we shall find many adversaries and stays [hindrances]. Yet if we (whose sufferance and persecutions are certain signs of our Sound doctrine) hold fast together, it is most certain that the enemies shall have less Power; offences shall sooner be taken away; and Religion best proceed and flourish.

For what can the Papist wish more than that we should dissent one from another; and, instead of Preaching JESUS CHRIST and profitable doctrine, to contend one against another, either for superfluous Ceremonies, or other like trifles; from the which, GOD, of his mercy, hath delivered us.

Therefore, dear Brethren! we beseech you (as we doubt not but your godly judgements will think it so best) that whatsoever offence hath been, heretofore, either taken or given; it may so cease and be forgotten that hereafter GOD lay it not to our charges, if thereby his blessed Word should be anything hindered.

And as we, for our Parts, freely remit all offences, and most entirely embrace you, our dear Brethren! so we be-seech you in the Lord that unfeignedly you will do the like on our behalf: whereof albeit we assure ourselves as both by good experience we have proved, and also have received by your Letters: yet (to cut off all occasions from Papists and other cavillers) we thought it best to renew the Same amity, and to confirm it by these Letters.

Most earnestly desiring you, that we may together reach and banishment, and by GOD's merciful Providence seen in the best Reformed Churches, That (considering our neg-ligence in times past; and GOD's punishment for the Same) we may, with zeal and diligence, endeavour to recompense it: that GOD, in all our doings, may be glorified; our con-sciences discharged; and the members of JESUS CHRIST relieved and comforted. The which thing the Lord GOD (who hath mercifully visited and restored us) grant and per-form. To whom be all honour, praise, and glory, for ever and ever.

Your loving friends,
and in the name of the whole Church,

CHRISTOPHER GOODMAN
WILLIAM WILLIAMS   JOHN POULLAIN
MILES COVERDALE   ANTHONY GILBY
WILLIAM BEVOYES   JOHN KNOX
FRANCIS WITHERS   JOHN BODLIEGH
WILLIAM WHITTINGHAM   WILLIAM FULLER

The Answer returned from Frankfurt, by W. Kethe
The Frankfurt congregation was not slow to reply and they too, though showing some caution regarding the definition of 'ceremonies' replied in the same brotherly spirit:

> The Grace of GOD and the assistance of the HOLY GHOST lighten and strengthen you, to the understanding and constant retaining of his Truth, to the furtherance of his honour and glory, and to the edifying and maintenance of his Church in CHRIST JESU our Lord.

> DEARLY BELOVED! as your Letters were most welcome unto us, both for that ye rejoice at the preferment of our godly Queen; and also that ye study how to promote the glory of GOD: so are we right sorry that they came not afore the departure of such as ye seek a charitable reconciliation withal. For where as ye require that all such offences as have been given and taken between you and us may be forgotten hereafter: there be not here past four left which were then present when ye dwelt here (in 1554-1555); and not one of the learned sort, saving Master BEESLEY. Yet we doubt not but, as they promised in their former Letters, to forget all displeasures afore conceived; so they will perform the same, and esteem you as their brethren.

As for our Parts, as we have had no contention with you at all afore time; so we purpose not, as we trust there shall be no cause, to enter into contention with you hereafter. For Ceremonies to contend (where it shall lie neither in your hands or ours to appoint what they shall be; but in such men's wisdoms as shall be appointed to the devising of the same, and which shall be received by [the] common consent of the Parliament), it shall be to small purpose. But we trust that both true Religion shall be restored; and that we shall not be burdened with unprofitable Ceremonies. And therefore, as we purpose to submit ourselves to such Orders as shall be established by Authority, being not of themselves wicked; so we would wish you willingly to do the same.

For where as all the Reformed Churches differ among themselves in divers Ceremonies, and yet agree in the unity of Doctrine; we see no inconvenience, if we use some Ceremonies diverse from them, so that we agree in the chief points of our Religion. Notwithstanding, if any shall be intruded that shall be offensive; we, upon just conference and deliberation upon the same, at our meeting with you in England, which we trust by GOD's grace will be shortly, will brotherly join with you to be suitors for the reformation and abolishing of the same.

In the mean season, let us, with one heart and mind, call to the Almighty GOD, that of his infinite mercy he will finish and establish that work that he hath begun in our country; and that we may all lovingly consent together in the earnest setting forth of his Truth that GOD may be known and exalted, and his Church perfectly builded up, through CHRIST our Lord.

From Frankfort, this 3rd of January 1559.

Your loving friends,
in the name of the rest of the Church,

JAMES PILKINGTON	JOHN BROWNE
RICHARD BEESLEY	JOHN MULLINGS
HENRY KNOLL[Y]S	JOHN GRAY
HENRY CAROWE[15]	FRANCIS WILFORD
CHRISTOPHER BRICKBATE	
EDMUND ISAAC	ALEXANDER NOWELL

As those brethren remaining at Frankfurt or later joining that church have been branded by later writers as being as near as one can get to Roman Catholicism and, indeed, criminality, it is necessary that we look briefly at these signatories so that false accusations may be dismissed. Of the signatories James Pilkington made a sure place for himself in English history by his early clash with Queen Elizabeth who wished to rob the churches of income otherwise used for the maintenance of the parochial ministry. After rejecting an offer of Winchester, which was then given to Robert Horn, Pilkington became Bishop of Durham, one of eight leading Puritans to be given bishoprics in the early part of Elizabeth's reign. Pilkington remained closely associated with his Frankfurt and Genevan fellow exiles and was one of the relatively many who had left Geneva for Frankfurt, thus exposing the myth that the exodus of Puritans was all the other way. Pilkington never regarded himself as anything 'Lordy' in his bishopric, always arguing that 'God's commission and commandment is like and indifferent to all, priest, bishop, archbishop, prelate, by what name soever he be called.'[16] Wherever we find Pilkington, he is striving to further the Reformation in England and maintaining a sound witness.

John Mullings (or Mullins), became archdeacon of London, and was one of the twenty clergymen, along with Humphrey, Sampson, Whittingham, Lever, Nowell, Cole, Coverdale and Fox who on 20 March, 1565 appealed to the Ecclesiastical Commissioners for leniency regarding Nonconformity. Here, too, we see that the sup-

---

[15] I have not been able to find information regarding this person.
[16] See Collinson's *The Elizabethan Puritan Movement*, p. 103.

posed permanent gulf between the 'Anglicans' and 'Puritans' at Frankfurt is but a myth as these brethren stood and campaigned together throughout their remaining lives though they had stood on different sides regarding their relationship to John Knox. Mullings deplored the low standard of education prevalent amongst the clergy and held half-yearly seminaries of four or five days duration in which he taught the clergy the fundamentals of their faith and gave them instruction in how to carry out their pastoral duties.

Edward Isaac of Patricksbourn, Kent was certainly no Knoxian as he and Parry were instrumental in having Knox leave Frankfurt. Here, however, Prof. Arber shows real sympathy with Isaac. After Knox's 'sermon' in which he denounced the moderate Prayer Book men for sins they were never guilty of, Isaac visited the Scotsman to ask him to stop exaggerating in such a way and regard the Prayer Book with more balanced criticism. Knox who formerly, according to his own confession, had respected the Prayer Book, now told Isaac that he wished his name to perish rather than to show such moderation. He then accused Isaac of plotting to put him in prison, which again, as the facts are there for all to read, was a nice bit of exaggeration. Knox added, 'The which dart the Devil doth ever shoot, by the craft of the Priests, against true Preachers!' This 'dart' being, Knox explains, the fact that his enemies could not reprove him for his doctrine or life so they must use subterfuge.[17] Knox was always blunt if not always modest. He goes on to relate how idolaters 'by the express command of God' ought to be put to death. Initially, the only 'punishment' Knox received was to be advised by the Senate via his closest friends not to preach. It was only after Knox and Whittingham continued to be offensive that the magistrates requested Williams and Whittingham to ask Knox to leave the city. One must force back a smile when one reads Knox's reaction here, 'I went to the Church the next day; not thinking my company would have offended any!'[18] Isaac, however, was on good terms with the French and Flemish brethren and also with the Sen-

---

[17] Knox's Account of His Banishment, *The Troubles at Frankfort*, pp. 66-67.
[18] Ibid, p. 68.

ate and he was supported by them in the later controversy over the order of discipline. Isaac objected to a plurality of pastors in the church but claimed that he would not make an issue of it as there was no clear Biblical guidance on the subject. Not all the brethren agreed with him. In September, 1557, Isaac with Horn, Chambers, Binks, Brickbek and Escot laid down their offices and a new pastor, preachers, elders and deacons were elected. It is interesting to note that the Senate did not apply to any of the Knoxians to arbitrate in the ensuing controversies at Frankfurt but they wrote to Cox, Sandys and Bertie (or Bartue) and asked them to return to Frankfurt and referee the debates. In the ensuing peace, Isaac once again became a 'Senior'. Edward Isaac showed great stubbornness at times but he certainly showed no High Church traits and managed to remain in office, with tiny ups and downs, until the reconciliation with Geneva and the other churches was effected. There is no reason to doubt that he stood four-square in true Puritan doctrine and way of life.

John Browne, whom Collinson calls a Neo-Calvinist, became chaplain to the Dowager Duchess of Suffolk. The Duchess, otherwise known as Catherine Bertie, went into exile with her husband Richard Bertie and served the English exiles in Holland, Germany and Poland, assisting those in particular who were in financial need. Throughout this time and later under Elizabeth, they remained very close to Miles Coverdale. Browne was a true Puritan but criticised severely the influence of the Precisians in his neighbourhood who split four or five local churches down the middle because of their bickerings over externals. Sadly Browne had his enemies and forged letters alleged from his and Cartwright's pens were placed before Archbishop Parker by a ruffian named Humphrey Needham in an effort to discredit them. The scoundrel was put in the Tower and Parker insisted that the wronged Puritans received compensation.

Three members of the influential Knollys (or Knolles) family joined the brethren at Frankfurt, these were Sir Francis, related through his wife to Queen Elizabeth, Thomas and Henry Knollys. They appear to have been still in their youth as the Earl of Bedford refers to Francis as 'a young man' in 1561 when he wrote to Rudolph

Gualter.[19] These brethren were not clergymen but politicians and statesmen, yet they supported the Reformation with all their combined powers and usually sided with the more Nonconformist elements. Francis became Vice-Chamberlain, Captain of the Guard, the Queen's Treasurer and a member of the Privy Council. Other letters to Gualter from various Englishmen praise Knollys' active faith and witness. Again, Knollys puts to flight the idea that the Frankfurt brethren were and remained High Churchmen and lovers of 'abundance of ceremonies'. Knollys used all his personal connections and friendship with the Queen to bring in further reforms and is thus termed by W. H. Frere 'a typical Nonconformist' and of a 'Presbyterian mind'.[20] The lesser-known Henry also entered the Queen's service becoming her agent in Germany in religious matters with a special commission to unite the Protestant countries against any possible Roman Catholic threat. Henry Knollys was highly respected by Zanchius who dedicated his treatise on the Lord's Supper to the English statesman. Knollys, now Sir Henry, became sponsor to Zanchius' daughter and a most friendly letter from Zanchius to Knollys is preserved in the *Zürich Letters*.[21] Knollys was one of the committee of eleven who strove to reconcile the two parties at Frankfurt in September, 1557.

Francis and Thomas Wilford joined the Frankfurt church and their kinsman John in 1557. The New Discipline was then under review and the Wilfords all backed Whitehead and the majority in accepting the new order. Francis with Knollys, Sandys, Browne, Turner and seven others drew up *The Form of Reconciliation* so that peace might reign between Horn and Chambers and the church majority. Sadly the move failed and the two men left for Geneva. Isaac, who had taken a critical stance with Horn and Chambers, remained popular with all the brethren and carried out his duties as before.

---

[19] *Zürich Letters*, Parker Society, p. 54. Though other sources say that Henry was Francis' son.
[20] *A History of the English Church in the Reigns of Elizabeth and James I*, pp. 226, 231, 276, 277, 405.
[21] Pp. 112-114.

Alexander Nowell was one of the greatest Puritans in the history of the English Reformation though he was totally without ambition and refused all offers of preferment, such as Coventry and Lichfield, believing he could work more effectively for the gospel as an ordinary dean. In this he stood four-square with his most gifted fellow exiles Humphrey, Cole, Sampson and Whittingham. The author of *Troubles at Frankfort* shows Nowell as a peacemaker and spokesman for the majority party in their efforts to debate in brotherly harmony. In church order, Nowell always came down on the side of those who saw the danger, manifested in the pope, of a single church leader and pleaded for a plurality of equal church officers, though with different functions. Here he differed from many Anglicans who taught that Scripture clearly teaches a limited hierarchy of utility as seen in the Twelve and Seventy. Once back in England, Nowell used his good reputation to make sure that sound gospel men received parishes.[22] The dean strove to have kneeling abolished as also 'curious' singing and organ playing, the sign of the cross in baptism, vestments and observance of saints' days. Baptism, he argued, may be performed by ministers only. In other words, Nowell's ideas of church order were very similar to Knox's but Nowell did not make a major issue of them as if they were soteriological doctrine. Nowell has the interesting reputation of being the only minister to be shouted down at during his sermon by Queen Elizabeth who found his preaching touched her too personally. Nowell was one of the men who used all his possible influence to have his friend Grindal made Archbishop of Canterbury. Nowell's greatest contribution to the history of the Reformation is no doubt his famous *Catechism or First Instruction and Learning of Christian Religion*, first published in 1571. The work was obviously built on and a continuation of that started by Bishop Ponet in the reign of Edward VI. Ponet, however, had died in exile and Nowell was his worthy successor in the work. Nowell specifically edited and extended the work for school use and to present a summary of Reformed doctrine. It is a fine testimony to the spiritual health of both Church and State in England that the work was

---

[22] Collinson calls the ministers whom Nowell supported 'the more radical protestants'.

accepted unanimously by both Archbishops, Convocation and Parliament. Sadly the Precisians under Cartwright protested at the use of the catechism because it proscribed that ministers should also be catechised, which Cartwright thought beneath his dignity. Whitgift told him, 'That catechism which you in derision quote in the margin is a book fit for you to learn also. And I know no man so well learned, but it may become him to read and learn that learned and necessary book.'[23] Happily the catechism was well received by such as Twisse and Joseph Mead and served as a guide in the setting up of the Westminster Confession. This was only to be expected as Nowell incorporated much of Calvin's work into his catechism. In spite of his Nonconformity, Nowell was a staunch supporter of the Reformed Church of England, to which his apologetic works against Harding and Dorman testify.

Richard Beesley and John Gray were founder members of the Frankfurt church and remained there until the exiles returned to England in 1558-9. The name of Christopher Brickbate (or Brikbeke/Brikbek) occurs often in the compilation of documents under the title *Troubles at Frankfort*. Brickbate, who appears to have been an elder, was appealed to in order to help solve the differences between Robert Horn and Thomas Ashley in 1557. Like Beesley and Gray, Brickbate does not appear to have taken any leading part in the Elizabeth Settlement but as names varied enormously in their spelling in those days, it is difficult to trace the subsequent histories of many of the British exiles. Often, too, the exiles took on pseudonyms to avoid government spies.

In commenting on this letter, Prof. Arber says:

The answer to this (the letter from Geneva), of the Frankfort Anglican Church was very sensible. That the reform of Ceremonies at home (in England) was a matter for Parliament: and not for them.

And then they hit the weak point in the Puritan argument:

[23] See *The Fathers of the English Church*, Vol. VIII, pp. 3-6. The full catechism is included in this volume.

For where as all the Reformed Churches differ among themselves in diverse Ceremonies, and yet agree in the unity of Doctrine; we see no inconvenience, if we use some Ceremonies diverse from them, so that we agree in the chief points of our Religion.

The Puritans, in their outcry against Ceremonies, forgot that they had them themselves.[24]

Here however, the weakness in Prof. Arber's argument throughout his editorial comments becomes most clear. He argues that with the advent of March 26, 1555 when the Senate consented to giving the exiles a free hand with their own order, 'the Calvinistic Church there may be regarded as destroyed.'[25] From then on, he speaks of the Frankfurt church as 'Anglican' and the Genevan church as 'Calvinist' or 'Puritan'. As Arber obviously believed that both the Frankfurt and Genevan churches had the same faith and doctrine, one can only conclude that his definitions of a 'Calvinist' or 'Puritan' is one who is against a moderate use of the Prayer Book. Such a definition, however, has no basis whatsoever in real life Calvinism and Puritanism which refers to the Christian's spiritual life and testimony and his calling within the Great Commission. But even this strange definition of 'Calvinist', 'Puritan', and 'Anglican' does not apply in the least to the life of the two churches as there was a continuous movement of exiles from Geneva to Frankfurt and back and the brethren, particularly after 1556, were happy to fellowship and worship under the various orders which never differed anywhere near as much as Knox had foretold. For instance, the Polish Reformer à Lasko (Jan Laski) who was very much a Nonconformist, joined the Frankfurt church *after* Knox had left.[26] Furthermore, these brethren had also worshipped in Poland, France, Denmark, Holland

---

[24] *The Troubles at Frankfort*, p. xxiv.
[25] Ibid, p. xv.
[26] Laski stayed at Frankfurt after being forced to leave Denmark and Holland. He became dangerously ill there and on his recovery proceeded back to Poland.

and even Italy with brethren of most varied orders which had never compromised their standing as Calvinists and Puritans.

Knox however, held so rigidly to his ceremonies down to their finest detail that he proscribed the death penalty for those who disagreed with him. It is also odd to note in Arber's comments, that whenever the so-called 'Anglicans' diverted from the so-called 'Calvinists' whether in their insistence on oral responses, the public reading of the word or in their few ceremonies, Arber argues that the validity of their views needed no argument as they were self-evident.[27] Indeed, he clearly states that the 'Anglicans' were well able to hold their own against Calvin's criticisms.[28] Finally, Arber argues that it was not the 'new Anglican Church as a whole' (i.e. in Frankfurt) who moved for Knox's dismissal but 'entirely the act' of two individuals.

So one must surely ask, why then, does Arber take such a biased stand for Knox against his brethren of the Reformation? This question is all the more necessary as Arber announces in his *Introduction* that his policy is 'absolute fair play for everyone',[29] yet his subsequent denigration of the Frankfurt 'Anglicans' as anti-Calvinists, Conformists and anti-Puritan and his claim that 'Puritans' are anti-Anglican, Nonconformist and stickers for ceremonies and liturgies, cannot be validated by the selected documents he edits. Perhaps mere personal preference plays the major role in such matters and not academic objectivity, which is all the more reason why balanced mutual understanding and tolerance should reign.

Thomas Lever's letter of reconciliation

As Thomas Lever had been one of the major instruments of reconciliation for the scattered brethren and had helped keep the churches of the exiles in touch with one another, it will be profitable to see how Lever fared after Knox left Frankfurt. Lever must have been most upset to have reaped Knox's wrath as he did, which might help

---

[27] See, for instance, ibid, p. xiv, §s 5 and 9.
[28] Ibid, p. xiv.
[29] Ibid, p. xxvii.

to explain why he kept up an intensive correspondence with Geneva and his former brethren at Frankfurt. It appears that Lever spent some brief time at Wesel but the church there, now weakened because of the absence of Coverdale and the Berties and the Frankfurt contingent, could not stand up to Lutheran opposition and eventually the magistrates forbade the remnant church to celebrate the ordinances. Lever thus travelled to Berne to obtain permission from the Bernese lords to allow the Wesel brethren to set up a church there. On gaining such permission, Lever was suddenly called back to Wesel. The brethren informed him that they had elected him by common vote as their pastor and they were calling him to return to shepherd the flock and to petition the authorities for permission to celebrate the Lord's Supper and baptism. By this time (January, 1556) Lever was at Geneva where he wished to do some research and hear the great Swiss preachers. Nevertheless, he dashed off to Wesel but this was the start of a 'long and wearisome tossing about'[30] due to strong Lutheran opposition, so that in August, 1557, those of the Wesel church who did not move to Frankfurt, followed Lever to Switzerland staying first at Basle. With Bullinger's help, Lever found a limited number of lodgings and work in the wool trade at German speaking Aarau and French speaking Vevey and a number of the brethren settled there, taking over seven houses, in order to prepare a work for others to join as premises and work became available. Lever stayed in Aarau to shepherd the flock, writing:

> And thus we English, driven from our country by popery, and from Wesel by Lutheranism, are now, most of us, by our mutual wishes, counsels, and assistance, tending to one spot, where it is still permitted us freely, sincerely, and openly to acknowledge and worship Christ.[31]

At Aarau, Lever was joined by Horn and Chambers, formerly of Frankfurt, for a time, but they proceeded to Geneva as the old grudge (according to *Troubles at Frankfort*) 'had been clean forgotten'.

---

[30] *Original Letters*, Vol. I., p. 166.
[31] Letter to Rudolph Gualter, dated Aarau, August 11, 1557.

Here we may note that according to Prof. Arber, the money which was given to Geneva by Horn and Chambers as a token that the 'old grudge had being clean forgotten', had been collected at Frankfurt.[32] Indeed, Arber even hints that the fifteen or so who departed for Geneva from Frankfurt in 1555, took the church kitty with them.[33]

When Lever received the letter of reconciliation from Geneva, he was overjoyed and replied at once in the most heartfelt tones, thankful to God that past troubles were over and unity was now a reality. He sent Kethe off with the following rousing words:

> The Father of mercies and GOD of all consolation confirm, increase, and continue you always in the love of his son JESUS CHRIST our Lord.
>
> PRAISED BE GOD, through our Lord JESUS CHRIST, which pulled down MARY that did persecute, and hath set up the godly Lady ELIZABETH, Queen of England, to restore and maintain there the pure preaching of his Word.
>
> And for that it hath pleased GOD to move your good hearts, for the furtherance of the same, with godly zeal and charitable desire, by your Letters, to shew unto us your advice and purpose; and also to require ours to be returned and sent to you, by our brother KETHE. We do, with most hearty thanks, unfeignedly afore GOD, certify you, That to your counsel and conference with us, we do consent willingly concerning your most godly request: for that we acknowledge that the same shall be to the advancement of his glory and quietness of his Church.
>
> Also we desire you that, as oft as we may find hereafter any occasion to consult and confer, by word or writing, that then both you and we so take and seek the same as may be most to our unity in minds, and diligence to do good in the Lord's work.

---

[32] *The Troubles at Frankfort*, pp. xxi, 222.
[33] Or how are we otherwise to take his statement on p. xvi that the 'Calvinist migration' caused the Frankfurt church to be low in funds?

And, farthermore, for the forgetting and putting away all occasions of offences; we do likewise consent unto your good ensample and request.

And so, finally, for the Preaching and Professing of sincere Doctrine, so as we have seen and learned [it] in the best Reformed Churches, we do gladly hear your advice to be so agreeable to our purpose, that we beseech you to pray with us, that you and all we together that be faithful, may continue, proceed, and prosper, in godly zeal, charitable concord, and earnest diligence to honour and serve GOD; and to comfort and edify his Elect [at] all times and in every place, and especially now in England.

O, Lord! not unto us; but unto thy name be honour and praise for ever!

From Aarau, this 16th day of January 1559.

Your loving friends of the Ministry, in the name, and by the consent, of the whole Church,

THOMAS LEVER RICHARD LANGHORNE
THOMAS TURPIN ROBERT POWNALL

The Return to England

Now that Mary the Bloody, that gruesome symbol of the Scarlet Woman, fell with all her Babylon around her, the English exiles began their pilgrimage to the new Zion which they were called to build on the ashes of the martyrs. Those who were too poor to make the journey were helped on their way by their more wealthy brethren. Few of them found it a great struggle to reach the shores of a country crying out for Reformation and the gospel's healing powers to restore peace, prosperity and liberty in a once suppressed land. Few now felt any inclination to stay on the Continent but those who did such as Edwin Sandys were soon persuaded by such as Edmund Grindal to move forwards in order to help build the New Jerusalem on England's green and pleasant land. Both were to become arch-

bishops and lay great corner-stones for Zion. A few did remain on
the Continent but even they had the final triumph of the gospel in
England in view. Coverdale, Goodman, Sampson, Cole, Gilby and
Whittingham[34] stayed behind to finish off their translation of the
Bible into English. It is a fitting close to this vindication of the English Reformers that these great men, now earnestly translating the
Bible together, had been on opposite sides in the troubles at Frankfurt. Now their call to 'rightly divide the word of God' had rescued
them from all petty, human quarrels. May we pray for the day when
once again Anglicans, Presbyterians and Dissenters will put Church
before denomination and the gospel before statutes and constitutions and unite their energies in rightly dividing the word of God and
building once again the much neglected work of Zion in unison and
joint worship of their Saviour.

But what was Knox doing at this momentous time? He was busy
writing his defence of Old Testament case law in *The Appellation
of John Knox from the cruel and most injust sentence pronounced
against him by the false bishops and clergy of Scotland* and looking for a publisher for his *The First Blast of the Trumpet Against
the Monstruous Regiment of Women*. He had been called back to
Scotland by the lords who had asked him to set about reforming
Scotland. Knox cannot have been too pleased. He was commissioned to do this by the secular authorities on the basis of the Edwardian Book of Common Prayer!

Once the Reformers were back in England, they were at first
ignored as the popish powers were still in authority.[35] Gradually,
mostly through itinerant preaching and using the age-old facilities
of St Paul's Cross which speedily became open to them, and public
disputing led by Jewel, they again preached the Reformation of
religion leading to the New Birth in Christ and the setting up of a
gospel church. Spear-heading this strategy were Lever, Jewel and
Cox who, in their various ways pressed on Elizabeth the need for
her example to the people. They very easily persuaded the new
Queen to drop the title of Supreme Head of the Church which Henry

---

[34] The Life of Dean Whittingham in *Troubles at Frankfort*, pp. 3-4.
[35] See Chapters VII and X in Strype's *History of the Reformation*.

had used and also Mary for a period of time. Gradually, the church was reformed again and all the popish prelates save one left the restored church. No less than 17 out of the 25 bishoprics were gradually filled by former exiles. Instead of burning the outgoing papists to ashes as Mary had burned the Reforming bishops, Elizabeth, backed by the Reformers, allowed the former papist priests to live in peace and a number of them even in affluence. This great strength shown by the Reforming party, was interpreted as a sign of weakness by the Precisians who had persuaded themselves that Mary's policy was correct – she had only chosen the wrong people to burn.

Knox decided to give tit for tat to the papists and was far harder on them than his English counterparts. Schoolmaster Ninian Winzet, who was as close to a Protestant as one can perhaps get and remain a papist, challenged Knox time after time to a public disputation as to the Scriptural nature of his position. Knox refused to have his doctrines openly challenged. Thus Winzet published a pamphlet called *The Last Blast of the Trumpet of God's Word against the Usurped Authority of John Knox and his Calvinistic Brethren Intruded Preachers*. When Knox heard of this he commanded the Edinburgh Town Council to seize and destroy the manuscript which was already at the printer's. Then Knox had Winzet dismissed and exiled. If Winzet had been allowed to argue according to God's Word, Knox might have gained a friend within the Reformation rather than an enemy outside of it. Winzet fled to Antwerp and quickly published his *The Book of the Four-score and Three Questions Touching Doctrine, Order, and Manners, Propounded to the Preachers of the Protestants in Scotland*. Winzet was fond of pulling Knox's leg for giving himself English airs and using Latin when the common people were in need of the mother tongue which Knox appeared to have forgotten. Winzet thus teased Knox with the words. 'If you, in zeal for novelty, have forgotten our old plain Scots which your mother taught you in times past, I shall write you my mind in Latin, for I am not acquainted with your Southron.'[36] As Knox brought out works in Latin, Winzet published in Broad Scots, though

---

[36] See Watt, p. 30.

he did write in Latin against the Latin works of Buchanan and other Scots Reformers who apparently could not speak their mother tongue.

It was then that Knox[37] interfered radically in the affairs of the new monarchy and restored Church of England, damning both in most far-fetched and arrogant terms. Not knowing of what spirit Elizabeth was and ignoring the fact that she had been brought up by Genevan tutors and was in close correspondence with the Continental Reformers besides most open to the wishes of the exiles and also showing a grave lack of respect for English law, Knox gave her an ultimatum. She should publicly proclaim that the laws of England were null and void regarding female inheritance and rights of women as, so Knox argued, by God's law women could take on no such inheritance and had no such rights. Instead, she must tell her nation that she ruled purely as the single exception in the whole world of a woman appointed particularly by God for the office. If she ever stopped serving God as His single exception and claimed powers that were given her by English law, God would punish her. Elizabeth's reign would be short and her doom long. 'Thus,' says Strype, 'he took upon him to play the Prophet, to uphold his own Conceit.'[38] This outburst caused Knox much trouble in Scotland as he had to own allegiance to Mary of Guise and Mary Stuart, whom he could not pronounce 'unique exceptions' because he had pronounced Elizabeth the only possible such. Soon Knox was eating humble pie and asking Elizabeth, in her capacity as a mere head of state and not God's exception, to send troops to Scotland to help him with his reforms there.

Turning to the Reformed and Restored Church of England, now led by most of Knox's fellow exiles, Knox exercised his 'hot spirit' and with 'a mind sufficiently embittered against the English Reformation' (so Strype) castigated them for bearing the mark of the Beast and the dregs of popery. The form of worship for the Lord's Supper, he argued, was 'devised for the upholding of Massing Priests' and

---

[37] Ibid, Chapter IX.
[38] Ibid, p. 123.

performed by ministers 'for the most part'(again his fellow exiles at Frankfurt and Geneva) 'without the soul'.[39]

Now turning to the English people, he told them that any oath or declaration of allegiance that they made to the English Queen and her government would be rendered null and void if Elizabeth ruled according to English law and not according to his own most questionable view of Scripture. The powers that be, he argued, were only ordained of God if they followed Christ in all things, as proscribed by himself. So Knox joined the Papists in slandering the Queen, the Church and the English nation and presented an understanding of the Bible that was radically different from that of the New Testament writers. When Paul appealed to Caesar, he most obviously did not do so because he knew him to be a fine, godly Christian. He did so because he believed that in all his paganism, the Roman Emperor was still appointed by God.

After presenting some of Knox's extraordinary exaggerations and before going on to list several pages more, Strype says. 'This is enough to show the Hot Spirit of this Man, and the Prejudice he had, for some Cause or other conceived against this Church and Kingdom: where he had once been kindly harboured.'[40] Commenting of this megalomania of Knox when the 'rude vehemencie and inconsidered affirmations'[41] came upon him, which was whenever he thought of Elizabeth and the Reformed Church of England, Lang concludes:

> The truth is that Knox contemplates a State in which the civil power shall be entirely and absolutely of his own opinions; the King, as 'Christ's silly vassal' to quote Andrew Melville, being obedient to such prophets as himself. The theories of Knox regarding the duty to revenge God's feud by the private citizen, and regarding religious massacre by

---

[39] Ibid, p. 121.
[40] Ibid, p. 121.
[41] See Laing, *Knox's Works*, Vol. V, p. 5. Knox is writing to Fox who had criticises Knox's politcal and revolutionary ideas as signs of 'coler'.

the civil power, idea which would justify the Bartholomew horrors, appear to be forgotten in modern times.[42]

All this now made Elizabeth, and the Reformers who had remained in hiding in their home-country or had been ignored, most suspicious of the incoming exiles, suspecting that any one of them might turn out to be a Knoxian hot-head. This was especially because Knox had animated a small group of men who now were claiming that Knoxianism was equivalent to the true Reformed faith. They thus began to broadcast that as the Church of England worshipped in several ways different to the Genevan churches, they were unreformed to the degree in which they differed, taking of course the Genevan order as the supposed 'norm'. Perhaps they did not realise that Knox himself was in a number of areas, far from the Genevan norm.

This was too much for the Continental heroes of the Reformation and both Zürich and Geneva decided it was high time to show their true colours and break with the Precisians who were now striving to destroy the English church as they had striven to destroy the Continental churches and the so-called 'Strangers' churches' (i.e. foreigners' churches) in England.[43] Their reaction did not come a moment too soon, though, for many, it came almost too late. Bullinger appears to have found out first what was happening. As Knox had sent Calvin a most garbled version of the Prayer Book order, so Bullinger found out that more radical anti-vestiarians as Sampson and Humphrey were adopting the same method. This method, according to William Turner, who practised it himself, was called 'literary exercise'.[44] An extreme situation was postulated and described in highly exaggerated terms so as to frighten people off from every attempting anything approaching this exaggerated pic-

---

[42] Lang, *John Knox and the Reformation*, p. 85.

[43] See Chapters XXI and Chapter XLII in Strype for above mentioned correspondence. Chapters are given rather than pagination as there are repetitions of the same page numbers in Strype's 1709 edition used by this author.

[44] See William Turner's most critical letter to Bullinger, accusing him of 'literary exercise', in condemning the Precisians use of the same. *Zürich Letters*, 2nd Series, pp. 124-126.

ture. It was a misguided way of telling lies in order to drive the people to the truth. This kind of genre had been practised since the most ancient times in secular drama and literature, and had been preserved in the university drama and debating societies as it is still in use today.[45] It had led to the idea that all poets and writers are liars, which was the major reason why that master of literary critics, Dr Samuel Johnson, denied that religion was a fitting subject for literary poetry and prose. The Precisians now began to apply this method of displaying imaginary sin so that it would shock a person into fleeing to God for true salvation to their religious and political propaganda. Thus Bullinger had been given the impression that the new English bishops, most of whom he knew personally from the Maryan period, celebrated mass at altars with silver crucifixes on them, wearing fully-fledged Roman vestments with large crosses embroidered on the backs of their priestly garments. Looking into the matter, Bullinger found that the said bishops shared the Lord's Supper with the people at a simple table and they were dressed in a plain white shirt. This dress was far more simple than that worn by their Continental counterparts. Bullinger gave the English Precisians a nice telling off in several letters, warning them that they had no grounds whatsoever for leaving their churches and congregations because of silly debates over whether a cap should be round or square or a shirt black or white. Furthermore, Bullinger confessed that though he, as a Swiss Reformer, preferred other clerical garments, there was no case for the complaint that the habits used in England were of Roman Catholic origin. To demonstrate their strong affinities with the Reformed church of England, both Bullinger and Gualter, Zwingli's successors, sent their sons to be trained in theology in England.[46]

---

[45] Thus Arthur Miller wrote his *The Crucible* to display saintly Cotton Mather (with name changed in the play but broadcast in his commentaries on it) as 'absolute evil' in order, he says, to force people to flee to the truth.

[46] After the debate, Humphrey conformed but Sampson still refused. Though Sampson lost the Deanery of Christ's Church, he was made Master of Whittington College and allowed to officiate without a gown. See Strype's *Reformation of England*, Chapter XLIII entitled Some Account of Humfrey and Sampson.

Beza also joined the fray, complaining of Knox's and Goodman's subversive and revolutionary works and challenging the authors for their deceit in having them published clandestinely in Geneva without informing their spiritual mentors there. Strype records how the former exiles, too, 'utterly disliked the books' and how Goodman recanted publicly his writing such worldly works. Beza now made it clear through his correspondence with Grindal that he, like Bullinger, had been misinformed as to the state of the English church. When a group of separatists demonstratively gave Grindal and his Commissioners a copy of the Genevan book and said that if they proved that wrong by the Scriptures they would give up their opposition to Church and Queen, they were surprised to hear that the commissioners knew the book and thought highly of it. Grindal, reading letters to them from the Swiss Reformers, demonstrated clearly, however, how the men differed from their Continental mentors, especially Beza and Bullinger.[47] The dissidents appealed to Beza who distanced himself from their practices and complimented Grindal on his lenity and patience with them. Beza then stressed to the dissidents the need to respect the laws of their land and not grasp at church posts without due calling and ordination. If they wanted to impress the Queen, Beza advised, it must be as men of dignity and goodness and not as disobedient rebels. Then Beza told his supporters in no uncertain terms that if they wanted to change anything in the Church of England, it must be from within the Church and within the normal means of Christian debate. Furthermore, he adds:

> Those things which they cannot change, let them bear, rather than for this cause forsaking the churches, by greater and more dangerous evils, they yield an occasion to Satan, that seeks nothing else.[48]

---

[47] A full report is given in Strype's *Grindal*, Chapter XII.

[48] The complete letter entitled 'Theodore Beza, To certain Brethren of the English Churches, upon some Controversies in the Ecclesiastical Polity', is found in Book I, *Of Original Papers*, p. 37 bound with the 1710 edition of Strype's *The Life and Acts of Archbishop Grindal*.

At this time (1568), Beza asked the Reformed Church of England to pray for the precarious state of Geneva which was undergoing a severe attack of the plague and overfilled with refugees. This was one of many letters from the city asking the Anglican Church for assistance as Geneva moved steadily into bankruptcy. Grindal started collecting money for Geneva and the French Protestants who were suffering. By the time of Grindal's successor to the archbishopric, Whitgift, Geneva was in such straits due to natural disasters and mismanagement that the Roman Catholics were planning an immediate take-over. Through the donations of Anglicans, amongst whom Whitgift was the most generous, and Geneva's many other allies, the Reformed city was saved from the papist vultures. Throughout this period, the Precisians praised the Genevans for their orthodoxy and denounced the Anglican Reformers and doctrinal Puritans for their lack of what they called 'discipline' hardly taking note of the fact, it seemed, that the Anglican Puritans were helping to keep Geneva alive whereas the Precisian squabbles were helping to bring Geneva into disgrace.[49]

Meanwhile, Calvin shook off his long period of sitting on the fence which had left him appearing to back alternately the Precisians and the Reformation as the various 'sides' appealed to him for advice. In 1561, he discussed with his English brethren all the ceremonies and practices of the Reformed Church of England which had not been added to the Genevan Order, one by one, showing his full approval in every case and declaring that he would so like to move the Reformation in the way that the Reformed Church of England had succeeded but the weaker members of his own church made it impossible. He had to compromise with their weakness, Calvin confessed, so as not to lose them.

Calvin, and Beza, who worked alongside Calvin and later took over his responsibilities, found their churches in England an embarrassment to them. With Grindal's cooperation they had encouraged the setting up of Dutch, French and Italian congregations,

---

[49] Grindal also persuaded the Queen to give pensions to certain Continentals who had assisted the exiles during Mary's bloody reign.

especially in London. These churches originally looked to Geneva for their standards. Other elements, however, quickly altered the courses of the churches and the French, unused to the freedom found in England, found themselves in deep controversies related to their home problems. The Anabaptists of most extreme differences plagued the Dutch London Church and the Italian church became a school for scandal leading up to their 'Reformed' pastor deflowering a maiden, as an expression of his new 'Christian' liberty. Peter Martyr kindly and most brotherly assisted Grindal in sorting out all these problems but the strife in the Genevan churches which Beza had envisaged as part of a possible Genevan world church, led to so many splits and excommunications that the churches lost any claims they might have had to being model Reformed churches.

The pro Anglican declarations from Zürich and Geneva helped the English Reformation to gather momentum and be seen as a most worthy alternative to the Genevan model. Knox asked the Queen, shortly after insulting her in a personal letter, to give him permission to preach his system in England. He cannot have been surprised when such a request was refused. Thus Knox made off for Scotland, cursing the English church, the English Queen and her people. Arriving at his home country, he found that he had fallen out of the frying pan into the fire and had to battle with more women in power who had not a fraction of the Reforming faith and Reforming power that Elizabeth had. Furthermore, as in England, he was faced with lords who believed that the reforms of Edward's days ought to be used as a pattern for reforming Scotland.

A few Continentals wrote to Elizabeth asking her why she did not move her country to join their Reformation as a sign of unity with their cause. Elizabeth replied that unlike theirs, the Reformed Church of England was a free, independent Church and that the Continental state and national churches were limited in what they did by either Imperial or papist powers who had no jurisdiction in the realm of England. This was no ideal with which the freedom-loving English people could identify themselves. Thus they could not expect English church life to be bound by Continental political restrictions. Truly, none of the European churches outside of the

English and Scandinavian churches, including Scotland, had anywhere near the freedom of the Reformed Church of England at this
time. In Scotland, even after Knox had been striving to bring in the
Reformation for a number of years, French Roman Catholic influence was still very much present. This is witnessed by the riots of
September 1559 when the papists, led by Mary Queen of Scots and
her gentry proceeded through the streets of Edinburgh holding aloft
what Strype calls 'the Chief Idol of the City, one Giles.'[50] France,
backed by the pope, now claimed England as their own and prepa-
rations were made to invade England via Scotland many of whose
nobility were still papists and their Queen, the widow of the Dau-
phin, herself laid claims to England's throne. As late as 1563 Scotland was still ruled by deadly enemies of the Reformation and of
Queen Elizabeth and England. Charles V's powers now stretched
over vast areas of the Low Countries, Germany, France, Spain and
Italy at the time, and also extended into many Eastern European
states besides Scotland.[51] Nor was Switzerland free from his influence. It is said of Charles' Roman Empire that it's extent was so
great that the sun never set on it. In 1563, the Emperor was still
striving to put pressure on Elizabeth to allow papacy to flourish on
English soil as it was still doing in his own realms. So too, militant
Lutheranism plagued the Continent as Lutheran rulers strove to keep
their petty states and Lutheran theologians gave up the doctrines of
grace held by their founder. Geneva, Basle, Bern and Zürich could
not even find unity of witness in the tiny state of Switzerland. The
Continental churches were also at logger-heads with one another on
the question of state traditions, ceremonies, vestments, predestina-
tion and the Lord's Supper in a manner unknown in England. By
1569, church after church on the Continent was pleading with Elizabeth to send troops over to help them throw off the Roman yoke
which Edward and Elizabeth had succeeded in doing mainly by the
free preaching of the gospel. Thus, whereas the Reformation had
been enforced and defended very much with the sword in other countries, the English Reformation, in comparison, had been a far more

---

[50] The 'patron saint' of cripples.
[51] *History of the Reformation*, p. 185.

peaceful work of grace. Indeed, the era of Elizabeth ushered in a period of peace in the English Church which the combined efforts of the papists and Precisians failed to disturb to any great extent whereas the Continental churches continued to go through times of great unrest and church-splitting. On the Continent, the dark, foreboding clouds of the Thirty-Years War were gathering which were to sadly smother much of the Reformed life in those lands. So too, Arminianism was already casting its Pelagian shadow over the Reformed churches of the Continent sixty years before it darkened England's shores. Indeed, no one could perhaps sum up the work of God in England at this time better than John Jewel who had, to quote Strype, 'lived in the middle of these times, and bore a great part in them.' This gem of the Church preached on the peaceful process of the English Reformation, at a time when, humanly speaking, it would have been impossible to imagine such a miraculous change. There is thus no better note on which to end this study than Jewel's depiction of the glorious nature of the truths for which the English Reformers lived and died:

> All these came to pass at such a time, as to any man's reason it might seem impossible, when all the world, the people, priests and princes were overwhelmed with ignorance; when the Word of God was put out of sight; when he (the pope) took upon him the great rule of all together, was crept into the holy place, and had possessed the consciences of men, as if he had been God, and had set himself above the Scriptures of God, and gave out decrees, that whatsoever he should do, no man should find fault with him: When all schools, priests, bishops and kings of the world were sworn to him; that whatsoever he took in hand, they should uphold it: When he had chosen kings' sons and brothers to be his cardinals; when his legats and espies were in every King's Council; when nothing could be attempted any where, but he by and by must have knowledge of it; when whosoever had but muttered against his doings, must straightways have been excommunicated, and put to most

cruel death, as God's enemy: When no man could have thought there had been any hope that even these days should have been seen, that God of his mercy hath given us to see: When all things were void of all hope, and full of despair; even then, I say, even contrary to all men's reasons, God brought all these things to pass. Even then God defeated their policies; not with shield and spear, but only with the Spirit of his mouth; that is, with the preaching of the gospel. And therefore this is the Day that the Lord hath wrought.

And the Power of God was as remarkable, that all the bloody, cruel and inhuman Methods, to destroy all that would not submit to their errors, could not prevail. No persecution, no torments, no fire, no faggot did ever weaken the cause of the gospel. This must be acknowledged the Lord's doing, and marvellous in our eyes.[52]

---

[52] Quoted from Strype's Preface to his *History of the Reformation.*

Steinerne Haus Frankfurt

Appendix 1
List of British Exiles in the Frankfurt Church 1554-59

The year of the first entry of the British members in the city records is given in the list below. This does not exclude an earlier sojourn in the city. Many women arrived in 1554-5 with their husbands accompanied by their children born in England. They were first recorded, however, in the 1557 Frankfurt census of 10 June, 1557 (*Numerus Anglorum in ista inclyta civitate Francoford. ad Moenum*). Anne Hooper and her son Daniel, for example, are first mentioned in the 1557 census, but we know from Anne's letters to Bullinger that she arrived in Frankfurt in the spring of 1554 and Daniel was brought by a maid soon afterwards. Sadly, the names of most of the children are not extant. Sons and daughters are indicated where the sex is known, otherwise offspring are merely entered in the records as 'children'. Though many of the members stayed in Frankfurt for an average of approximately three years, only four original members were there in 1559. Many members left Frankfurt immediately on hearing the news of Mary's death in November 1558. The 1557 list seems to have been a loosely controlled census as, according to Jung, though it is written on official Senate paper, one of the English filled it out and it may reflect merely those present in the church when the officials paid a surprise visit and asked someone to write down the names. Though 39 servants are listed, only four are named, thus these missing names would have extended the list. The total of the known British citizens who attended the Frankfurt church amounts to 342. This still gives no indication of the actual size of the congregation as not all the English were recorded in any way. We look, for instance, in vain for any mention of Knox in the city records, but his name is recorded in dated letters sent from the church. Furthermore the Dutch members are not listed, nor are German citizens who attended the services. Registration was sporadic and some of the Magistrates such as Glauburg are known to have kept lists of the British refugees which are now lost. There were also, most probably, English still worshipping at the Walloon church and possibly English supporters of Laski worshipping at the Dutch church. It is not known for certain whether any of the English worshipped in the German churches but as at least two English exiles became ministers of such churches, this is also probable. It also appears that the ministers of the Walloon church played an authoritative, though limited, role in the English church which was never granted permission to act as a separately constituted ecclesiastical body.

Abell, John, 1557.
Acworth, Thomas, 1557.
Ade, John, 1555.
Adishe, Philipp, 1557.
Alford(e), Hugh, 1554.
Alford, Mrs, (widow of a Frankfurt citizen, married Hugh c.1555)
Alvey (Alvay, Alveus), Richard, 1555.
Alvey, Mrs, wife of above, 1557.
Asheley (Ashley, Aschley, Astleius, Astelius), Thomas, 1557.
Augustinus Walterus, 1555.
Bagster, Thomas, 1557.
Baker, Reignold(e), 1557.
Bale, John, 1554.
Batus, Thomas, 1555.
Beauper, Margareta; 1557.
Beauper, son of Margareta, 1557.
Becon, Thomas, 1555.
Bedell (Bidell, Bidellus), John, 1554.
Beesley (Byselaeus, Biseley), Richard, 1555.

Beesley, Mrs, wife of above, 1555.
Beesley, child 1 of above, 1557.
Beesley, child 2 of above, 1557.
Bentham, Thomas, 1557.
Berkeley (Berckle), Gilbert, 1556.
Bertie (Bartue), Catherine, Duchess of Suffolk, 1557.
Bertie (Bartue), Richard, 1557.
Best, Robert, 1555.
Best, Mrs, wife of above, 1557.
Best, son of above, 1557
Bink(e)s (Byntzss, Binkus), John, 1555.
Birsch (Bierss), Jacobus, 1556.
Birsch, Elizabeth, wife of above, 1556.
Boyes, Edward (Edouardus), 1557.
Boyes, Mrs, wife of above, 1557.
Boyes, child 1 of above, 1557.
Boyes, child 2 of above, 1557.
Boyes, child 3 of above, 1557.
Brikbeke (Brickbek, Byrkebeke, Brickbate), Christopher, 1555.
Brikbeke, Mrs, wife of above, 1557.
Brikbeke, child 1 of above, 1557.
Brikbeke, child 2 of above, 1557.
Brikbeke, child 3 of above, 1557.
Brokus, Sigismundus, 1557.
Browne, Elisabetha, 1557.
Browne, John, 1557.
Carel(l), Thomas, 1557.
Cariar (Carrier), Anthony, 1554.
Carowe, Henry, 1559.
Carvell (Carvile), Nicholas, 1555.
Caunt, Edouardus, 1557.
Caunt, Mrs, wife of above,, 1557.
Caunt, child of above, 1557.
Chambers, Richard, 1554.
Chidley, George, 1554.
Chittington, Mrs, 1557.

Chittington, son of above, 1557.
Cockroft (Cockrafft), Henry, 1555.
Cockroft, Mrs, wife of above, 1557.
Cockroft, child 1 of above, 1557.
Cockroft, child 2 of above, 1557.
Cockroft, child 3 of above, 1557.
Coke, Mighell (Michael), 1557.
Cole, Thomas, 1554.
Col(e), William, 1556.
Colton, Edward, 1557.
Cottesford (Cottisford), Thomas, 1555.
Cox, Richard, 1555.
Crafton (Crofton), Thomas, 1555.
Crawley (Crauulaeus, Craulaeus, Graulerus), Thomas, 1555.
Crowley (Crowleus, Krole, Crowlaeus), Robert, 1555.
Crowley, Mrs, wife of above, 1557.
Crowley, child of above, 1557.
Davage, William, 1557.
Dakies, Master, 1557.
Davies (Davis, Davids ?), Richard, 1555.
Davies, Mrs, wife of above, 1557.
Dixson, Gawin (Gawen), 1557.
Donnell (Donell), Thomas, 1557.
Donninge (Donnings), Anthony, 1557.
Dyxsonn, Thomas, 1556.
Eaton, Thomas, 1557.
Elizabetha Lucia (no surname given), 1557.
Elyot, Magnus, 1557.
Escot, John, 1555.
Escot, Mrs, wife of above, 1557.
Escot, daughter of above, 1557.
Fauconer (Fagener, Falconer), John, 1556.
Fox(e), John, 1554.
Frank, Walter, 1557.
Fynchaeus, Johannes, 1555.
Geofrie (Geoffrey, Geffray, Geoffrye), John, 1554.

Gilby, Anthony, 1555.
Gilby, Elizabeth, wife of above, 1555.
Gilby, Goddred, son of above, 1555.
Gill, Michael, 1554.
Goodman, Christopher, 1555.
Graie (Gray), John, 1554.
Grindal, Edmund, 1554.
Hales, Christopher, 1556.
Hales, Mrs, wife of above, 1557.
Hales, John (brother of Christopher), 1555.
Hammon, William, 1554.
Haries (Harries), Edmond, 1557.
Harrington, Percival, 1557.
Harrington (Harrintonus), Robert, 1555.
Harrington, Joanna, wife of above, 1556.
Harrington, daughter of above, 1557.
Herald, Mrs, 1557.
Herald, child 1 of above, 1557.
Herald, child 2 of above, 1557.
Hilles, Johannes, 1557.
Hilton, John, 1555.
Hobbes, Joannes, 1557.
Hobbes, Leonardus, 1557.
Hodgston, Robert, 1557.
Hollingham, John, 1554.
Hollingham, Elene, wife of above, 1555.
Hollingham, Daniel, son of above, 1555.
Hooper, Anne, wife of Bishop Hooper, 1554.
Hooper, Daniel, son of above, 1554.
Hornbeus, Nicholaus, 1555.
Horn(e), Robert, 1555.
Horn(e), Mrs, wife of above, 1557.
Horn(e), daughter of above, 1557.
Horneby (Hornbeus), Robert, 1557.
Horton, Thomas, 1556.
Irlandus, Guilielmus, 1555.

Isaac, Edmond, 1559.
Isaac, Edward, 1555.
Isaac, Mrs, wife of above, 1557.
Isaac, daughter 1 of above, 1557.
Isaac, daughter 2 of above, 1557.
Isaac, daughter 3 of above, 1557.
Jackson, Mrs, 1557.
Janson, Johannes, 1556.
Jewel, John, 1555.
Jong, Guilihelmus, 1555.
Joyner, Robert, 1557.
Kelke, John, 1555.
Kelke, Mrs (wife of above), 1557).
Kent (Kendt), Laurence, 1554.
Kent, Mrs, wife of above, 1557.
Kent, child 1 of above, 1555.
Kent, child 2 of above, 1557.
Kent, child 3 of above, 1557.
Kent, child 4 of above, 1557.
Kent, child 5 of above, 1557.
Kent, child 6 of above, 1557.
Kethe, William, 1554.
Knoll(e), (Knols, Knollys ?) Thomas, 1556.
Knolle, Johanna, wife of above, 1557.
Knollys, Henry, 1557.
Knollys, Sir Francis, 1557.
Knollys, Lady, wife of above, 1557.
Knollys, child 1 of above, 1557.
Knollys, child 2 of above, 1557.
Knollys, child 3 of above, 1557.
Knollys, child 4 of above, 1557.
Knollys, child 5 of above, 1557.
Knot, Thomas, 1557.
Knox, John, 1554.
Langhorne, Richard, 1555.
Leaeverus, Joannes, 1555.

Letler (Littler), Richard, 1557.
Letler, Mrs, wife of above, 1557.
Letler, daughter of above, 1557.
Lever, Thomas, 1554.
Luck, Joannes, 1555.
Luddington, Richard, 1555.
Luddington, Mrs, wife of above, 1557.
Luddington, child 1 of above, 1557.
Luddington, child 2 of above, 1557.
Lynbrought (Lynbroughe), Richard, 1557.
Machet, John, 1555.
Machet, Mrs (wife of above), 1557.
Mahewe, Anthonie, 1556.
Makebray (Makebraie), John, 1554.
Mason, Richard, 1557.
Master (Maister), William, 1557.
Master, Mrs, wife of above, 1557.
Maynard, Egidia, 1557.
Molyns, John, 1555.
Nagors, Richard, 1557.
Nowell, Alexander, 1556.
Olde, John, 1557.
Olde, Mrs, wife of above, 1557.
Oldsworth (Oldissworthus), Edward, 1555.
Oldsworth, Thomas, 1557.
Parker, Roger, 1557.
Parpoint, Edward, 1557.
Parry (Parrie, Perryus ?), Henry, 1555.
Parry, Mrs, wife of above, 1557.
Parry, son 1 of above, 1557.
Parry, son 2 of above, 1557.
Parry, son 3 of above, 1557.
Parry, son 4 of above, 1557.
Parry, Leonarde, 1557.
Pedder, John, 1555.
Peers, James, 1555.

Peers, Mrs, wife of above, 1557.
Peers, child of above, 1557.
Penteny, John, 1557.
Pilkington, James, 1559.
Porter, Richard, 1557.
Purfoot, Nicholas, 1555.
Railton, Gregorius, 1556.
Railton, son 1 of above, 1557.
Railton, son 2 of above, 1557.
Rawlins (Raulins, Rawlyns), Erkenwaldus, 1555.
Rawlins, Mrs, wife of above, 1557.
Rawlins, child 1 of above, 1557.
Rawlins, child 2 of above, 1557.
Rawlins, child 3 of above, 1557.
Rawlins (Raulings, Raulinges, Rawlyns), William, brother of above, 1555.
Rawlins, Mrs (wife of above), 1557.
Reignoldes (Reinolldus, Reinoltt), Henry, 1555.
Reignoldes, Mrs (wife of above), 1557.
Rogers, Daniel, 1557.
Rogers, Richard, 1557.
Sade, Peter, 1557.
Salkins, Wilhelmus, 1558.
Samford, John, 1554.
Sampson, Thomas, 1555.
Sandell, Richard, 1557.
Sandes (Saunders, Sanders), Thomas, 1557.
Sandes, (Saunders, Sanders) Mrs, wife of above, 1557.
Sandes, son of above, 1557.
Sandys, Edwin, 1557.
Saul(e), Arthur, 1557.
Selye, Ralf, 1557.
Soothous, Christopher, 1555.
Sorby (Sowerby ?, Soerby, Sorbeus, Serbis ?), Thomas, 1554.
Springheim, Richard, 1559.
Staunton (Stanton), John, 1554.

Steward, Thomas, 1554.
Sutton, Edmund, 1554.
Swyft (Swift), Jasper, 1554.
Taverner, John, 1557.
Todchamber (Tod Chamber), Thomas, 1557.
Tomson (Thombson), Edmund, 1557.
Traheron, Bartholomew, 1555.
Turner, John, 1557.
Turner, Richard, 1555.
Turpin, John, 1557.
Upcheare (Upchair), Thomas, 1557.
Upcheare, Mrs, wife of above, 1557.
Upcheare, child 1 of above, 1557.
Upcheare, child 2 of above, 1557.
Vates, John, 1557.
Walker, Thomas, 1555.
Walker, Mrs, wife of above, 1557.
Walker, child of above, 1557.
Walton William, 1554.
Warcope (Warcapp, Warcup), Cutbert, 1556.
Warcope, Mrs (wife of above), 1557.
Warcope, child 1 of above, 1557.
Warcope, child 2 of above, 1557.
Warcope, child 3 of above, 1557.
Warcope, child 4 of above, 1557.
Warcope, child 5 of above, 1557.
Warcope, child 6 of above, 1557.
Warcope, child 7 of above, 1557.
Warcope, child 8 of above, 1557.
Warcope, child 9 of above, 1557.
Warcope, child 10 of above, 1557.
Water (Wather), Thomas, 1557.
Watts (Wats, Wattes, Watzs), Thomas (Thomasen), 1556.
Weller, Joannes, 1555.
Weller, Mrs (wife of above), 1557.
Weller, son 1 of above, 1557.

Weller, son 2 of above, 1557.
Weller, son 3 of above, 1557.
Weller, son 4 of above, 1557.
Weller, son 5 of above, 1557.
Whetnal, George, 1554.
Whetnall, Thomas, 1554.
Whitehead (Whitedus), David, 1554.
Whitehead, Anna, wife of above, 1556.
Whitehead, child 1 of above, 1557.
Whitehead, child 2 of above, 1567.
Whittingham, William, 1554.
Wilford, Francis, 1557.
Wilford, Mrs, wife of above, 1557.
Wilford, child 1 of above, 1557.
Wilford, child 2 of above, 1557.
Wilford, child 3 of above, 1557.
Wilford, child 4 of above, 1557.
Wilford, John, 1556.
Wilford, Mrs (wife of above) 1557.
Wilford, child 1 of above, 1557.
Wilford, child 2 of above, 1557.
Wilford, child 3 of above, 1557.
Wilford, Thomas, 1557.
Wilkinson, Jane (Joanna?), 1556.
Williams, William, 1554.
Willobie (Wilobaeus, Willogbe), Thomas, 1555.
Willobie, Mrs (wife of above), 1557.
Willobie, son of above, 1557.
Wilson, Thomas, 1555.
Wisdom, Robert, 1555.
Wood, Henry, 1557.
Wood, John, 1554.
Wood, Thomas, 1554.
Wood, Anne (wife of above), 1555.
Wood, Deborah, daughter of above, 1555.
Wroth, Sir Thomas, 1557.

Appendix 2
A. C. Dickens and
The Troubles at Frankfurt

An unsatisfactory account

A. C. Dickens is one of the most respected and renowned students of Reformation history. His works have been of great help to this author, in particular his *Lollards and Protestants in the Diocese of York*, OUP, 1959; *The English Reformation*, Batsford, 1964, and his various collections of original documents. Dickens has been praised by G. R. Elton in the *Listener* as an unrivalled, champion researcher and the *Times Literary Supplement* wrote of his 1964 study of the English Reformation as a 'masterly book by a master of the subject.' Reviewers of Dickens works have invariably used such words as 'incomparable', 'definitive', 'superb', 'mature' and 'authentic'. It would therefore be considered presumption indeed for anyone to question Dicken's findings. Yet this must be done regarding Dicken's lengthy presentation of the troubles at Frankfurt in chapter twelve of his book *The English Reformation*. The blurb on the dust-jacket of the 1965 edition of this work quotes Harold Kurtz of *The Daily Telegraph* as saying that Dicken's account is 'exceptionally rich, comprehensive and unbiased.' This would appear to be the case concerning much of this work but his handling of the troubles at Frankfurt certainly does not come under these categories but shows a poverty of source-usage, a highly limited approach and an obvious bias which comes down to the level of sarcasm.

Back-projecting controversies

In this chapter entitled *The Foundation of Elizabethan England*, and under the subtitle *The Troubles at Frankfurt*, Dickens begins by saying 'The most controversial and best-documented of the settlements abroad we have left to the last. *The Brief Discourse of the Troubles Begun at Frankfurt*, first published by a group of English Puritans in 1574-5. Thereafter Dickens bases all his account of the troubles on certain, unnamed, passages out of this book, ignoring the numerous further primary sources and the fact that the 1574 collection itself contains quite contradictory accounts. Furthermore, Dickens falls into the trap of back-projecting the controversies of a later generation onto the Frankfurt congregation, for which propaganda purposes the 1574 accounts were compiled and later used as the 'definitive' account over a long period of time.

Starting off on the wrong historical footing

Dickens sees Whittingham arriving at Frankfurt in June, 1554 as if he were the first English exile there but the records show clearly that the first English refugees arrived in Frankfurt during the winter of 1553-4 and continued to arrive throughout the Spring. Furthermore, he writes as if the Franco-Belgian church in Frankfurt had been established for some time,[1] though it, too, was in the first stages of formation and included a number of English refugees. He then states that the earliest order of worship drawn up for use by the English was a remodelled Prayer Book which was compiled by Whittingham alone. This contradicts the evidence given in the source Dickens mentions which emphasises that Whittingham arrived with Edmund Sutton, William Williams and Thomas Wood who were led in the initiative to separate from the French-speaking church by Morellio, their co-pastor, by Elder Castalio and a man called Adrian of whom we hear nothing further. As Whittingham signed the French church

---

[1] See also Warren's *John Knox and His Times*, p. 64. Warren says "A French Protestant church had for some time existed at Frankfurt," as if it were a long established work. Actually, the Franco-Belgians left England for Frankfurt at roughly the same time as the English refugees and for the same reason – to get out of Mary's way.

order in September, 1554, it would appear that he was then in fellowship with the French church, though the English church had already been formed.

The actual working out of an English order of service based on the Second Prayer Book of Edward VI is expressly stated as the work of the gathered English congregation which, three days after the initial supplication for a separate English church building, appears to have been numerous enough to enter into debates on worship, church order and discipline and to appoint provisional pastors and elders.[2] It was, however, this modified form of the Prayer Book for which the so-called Coxians pleaded for all along and the one which they used when Knox left for Scotland. Moreover, Whittingham obviously opposed this Prayer Book version along with Knox. The records are clear that the first pastor to be called was not Whittingham, who was an anti-Prayer Book man but Whitehead, a moderate Prayer Book man who resumed his pastorate after Knox left. In order to understand the church situation in Frankfurt, the three refugee congregations, Anglo-French-Belgian, English and Dutch,[3] had never a separate legal standing and were not considered separate constituted churches but merely tolerated because the British, including the foreign churches exiled from Britain, had been given freedom of the city by the Emperor. The Senate always classified the 2,000 refugees in Frankfurt together. If they paid their taxes and were peaceful, they could stay. If they were troublesome, as was Knox, they were asked to leave. If they did not leave, their goods were confiscated and, according to Frankfurt law, their lives could be forfeited.

Dickens' account of the call for pastors is inaccurate

Dickens tells us that 'instead of working out their own experiment the Frankfurt leaders soon issued letters in English in Strassburg and Zürich, inviting them to come and join the enlightened pro-

---

[2] *Troubles at Frankfort*, pp. 23-25.
[3] The Dutch originally worshipped with the English until Jan Laski formed a separate church in 1555-6.

ceedings at Frankfurt.' Thus it would appear that Dickens believes
the Frankfurt church dropped one experiment to take up another.
However, the idea of the first 'experiment' was to make Frankfurt
the central meeting ground for all the British refugees. This, they
put into practice as soon as they were enabled by the Frankfurt city
authorities. Not only did the Frankfurt church never give up this
initial 'experiment', they remained by far the largest congregation
of British refugees on the Continent.

Apart from the fact that Dickens gives the impression that such
as Bale was recommended by Strasburg in opposition to what became the Knox faction, it was Bale who headed the signatories in
inviting Knox to the city. Here, however, Dickens writes as if Knox
was the one and only choice of the Frankfurt congregation but the
records Dickens gives, but does not follow, inform us that the Anglican Prayer Book man James Haddon was the first choice but he
refused the offer. Nor does Dickens tell his readers that Lever was
also invited from Zürich to co-pastor the church but deals with him
as if he were some Prayer Book upstart from within the Frankfurt
congregation.[4] Nor does Dickens relate that Knox refused to take
up pastoral duties in the Frankfurt congregation. Indeed, though
Dickens has only written two paragraphs, he has already involved
himself in self-contradiction. Though he argues that the original
plan of the church was to have a remodelled Prayer Book, which
was accepted by a general majority, he now writes as if those in
favour of the majority decision were rebels and the majority were
anti-Prayer Book men. However, the lists of members from these
early stages show that the moderate Prayer Book men were in a
majority, a majority which continually increased as the church grew.

Knox's and Whittingham's subterfuge not questioned
Concerning Knox's and Whittingham's Latin fantasy version of
the modified Prayer Book Order used, Dickens does not question
the nature of this subterfuge, nor does he query the faulty rendering of Calvin's letter given. Nor did it lead to a 'complete victory'

---

[4] *The English Reformation*, p. 290.

for the Whittingham-Knox minority as Dickens boasts – as if the vast majority of the church had now become yes-men to the Knoxians. If this had been the case, the troubles at Frankfurt would not have continued and the Liturgy of Compromise never drawn up.

Cox described in highly exaggerated language

Dickens loses all trace of objectivity in his highly exaggerated language regarding Cox, whom he gives far too much pre-eminence as the 'baddy' who came to disturb a pre-fall Eden of 'goodies'. Cox does not 'arrive' at Frankfurt, but we read that 'the *new* and *formidable* figure of Dr. Richard Cox *erupted*[5] upon the Frankfurt scene.

First of all, Cox was well-known to most of the Frankfurt men and, as Dickens had already indicated, had been mentioned in correspondence with Frankfurt, secondly, he had come as a man of peace, as we know from trustworthy Edward Grindal.[6] Thirdly, Cox never gave himself pre-eminence and did not present himself as a candidate for any church post. Dickens admits that he knows of no commission Cox had from 'the Prayer Book parties at Strassburg and elsewhere' but still affirms, 'At all events, he came with John Jewel and other followers, and as befitted a former Prayer Book commissioner he had but one thought – to smash the Knox-Whittingham ascendancy at Frankfurt.'[7]

Again, this is exaggerated language that ignores the facts. Cox did not travel to Frankfurt with Jewel as we have seen,[8] nor was his purpose to 'smash' anything but to arrive at a practical and peaceful consensus. Indeed the main futile attempt at ascendancy practised by Whittingham and Knox was still to come. Furthermore, in the way he speaks of the ascendancy of these two men, Dickens indicates that, in reality, Knox and Whittingham separated themselves from the majority, as, indeed, they did.

---

[5] My emphasis.
[6] A Letter of Master Edmund Grindal, 6th May, 1655, from *Godly Letters of the Martyrs*, Miles Coverdale, John F. Shaw, 1837.
[7] *The English Reformation*, p. 290.
[8] See p. 153 of this work.

The Litany controversy not handled objectively

This disinformation is continued by Dickens saying that 'Cox created a disturbance by interjecting responses to the officiating minister.' Again, this claim must be treated with caution. Although one of the authors of the accounts Dickens uses claims that in a service 'Doctor Cox with his company answered aloud,'[9] presumably as against answering in a murmur or in silence, no source blames Cox for reading the Litany to which such responses were necessary. Indeed Knox himself tells us that this was the work of Lever in his capacity as pastor of the church.[10] Furthermore, Knox's account shows that he had taken up this matter with Lever prior to the service Dickens mentions and that Lever 'began to treat (solicit) that the Litany, which answered (with responses), might be used.'[11] In his account, Knox admits that Lever was the duly elected pastor but that he was not willing to support him because the pastor had not bowed to his personal requests. Looking further into the account of the use of the Litany, we find, as documented in the main body of this work,[12] that it was John Jewel, the friend of Nonconformists, who read the Litany and that this Edwardian liturgical form contained Reformed statements hardly paralleled elsewhere in the Frankfurt Order of Worship and which were later removed in the Elizabethan Settlement. If any disturbance was caused, it would have been more by the reading of the Litany than the responses which naturally accompanied it and this was the work of Lever, the appointed pastor and Jewel whom he asked to conduct the service. The records show that the vast majority were much moved by Jewel's conduct and that Jewel won the hearts of his hearers. Thus Dickens' claim that 'On the second Sunday Cox put one of his backers into the pulpit to read the Litany, while he and his faction made the responses from the body of the church'[13] does not fit the facts. Fur-

---

[9] *Troubles at Frankfort*, p. 54.
[10] See John Knox's Account of his Banishment from Frankfurt, pp. 62-69 in *Troubles at Frankfort*.
[11] Ibid, p. 63.
[12] See pp. 151ff., p. 163, p. 164 of this work.
[13] *The English Reformation*, p. 291.

thermore, it is an exaggeration to claim that Jewel was one of Cox's backers as Jewel had made his own way to Frankfurt, was quite new to the controversy, but was supported there by a broad selection of 'moderates'. It is interesting to note that Cox's critics, such as Whittingham and Knox, do not give the name of the person who conducted the liturgy, most likely because if he were known to be Jewel, opposition would crumble as Jewel was generally honoured and respected by all sides. As the Litany was used both in England and Scotland up to the death of Knox and beyond by the most stalwart of Puritans, one wonders what all this fuss was about!

An English church criticised for being English
Dickens emphasises that Cox maintained 'They would do as they had done in England and they would have the face of an English church.'[14] The author refers to this quite reasonable remark as if it were a thing to be despised. Again, this statement needs qualifying as we have no direct records of Cox ever saying such a thing. These are words put into Cox's mouth, and those of the other Frankfurt members, by Dickens and obviously taken from an extremely polemic text written by Knox years later which does not even mention Cox. Yet this supposed quote has been cited by almost every pro-Knox writer ever since as coming verbatim from Cox's mouth. Knox however, is here summing up the opposition against him, giving his most subjective interpretation of what the other side might have thought, irrespective of the fact that the majority he is criticising were all for a modified Prayer Book of the kind used by the original church members. All, including Cox, had agreed to put nothing in the order of worship that would offend the host country. Cox, of course, even moved the congregation to accept the French Order which had been refused by Knox himself.[15] Yet Dickens 'reconstructs' a conversation between Knox and Cox where Cox speaks and Knox replies,[16] which obviously from Knox's account

---

[14] Ibid, p. 290.
[15] Ibid, pp. 59, 62-63.
[16] *The English Reformation*, p. 290.

never took place, or at least not in the form Dickens would have us believe it did. Dickens maintains that Knox wanted 'to convert Englishmen to an international creed', but as yet, Knox, though showing signs of intolerance towards English ways, had not developed anything like an 'international' order of his own and had, indeed, rejected several international orders which had been quite acceptable to the Frankfurt men he opposed. In the end, on being called to Geneva, Knox was forced to accept an order based on the Frankfurt compromise and Calvin's order, both of which appear to have been formed without Knox's cooperation and, in the case of the Genevan order, in his absence. In other words, Knox's protests and bitterness had not changed matters at all, apart from causing a great deal of unnecessary trouble. When Knox took up his pastorate in Geneva, he was back at peg one, i.e. as at the commencement of his brief sojourn in Frankfurt. At Geneva, however, Calvin made sure that the English Genevan Order carried his imprint, sanction and authority, against which Knox was powerless.

Cox, not Knox persuaded the English to accept the French forms
Dickens again exaggerates when speaking of tempers rising to little short of violence and shows surprise when Knox finally accepted the majority opinion, saying that this was 'utterly out of keeping with his normal fanaticism.' He then relates how Cox 'redoubled his efforts to undermine the position of his chief antagonist', though he has not shown at all that Cox now demanded any further concessions. Nor do the records which Dickens cited at the beginning of his essay on Frankfurt. On the contrary, Dickens argues that Knox now called for the 'abolition of the Litany, the responses, the Te Deum and other parts of the Prayer Book, as if he were making fresh demands, as, indeed Knox was - and continued to do so during the entire period he spent in Frankfurt.

When the Frankfurt authorities urged the English to take over the French forms, it was Cox, not Knox who persuaded the English to accept the Senate's ruling. We must not forget here that Knox had, just a matter of weeks before, refused to use this form and now he kept out of the debate. This was Cox's day, and he used his persuasive powers to unite the church in peaceful acceptance of the Senate's wish. The author of this section of *Troubles at Frankfort* writes:

> Doctor Cox then spake to the Congregation in this wise. 'I have,' said he, 'read the French Order; and do think it to be both good and godly in all points'; and therefore wished them to obey the Magistrate's commandment. Whereupon the whole congregation gave consent. So as, before the Magistrate departed the Church; Doctor Cox, Lever, and Whittingham, made report unto him accordingly.
>
> Dr Cox, also, at that present, requested, That it would please him, not withstanding their ill behaviour, to shew unto them his accustomed favour and goodness: which he most gently and lovingly promised.
>
> At the next meeting of the Congregation, that Order was put in practice; to the comfort and rejoicing of the most part.[17]

When we understand that this writer was, for the most part, antagonistic to Cox, which has obviously coloured the account somewhat, it is the more remarkable how he fully acknowledges Cox's part in bringing peace to the church. It must be also noted that here we find Cox, Lever and Whittingham united, but there is no mention of Knox as being a worker of peace or of having taken any initiative whatsoever in the agreement. Yet, strangely enough, Dickens looks on this move, not as a defeat for Knox but as a defeat for Cox. This was certainly no defeat for the ex-university chancellor who had all along agreed that private baptisms, saints' days, surplices, bishops, crosses and even kneeling at communion should be dropped. For Cox, the church, torn apart by Knox who could never come up with a peaceful solution himself, now could worship in a 'good and godly way'. As Knox is not mentioned in this venture for peace, one cannot help thinking that he was still in disagreement

---

[17] *The Troubles at Frankfort*, p. 59.

over using the French forms and adhered to those few on both sides who did not wish to follow the Magistrates' ruling. Indeed, from now on, until the end of the account describing Knox's departure from Frankfurt, the author emphasises the Knoxian opposition to the Coxians and Knox's alleged political treason, but does not mention any support of the French forms by Knox at all.

Cox blamed wrongly for Knox's departure
Dickens believes that it was Cox's stratagem that persuaded the Senate to ask Knox to leave the city. Thus, he maintains, 'inside a fortnight' Cox gained 'outright victory'[18]. However, the sources give Cox either no blame or a mere part blame but none give him the full blame and it is obvious that the trouble started with Knox in November 1554, four months before Cox arrived. Furthermore, the Senate did not ask Knox to leave because of any theological controversy but because of Knox's political activity with which none of the Frankfurt men agreed. Even Whittingham could not follow Knox in this respect. Indeed, the Senate did not approach Cox at all in the matter but they took Whittingham into their confidence and also William Williams:

> ... willing them that Master Knox should depart the City. For otherwise, as they said, they should be forced to deliver him, if the Emperor's Council, which then lay at Augsburg, should upon like information, send for him[19]

The supposed September schism
Miss Warren, in her *John Knox and His Times*[20], tells the story of how after Knox failed to force his will on the Frankfurt church and had to leave, 'the congregation dispersed'. Most other pro-Knox writers do not go to this extreme but there are those who believe

---

[18] Cox arrived at Frankfurt on 13 March, 1555 and Knox departed on 26 March of the same year.
[19] *The Troubles at Frankfort*, p. 61.
[20] P. 65.

that when Knox left Frankfurt, most of the congregation moved with him. Actually, as has been shown in the body of this book, very few if any at all left with Knox.[21] Dickens is most sober on this issue but does see the handful of men who left Frankfurt six months after Knox as a 'rather belated' display of solidarity with the Scotsman. As we have seen, at this time the city authorities were putting pressure on the English to move and it says much for the unity of the church that so few left at all. As a relatively tiny group left Frankfurt so long after Knox, they can hardly be thought to have departed out of sympathy with him. Besides, Fox records that the reason for his own move was because of the young, know-it-all radicals in the church. Those who eventually left for Basle, Bern and Zürich were certainly not, or no longer, Knoxians. Bale, as we have seen,[22] though he called Knox to office, obviously changed his mind on obtaining first-hand experience of the fiery Scotsman. Indeed, Knox accused Bale, alongside Cox, Turner and Jewel of wanting to get rid of him at Frankfurt.[23]

Genevan Puritans and Prayer Book Puritans
After dealing with Knox's departure, Dickens gets down to more mature and arguable theories but, as in the first part, the Reformation historian does not give a hint as to the exact source of his information. However, Dickens is still guilty of reading back into the 1550s the controversies of generations ahead. He acknowledges that the Cox party were no 'Erastian prelatists', though he does not point out that, especially at this time, Knox most certainly was. From now on, until his death, Knox was to argue for a state monopoly in disciplining 'idiots', his word for Nonconformists, who did not follow his narrow liturgical course and his view of order and discipline.[24] Dickens concludes that whereas the Knoxians were 'Genevan Puritans', the Coxians were 'Prayer Book Puritans'. This is a major step forward as most pro-Knox church historians or po-

[21] See p. 227 of this work.
[22] See pp. 95ff., p. 107, p. 129, pp. 154-156 of this work.
[23] Ibid. p. 67.
[24] See pp. 183-184 of this work.

lemic writers such as Lloyd-Jones would not count Cox as a Puritan at all! However, this tidy distinction still will not do. As shown in the main body of this work, Calvin was often nearer the middle-of-the-road Anglicans than such as Knox and certainly far closer to them than the Precisians. Most of the Swiss Reformers including Calvin, Beza, Gualter and Bullinger urged the British Precisians, who boasted of being 'Genevan', to be less extreme and more tolerant.[25] This was echoed most strongly by Italian Peter Martyr. The most one can say is that the vast majority of the Frankfurt church held to a modified Genevan, Prayer Book Puritanism, not going to extremes either way. This is seen by Fox's, Grindal's and Whitgift's controversies with the supposed Genevan Precisian Puritans who were in danger, they argued, of becoming old Rome with a new name. The Frankfurt Anglicans would have argued that the Church of England was Calvinist long before Calvin and, indeed, more so, thinking of such as Bede, Greathead, Bradwardine and Wycliffe.[26] They obviously found Calvin a man to their liking, though they could not understand why he did not put his views more into practice in his own church.[27] However, in later years, they often looked at his successors, especially Beza, as having one foot in Rome.

---

[25] See pp. 306-309 of this work.

[26] Many scholars follow Lechler in arguing that Wycliffe did not believe in justification by faith. Actually, as this author has striven to show in his essay *The Reformation Candle That Is Never Extinguished, Part 3*, New Focus, Vol. 5, No. 02, Wycliffe was especially Reformed in his teaching on justification which even transcends that of Luther and Calvin.

[27] See pp. 309-312 of this work.

Appendix 3
The Frankfurt *Liturgia Sacra*

The entire 92 paged work is too long to be inserted here and the Latin might tire the patience of most readers. An overview might, however, not be amiss in order to give some indication of Reformed worship in the 16th century. The full title of the liturgy will be given and then the various subsections with their page references.

LITURGIA
SACRA
SEU
RITUS MINISTERII
IN
ECCLESIA PEREGRINORUM
FRANCOFORDIAE AD MOENUM
ADDITA EST
SUMMA DOCTRINAE
SEU
FIDEI PROFESSIO
EIUSDEM ECCLESIAE
PSALM CXLIX
Laudem Deo Canite in Ecclesia Sanctorum
Joan. I
Veni ac Vide

Francofordiae
1554

CHRISTANO LECTORI ECCLESIA PEREGRINORUM QUAE EST FRANCOFORDIAE COLLECTA S. PER CHRISTUM
Address to the Christian Reader, dated September, 1554.

LITURGIA DIEI DOMINICI (page 6)
8 am Sunday Morning Service. The precentor sings the Leve le cueur or the Ten Commandments in verse form.

One of the ministers (Kirchendiener) then sings 'Our help comes from the Lord who has made heaven and earth, Amen.' He then reminds the congregation that they are in the presence of the Lord.

Confessio Peccat: This is followed by the General Confession which the minister reads out line by line to be repeated by the congregation.

Absolutio: The Absolution. The people stand or kneel as they wish.

A text is then read and expounded and the sermon has not to last more than an hour and to be closed in prayer.

The notices are then given out and the congregation is informed that a collection will be taken at the door as the congregation leaves. This measure was obviously to save time as the Glastonbury church had taken a collection during the service.

Oratio: Prayer. Prayers are offered for the general state of the church; for those in political authority; for those in church authority; for the church universal; for mankind universally and the witness of the church to them. Likewise, the sick; the poor; those oppressed by war; all troubled in body and soul and those who are at death's door are prayed for. Then those who are suffering under the tyranny of the Antichrist are remembered. A special prayer is said on the first Sunday in each month to prepare the people for the communion service.

Benedictio Populi in Discessu Num. 6.
The blessing is given according to Numbers 6:24, 'The Lord bless thee and keep thee etc.'.

LITURGIA COENAE DOMINI (page 16)

The Communion Service. A prayer is offered by one of the ministers followed by the Apostles' Creed which is sung by the entire congregation.

Institutio Coenae Domini 1 Cor. 2.: The Lord's Supper is then celebrated according to the wording of 1 Corinthians 2. A prayer of warning against the misuse of the Lord's Table is given followed by a lengthy exposition of what the Lord's Supper entails.

Agamus Deo Gratias: After all have partaken of the elements, prayers of thanks are given.

LITURGIA POMERIDIANA (page 23)

The early afternoon service reserves an hour for catechetical work which is then immediately followed by the

LITURGIA VESPERTINA (page 24)

The evening service which starts at 2pm features a sermon, a prayer, a psalm and a blessing which should not take more than an hour in all. It is emphasised that the church officials need time after the service for consultation before the evening meal starts. The strange times for the meetings can be best understood when one realises that the English and the Dutch were using the same building and each had to await their turn.

LITURGIA QUOTIDIANA (page 24)

The midweek services were held on Tuesdays and Thursdays. A psalm was sung prior to the sermon which was followed by a prayer.

LITURGIA POENITENTIAE (page 25)

The Thursday meeting was followed by a meeting for prayer to which all the congregation were expected to come. This is one of the longest sections featuring six pages of set prayers prayed by the minister alone.

LITURGIA BAPTISMI (page 32)
The baptismal service may only be carried out in the church building before the entire congregation and after a sermon is given.

LITURGIA BENEDICTIONIS CONJUGII (page 41)
This is the liturgy for the marriage service and though the title merely refers to a blessing of the marriage, the ceremony is virtually a marrying of the couple. Later Precisians would not have agreed with the wording.

DE VISITATIONE AEGROTORUM (page 47)
Visiting the sick is described in general terms of Christian witness.

De Eucharisttia minstranda Aegrotis (page 49)
This is part of the *visitione aegrotorium* and should take place on the same day as communion in the church with fitting words from a minister.

IN FUNERE (page 50)
Here the deceased are accompanied to the grave by the entire congregation who assemble at the graveside where a minister gives a brief word and closes in prayer. This was a ministry which the later Precisians also felt very lax to carry out.

DE ORDINE MINISTRORUM ET EORUM INSTITUTIONE AC DISCIPLINA ECCLESIASTICA (page 50)
The ordination and discipline of ministers. This is divided into:
De Electione Ministri: Election of Ministers (page 51)
De Electione Seniorum: Election of Elders (page 53)
De Electione Diaconorum: Election of Deacons (page 53)

Elections were by blind vote at the recommendation of the clergy.

DE DISCIPLINA ET EXCOMMUNICATIONE (page 55)

The necessity of discipline which might even lead to excommunication is stated and illustrated in the following sections.

AD LECTOREM CANDIDUM PRO LITURGIA ADMONITIO (page 57)

Here, the strength and weaknesses of the liturgy and the effects of the church to find acceptance with the Senate and fellow believers are discussed.

PROFFESSIO FIDEI CATHOLICAE (page 70)

This is to be signed by all who wish to join the membership or share in the ordinances. In the Preamble, the church testifies that 'We are not born as Christians but must be born again.'

CREDO IN DEUM PATREM OMNIPOTENTEM CREATOREM COELI & TERRAE

I believe in God the Father, Maker of heaven and earth. The entire Apostles' Creed is stated and then expounded in four parts.

PARS PRIMA: CREDO IN DEUM PATREM CAUSAE CUR PATER DICATUR

The first part states that God can only be known through Jesus Christ, through whom God reveals Himself. It is explained why God is called Father in relation to his omnipotence, election and the new birth and why God decides on all things but is not thus the Author of sin. The way of obedience and abstinence from evil is outlined and the doctrine of sin expounded.

PARS ALTERA: DE FILIO JESU CHRISTO

The Incarnation is outlined and that Christ was born of the Holy Spirit in the virgin Mary and that He is both God and man, yet without sin. The reasons for Christ's suffering, death and resurrection are given, followed by His offices as Prophet, Priest and King. His place at God's right hand is described from whence He will come to judge the quick and the dead.

PARS TERTIA: DE SPIRITU SANCTO

The sanctifying work of the Spirit is explained and that all the power and efficacy in our ministry comes from the outworking of the Spirit.

PARS QUARTA: DE ECCLESIA

The Church is presented as one Holy Catholic Church (eine heilige allgemeine Kirche) i.e. the church universal. This church is composed of all elect believers which is the one Body of Christ and the communion of the saints. (sanctorum communionem). Those outside of this communion are lost so that one can truly say 'extra ecclesiam nulla salus' – 'outside the Church, no salvation.' The difference between the true church and local visible churches is stated. God has indeed founded a visible church for local fellowship but there are tares amongst the wheat which church discipline must root out through admonishing and, when necessary, exclusion from fellowship. The marks of a true Christian are then outlined at length.

The sacraments are then described. Baptism is seen as a sacrament of regeneration pointing to the promises in the Word. It is a symbolic washing depicting the mercies of God. Baptism is for all those entering into and born within the covenant and is thus for believers and their children only. The Lord's Supper is to remember Christ's death and the believer's sharing in His sufferings and death and the blessings which Christ has procured. Again, the need for church discipline is stressed and the membership is admonished to honour the secular authorities as part of their Christian service as they are ordained of God.

Finally, the congregation are pledged to reject all gatherings which falsely call themselves churches and other religions such as Islam, the Anabaptists, the Libertines, Mennonists, Daviditists, Marcionites, Arians and other heretical movements. They are then admonished to reject the pope as Antichrist, his teaching and worship such as the changing of the bread in the Lord's Supper, invocation of the saints, any trust in one's own works of righteousness or of others besides Christ, free-will, purgatory and any other satisfaction for sin apart from Christ's blood, worship of images or any human invention. At the end of the liturgy is a prayer that God will allow this faith to grow in the believer and keep with him to the end and that those who do not know the Lord will, through the witness of the church, receive the true light of faith and learn to know the one and only Saviour of the world, Jesus Christ, the Father's only-begotten Son and with them enter into blessedness.

The So-Called Knox Liturgy of 1556[1]

This is added in both its Latin and English forms which came out simultaneously in order to compare its structure with that of the *Liturgia Sacra* above.

RERVUM NOTATIO QUAE
in hoc libello habentur.

1. Confessio Christianae fidei
2. De conscribendis Pastoribus, Senioribus & Diaconis.
3. Ministerii conuentus, vnaquaque quarta die hebdomadae.
4. Formula interpretandi Scripturas, prima septimanae die obseruata.
5. Confessio totius Ecclesiae nomine paulò antè concionem habita, ac temporib. accommodata.
6. Altera ad omnia temporum & ordinum momenta pertinens.
7. Preces à concione, ad vniuersae Ecclesiae Christianae commodum factae.
8. Ratio administrandi Baptismi, ac Cenae Dominicae.
9. Modus instituendi matrimonii.
10. De visitandis aegrotis.
11. Ratio efferendi funus.
12. De Disciplina Ecclesiastica.

---

[1] Reproduced in Laing, Vol. IV, p. 149 ff.

THE CONTENTES OF THE BOOKE.

1. The confession of the Christian faythe.
2. Thorder of electinge Ministers, Elders, and Deacons,
3. Thassembly of the Ministery every thursdaye.
4. An order for the interpretation of the scriptures, and answeringe of dowtes, obserued euery mundaye
5. A confession of our synnes vsed before the sermon and framede to our state and tyme.
6. An other confession for all states and tymes.
7. A generall prayer after the sermon, for the whole estate of Christes Churche.
8. The ministration of Baptisme, and the Lordes Supper.
9. The forme of Mariage, the Visitation of the Sycke and the Maner of Buryall.
10. An order of Ecclesiasticall Discipline.
11. One and fyftie Psalmes of Dauid in metre.
12. The Catechisme of M. Caluyn. etcet.

The Latin translation and the lengthy Preface is attributed to Whittingham. A mention of the 'godly churches' at Emden, Wesell, Frankfurt and 'at this Citie', i.e. Geneva, indicating their sound ministry would indicate that Geneva was at peace with the other three. No reference is made to this order ever being used at Frankfurt, nor is there any reference to Knox. The Preface is dated, Geneva, 10 February, 1556. Knox arrived at Geneva on September of that year, the church being established in November of the previous year. During the baptism ceremony, the child is presented by the father and godfather. Concerning whether all sat at the Lord's Supper or not, the order prescribes that the minister is to officiate sitting but the rubric says rather ambiguously, 'every man and woman in likewise takinge their place as occasion best serveth.'[2] The actual liturgy of the services is not given but forms of prayers for home use are added.

---

[2] Ibid, p. 194.

Index of Names

(Further names are on the list of church members appended to this study)

Index of Places and Institutions

Index of Topics

Bibliography

Primary Documents

Anonymous, The Writings of John Fox, Bale and Coverdale, London, RTS, 1831.

Arber, Edward (Ed.), A Brief Discourse of the Troubles at Frankfort, privately printed, 1907.

Becon, Thomas, Early Writings of the Rev. T. Becon, 3 vols, Parker Society, 1842.

Bothe, Dr. Friedrich, Die Entwicklung der direkten Besteuerung in der Reichsstadt Frankfurt bis zur Revolution 1612-1614, Leipzig, 1906.

Bradford, John, The Writings of John Bradford, 2 vols, Parker Society, 1848.

Bullinger, Henry, Bullinger's Decades, 2 vols, Parker Society, 1849.

Cardwell, Edward (Ed.), Documentary Annals of the Reformed Church of England, 2 vols, OUP, 1844.

Collinson, Patrick (ed), Letters of Thomas Wood, Puritan, 1566-1577, Bulletin of the Institute of Historical Research, University of London, 1960.

Coverdale, Miles (ed.), The Letters of the Martyrs Collected and Published in 1564 with a Preface by Miles Coverdale, (Introduction by Edward Bickersteth), London, 1837.

Coverdale, Miles, Works of Bp. Coverdale, Parker Society, 1844.

Dathenus, Petrus, Kurtze und warhaftige erzelung, welche massen den Frantzösischen und Niderländischen der wahren Religion halben verjagten Christen in der Stadt Franckfurt im vier und fünffzigsten und etliche volgende jar die offentliche predig Göttliches worts und ausspendung der H. Sacramenten in ihrer sprach verstattet und auß was ursachen ihnen nachmals solches verbotten worden ist, Löw, Heidelberg, 1598.

De Beer, E.S. (ed.), The Diary of John Evelyn, OUP, 1959.

Dickens, A.G. and Carr, Dorothy, The Reformation in England to the Accession of Elizabeth I, Edward Arnold, 1967.

Duke, Alastair (ed.), Calvinism in Europe 1540-1610: A Collection of Documents, Manchester University Press, 1997.

Farr, Edward (Ed.), Select Poetry: Chiefly Devotional of the Reign of Queen Elizabeth, 2 vols, Parker Society, 1845.

Gardiner, Samuel Rawson, The Constitutional Documents of the Puritan Revolution 1625-1660, Clarendon Press, 1906.

Gee, Henry and Hardy, W.J., Documents Illustrative of English Church History, Macmillan, 1921.

Gibson, Edgar C.S., The Thirty-Nine Articles of the Church of England, 2 Vols., Methuen & Co., 1897.

Grindal, Edmund, The Remains of Archbishop Grindal, Parker Society, 1843.

Henderson, G.D. (Ed.), Scots Confession, 1560, Negative Confession, 1581 (Latin-Scots versions), Church of Scotland Committee on Publications, 1937.

Hooper, John, Early Writings of John Hooper, Parker Society, 1843.

Hooper, John, Later Writings of John Hooper, Parker Society, 1852.

Jewel, John, The Works of John Jewel (4 vols.), Parker Society, 1850.

Jung, Rudolf, Die englische Flüchtlings-Gemeinde in Frankfurt am Main 1554-1559, Frankfurter historische Forschungen, Baer, 1910.

Kriegk, Dr. G.L., Geschichte von Frankfurt am Main nach Urkunden und Acten, Frankfurt a. M., 1871.

Laing, David (Ed.), The Works of John Knox, 6 vols, Edinburgh, 1895.

Latimer, Hugh, Sermons by Hugh Latimer, Parker Society, 1844.

Meinert, Hermann (ed.), Die Eingliederung der Niederländischen Glaubensflüchtlinge in die Frankfurter Bürgerschaft 1554-1596, Verlag Kramer in Frankfurt am Main, 1981.

Original Letters 1537-1558, 2 vols, Parker Society, 1846.

Parker, Matthew, Correspondence of Matthew Parker, Parker Society, 1853.

Richmond, Legh (Ed.), Fathers of the English Church, 8 vols, London, 1807. (The collection includes the works of a number of exiled Anglicans such as Nowell, Jewel, Fox etc..)

Ridley, Nicholas, Works of Bp. Ridley, Parker Society, 1843.

Sandys, Edwin, Sermons of Bp. Sandys, Parker Society, 1842.

Sandys, Sir Edwin (Son of Archbishop), Europae Speculum; or a View or Survey of the State of Religion in the Western Parts of the World, etc., London, 1673.

Stempel, Walter, . . . under beider Gestalt . . . Die Reformation in der Stadt Wesel, Städtisches Museum, Statdtarchiv, Ev. Kirchengemeinde Wesel, 1990.

Whitaker, E. C. Martin Bucer and the Book of Common Prayer (*Censura* and *De Ordinatione* Legitima), The Alcuin Club, 1974.

Whitgift, John, The Works of John Whitgift, D.D., 3 Vols, Parker Society, 1851.

Withof, J. H., Duisburger Chronik (1740/42).

Withof, J. H., Wahrhafte Liturgie Und Bekänntniß Des Glaubens, Wie solche von den zu Franckfurt am Mayn Angekommenen Reformirten Vor 200 Jahren überreicht worden, Nach dem ersten authenticken Lateinischen Druck Auf Begehren wieder ans Licht gegeben, Und mit einer Teutschen Uebersetzung samt Vorrede versehen, Von Johann Hildebrand Withof, Professor der Universität zu Duisburg am Rhein. DUISBURG, Gedruckt bey Johann Sebastian Straube, Universitäts-Buchdrucker, 1754.

Withof, J. H., Wochentliche Duisburgische Adresse- und Intelligentz-Zettel (Nr. XII-XVI, 1752).

Wolf, Armin, Die Gesetze der Stadt Frankfurt am Main im Mittelalter, Verlag Kramer in Frankfurt am Main, 1969.

Wolf, Armin, Gesetzgebung und Stadtverfassung: Typologie und Begriffssprache mittelalterischer städtischer Gresetze am Beispiel Frankfurt am Main, Verlag Kramer in Frankfurt am Main, 1968.

Wotherspoon, H.J., and Sprott, George W. (eds), The Second Prayer Book of King Edward the Sixth (1552) and the Liturgy of Compromise, William Blackwood and Sons, 1905.

Zürich Letters 1558-1602, Second Series, Parker Society, 1845.

Biographies of Characters Mentioned in this Work

Addison, William, Worthy Dr. Fuller, J.M. Dent, 1951.

Anonymous, The Lives of the British Reformers From Wickliff to Fox, London, RTS, undated.

Barnett-Smith, G., John Knox and the Scottish Reformation, S.W. Partridge & Co., London, undated.

Bauer, Karl, Valerand Poullain, Elberfeld, 1927.

Bevan, Francis, William Farel, Alfred Holness, second edition, undated.

Blanke, Fritz and Leuscher, Immanuel, Heinrich Bullinger, Vater der reformierte Kirche, Zürich, 1990.

Bowen, Marjorie, Maria Stuart: Königin der Schotten, Gustav Kiepenheuer Verlag, 1934.

Brook, V.J.K., A Life of Archbishop Parker, Clarendon Press, 1962.

Bromiley, G.W., Thomas Cranmer, The Church Book Room Press, 1956.

Brown, P. Hume, John Knox (2 vols.), Adam and Charles Black, 1895.

Clarke, T.E.S. and Foxcroft, H.C., A Life of Gilbert Burnet, CUP, 1907.

Collinson, Patrick, Archbishop Grindal 1519-1583, Jonathan Cape, 1979.

Dalton, Hermann, Johannes a Lasco: Beitrag zur Reformationsgeschichte Polens, Deutschlands und Englands, Gotha, 1881.

Demaus, Robert, Hugh Latimer, Religious Tract Society, The Beacon Biographies, undated.

Ella, George M., Mountain Movers, Go Publications, 1999.

Firth, Sir Charles, Oliver Cromwell and the Rule of the Puritans in England, OUP, 1953.

Hill, Christopher, God's Englishman: Oliver Cromwell and the English Revolution, Purnell Book Services Ltd. 1970.

Innes, Taylor, John Knox, Edinburgh, 1896.

Jenkins, R.B., Henry Smith: England's Silver-Tongued Preacher, Mercer University Press, 1983.

Lang, Andrew, John Knox and the Reformation, Longmans, Green, and Co., 1905.

Lawson, Thomas, Calvin: His Life and Times, London, third, illustrated edition, undated.

Loades, D.M., The Oxford Martyrs, B.T. Batsford Ltd, 1970.

MacCulloch, Diarmaid, Thomas Cranmer, Yale University Press, 1996.

Marshall, Rosalind K, John Knox, Birlinn Limited, 2000.

Martin, Hugh, Puritanism and Richard Baxter, SCM Press, 1954.

McCrie, Thomas, The Life of John Knox, The Scottish Reformer, Glasgow and London, 1892.

McGinn, Donald J., John Penry and the Marprelate Controversy, Rutgers University Press, 1966.

Middleton, Erasmus, Biographia Evangelica, 4 vols, London, 1779.

Muir, Edwin, John Knox: Portrait of a Calvinist, London, 1930.

Olsen, V. Norskov, John Foxe and the Elizabethan Church, University of California Press, 1973.

Percy, Eustace, John Knox, Hodder and Stoughton, 1937.

Plowden, Alison, Danger to Elizabeth, London, 1974.

Rogers, Henry, An Essay on the Life and Genius of Thomas Fuller with Selections from His Writings, London, 1856.

Simpson, M.A., John Knox and the Troubles Begun at Frankfurt, private publication, West Linton, 1975.

Strype, John, The History of the Life and Acts Of the Most Reverend Father in God, Edmund Grindal, London, 1710.

Strype, John, The Life and Acts of Matthew Parker, London, 1711.

Strype, John, The Life of the Learned Sir John Cheke, Kt., Clarendon Press, 1821.

Strype, John, The Life of the Learned Sir Thomas Smith, Kt. D.C.L, Clarendon Press, 1820.

Tour, de la, Imbart, Calvin: Der Mensch – Die Kirche – Die Zeit, Callwey, 1936.

Warren, Miss, John Knox and his Times, James Nisbet, undated.

Watt, Hugh, John Knox in Controversy, Thomas Nelson and Sons Ltd, 1950.

White, F.O., The Lives of the Elizabethan Bishops, London, 1898.

Reformation and Puritan History

Abbott, Wilbur Cortez, A Bibliography of Oliver Cromwell, Harvard University Press, 1929, Kraus Reprint Co., New York, 1969.

Bainton, Roland H., The Reformation of the Sixteenth Century, Beacon Press, 1968.

Blunt, J. H., The Reformation of the Church of England, 2 vols, Rivingtons, 1882.

Brachlow, Stephen, The Communion of Saints: Radical Puritan and Separist Ecclesiology 1570-1625, OUP, 1988.

Burnet, Bishop Gilbert, The History of the Reformation, 4 vols, J.F. Dove, London, undated.

Campbell, Douglas, The Puritan in Holland, England, and America, 2 vols, New York, 1893.

Campbell, William M., The Triumph of Presbyterianism, The Saint Andrew Press, 1958.

Carter, C.S, The English Church and the Reformation, Longmans, Green and Co., 1925.

Clarke, Henry Lowther, Studies in the English Reformation, SPCK, 1912.

Cliffe, J.T., Puritans in Conflict, Routledge, 1988.

Collinson, Patrick, The Birthpangs of Protestant England, Macmillan, 1988.

Collinson, Patrick, The Elizabethan Puritan Movement, Clarendon Press, 1991.

Cragg, Gerald R., Puritanism in the Period of the Great Persecution 1660-1688, Cambridge University Press, 1957.

Curteis, George Herbert, Dissent in its Relation to the Church of England (Bampton Lectures), Macmillan and Co., 1906.

Daniel, Evan, The Prayer Book: Its History, Language and Contents, London, 1897.

Davies, Horton, The Worship of the English Puritans, Soli Deo Gloria Publications, 1997.

Dickens, A.G., Lollards and Protestants in the Diocese of York, The Hambledon Press, 1982.

Dickens, A.G., The English Reformation, London, 1965.

Dix, Kenneth, Faith or Force, Mayflower Christian Bookshop, 2000.

Elton, G. R., Reform and Reformation, England 1509-1558, Edward Arnold, 1977.

Elton, G. R., The Parliament of England, 1559-1581, CUP, 1989.

Frere, W.H., The English Church in the Reigns of Elizabeth and James I, Macmillan and Co., 1904.

Gairdner, James, Lollardy and the Reformation in England, 4 Vols, Macmillan, 1913.

Gairdner, James, The English Church in the Sixteenth Century From the Accession of Henry VIII to the Death of Mary, Macmillan and Co., 1904.

Gardiner, S. R., The First Two Stuarts and the Puritan Revolution, Longmans, Green, and Co., 1905.

Hardwick, Charles, A History of the Articles of Religion, Cambridge, 1859.

Heaton, W.J., The Puritan Bible, Francis Griffiths, 1913.

Heron, James, A Short History of Puritanism, T. &. T. Clark, 1908.

Hindson, Edward (Ed.), Introduction to Puritan Theology: A Reader, Guardian Press, 1976.

Knappen, M.M., Tudor Puritanism, University of Chicago Press, 1965.

Koenigsberger, H.G. and Mosse, L. George, Europe in the Sixteenth Century, Longman, 1979.

Lennox, Cuthbert (Ed.), The History of the Reformation of Religion in Scotland, Andrew Melrose, 1905.

Lewis, Peter, The Genius of Puritanism, Carey Publications, 1979.

Lindsay, T. M., History of the Reformation, 2 vols, T. & T. Clark, 1948.

Lloyd-Jones, D.M. (Ed), Puritan Papers, Vol. 1, P & R Publishing, Phillipsburg, 2000.

Lloyd-Jones, D.M., The Puritans: Their Origins and Successors, BOTT, 1987.

Lorimer, Peter, The Scottish Reformation, London and Glasgow, 1860.

MacCulloch, Diarmaid, The Later Reformation in England 1547-1603, Macmillan, 1990.

Macgregor, Janet G., The Scottish Presbyterian Polity: A Study of its Origins in the Sixteenth Century, Oliver and Boyd, 1926.

Marsden, J.B., The History of the Early Puritans: From the Reformation to the Opening of the Civil War in 1642, Hamilton, Adams & Co., 1850.

McGregor, J.F. and Reay, B., Radical Religion in the English Revolution, OUP, 1988.

Miles, Charles Popham, The Voice of the Glorious Reformation; or, An Apology for the Evangelical Doctrines in the Anglican Church, London, 1844.

Murray, Iain, The Puritan Hope, BOTT, 1975.

Neal, Daniel, The History of the Puritans (3 vols, Thomas Tegg, Klock & Klock reprint, 1979.

Niesel, Wilhelm, The Theology of Calvin, The Westminster Press, 1956.

O'Day, Rosemary, The Debate on the English Reformation, Methuen, 1986.

Packer, J.I., Among God's Giants: The Puritan Vision of the Christian Life, Kingsway publications, 1991.

Parker, T.M., The English Reformation to 1558, OUP, 1966.

Pennington, Donald and Thomas, Keith (Eds), Puritans and Revolutionaries, Clarendon Press, 1978.

Pettegree, Andrew, Foreign Protestant Communities in Sixteenth-Century London, Clarendon Press, 1986.

Renwick, A.M., The Story of the Scottish Reformation, IVF, 1960.

Rowse, A.L., The Elizabethan Renaissance, Sphere Books, 1974.

Shiels, W.J., The English Reformation 1530-1570, Longman, 1989.

Strype, John, Annals of the Reformation and the Establishment of Religion and other Various Occurrences in the Church of England, John Wyat, 1709.

Underdown, David, Pride's Purge: Politics in the Puritan Revolution, Clarendon Press, 1971.

Wendel, Francois, Calvin: The Origins and Development of His Religious Thought, Collins, 1965.

Westminster Conference Papers, Adding to the Church and Other Papers, 1973.

Westminster Conference Papers, The Christian and the State in Revolutionary Times, 1975.

Williams, George Hunston Williams, The Radical Reformation, The Westminster Press, 1975.

Wolters, Albrecht, Reformationsgeschichte der Stadt Wesel, bis zur Befestigung ihres reformierten Bekenntnisses durch die Weseler Synode, Bonn, 1868.

Books providing background information to the subject

Birt, Henry Norbert, The Elizabethan Religious Settlement, London, 1907.

Bicknell, E.J., The Thirty Nine Articles, Longmans, 1957.

Bothem Friedrich, Geschichte der Stadt Frankfurt am Main, Frankfurt a.M., 1913.

Daniel, Evan, The Prayer-Book: Its History, Language, and Contents, London, 18ᵗʰ edition, undated.

Darlington, R.R. et al., The English Church and the Continent, The Faith Press Ltd, 1959.

Davies, Horton, The English Free Churches, OUP, 1963.

Dietz, Dr. Alexander, Frankfurter Handelsgeschichte, Band I, Verlag Detlef Auvermann KG, Nachdruch der Ausgabe Frankfurt/Main 1910.

Dodwell, C.R. (ed.), The English Church and the Continent, The Faith Press, 1959.

Dowden, John, The Workmanship of the Prayer Book, Methuen & Co., 1904.

Eire, Carlos M., War Against the Idols: The Reformation of Worship from Erasmus to Calvin, CUP, 1990.

Fisher, George Park, History of Christian Doctrine, Edinburgh, 1902.

Fuller, Thomas, The Church-History of Britain From the Birth of Jesus Christ Untill the Year MDCXLVIII, 1656.

Garrett, C.H., The Marian Exiles, CUP, 1966.

Green, V.H.H., Renaissance and Reformation: A Survey of European History between 1450 and 1660, London, 1956.

Griffith Thomas, The Principles of Theology, London, 1945.

Guthrie, Charles John, John Knox and John Knox's House, Edinburgh, 1905.

Hardwick, Charles, A History of the Articles of Religion, Cambridge, 1859.

Koenigsberger, H.G. and Mosse, George L., Europe in the Sixteenth Century, Longman, 1979.

Lorimer, Peter, The Scottish Reformation: A Historical Sketch, London & Glasgow, 1860.

MacCulloch, Diarmaid, Groundwork of Christian History, Epworth Press, 1985.

Macnaughton, Samuel, The Gospel in Great Britain From St. Patrick to John Knox and John Wesley, Edingburgh, 1884.

Manthey, Franz, Polnische Kirchengeschichte, Bernward-Verlag, Hildesheim, 1965.

Moeller, Wilhelm, History of the Christian Church A.D. 1517-1648, 3 Vols, Swan Sonnenschein/George Allen & Company, 1898.

Philpot, J.C., Review of A Warning to Ministers by J.R. Anderson; A Day in Knox's Free Church by J.R. Anderson and John Knox Tracts, Gospel Standard Magazine, April, 1852, pp. 129-136.

Putzger, F.W., Historisher Weltatlas, Cornelsen-Velhagen & Klasing, 1978.

Sheldon, Henry C., History of Christian Doctrine, Vol. II, From A.D. 1517 to 1885, New York, 1886.

Thompson, J.M., Lectures on Foreign History 1494-1789, Basil Blackwell, Oxford, 1951.

Walker, James, The Theology and Theologians of Scotland, 1560-1750, Knox Press, 1982.

Walsh, Walter, England's Fight with the Papacy, James Nisbet, 1912.

Wedgewood, C.V., The Thirty Years War, Jonathan Cape, 1956.

Other titles by Dr George M. Ella published by Go Publications

A M Toplady — A Debtor to Mercy Alone
George M. Ella   large h/b 800 pp fully illustrated
ISBN 0 9527074 5 4
Biography and Anthology of the author of *Rock of Ages*. Foreword and recommendation by Mr Gerald Buss.

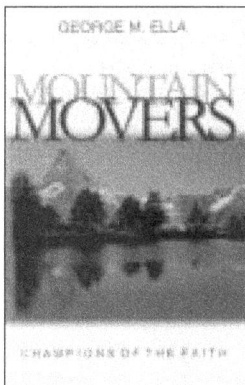

Mountain Movers — Champions of the Faith
George M. Ella   large h/b 448 pp fully illustrated
ISBN 0 9527074 4 6
Biographical sketches of famous (and some not so famous) reformers and puritans. Foreword and recommendation by Dr David Samuel.

John Gill & Justification from Eternity
George M. Ella   large h/b 236 pp
ISBN 0 9527074 3 8
A Tercentenary Appreciation researching and convincingly upholding Gill's doctrine of justification.

John Gill & Justification from Eternity

George M Ella

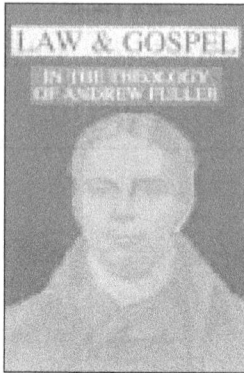

Law & Gospel in the Theology of Andrew Fuller

George M. Ella   large p/b 236 pp

ISBN 0 9527074 1 1

Analysis of Andrew Fuller's wayward theology and assessment of Fullerism's influence on today's church.

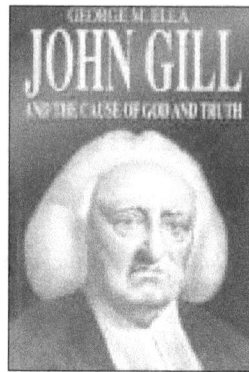

John Gill and the Cause of God and Truth

George M. Ella   large p/b 368 pp

ISBN 0 9527074 0 3

A highly readable and informative biography of Britain's greatest theologian & Bible commentator.

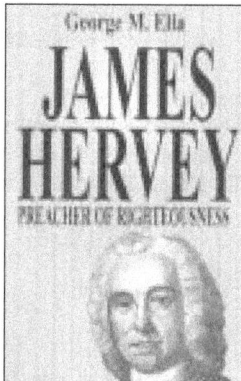

James Hervey — Preacher of Righteousness

George M. Ella   large p/b 368 pp

ISBN 0 9527074 2 X

Biography of Anglican writer, & theologian James Hervey.

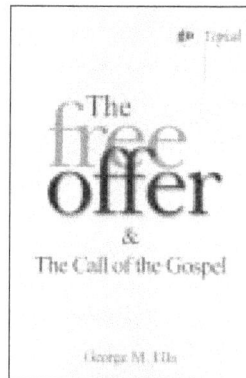

The Free Offer & the Call of the Gospel

George M. Ella   p/b 72 pp

ISBN 0 9527074 6 2

Critical appraisal of the free offer method of preaching.